The Force of Irony

Global Issues

General Editors: Bruce Kapferer, Professor of Anthropology, James Cook University and John Gledhill, Professor of Anthropology, Manchester University

This series addresses vital social, political and cultural issues confronting human populations throughout the world. The ultimate aim is to enhance understanding – and, it is hoped, thereby dismantle – hegemonic structures which perpetuate prejudice, violence, racism, religious persecution, sexual discrimination and domination, poverty, and many other social ills.

ISSN:1354-3644

Previously published books in the series:

The Force of Irony

Power in the Everyday Life of Mexican Tomato Workers

Gabriel Torres

Oxford • New York

English edition
First published in 1997 by
Berg
Editorial offices:
150 Cowley Road, Oxford, OX4 1JJ, UK
70 Washington Square South, New York, NY 10012, USA

Berg is the imprint of Oxford International Publishers Ltd.

Library of Congress Cataloging-in-Publication Data

A catalogue record for this book is available from the Library of
Congress.

British Library Cataloguing-in-Publication Data

A catalogue record for this book is available from the British Library.

ISBN 1 85973 936 9 (Cloth)
     1 85973 941 5 (Paper)

Typeset by JS Typesetting, Wellingborough, Northants

Contents

Acknowledgments

I have to thank the many people who made this book possible. I start by mentioning my mother, who died when I was organizing my fieldwork material in Holland. Although she cannot accompany me any longer, I am sure that her spiritual presence pervades all my efforts and that she is there in my bones. There are many tomato workers – the sisters Mily and Lety López, the brothers Juan and Raul Núñez and their father Don Manuel, Don Roberto and many more members of the Núñez family; Alejandro Hernández, Chimino Moya, Vicente Morán and Sandra Mata – who trusted me or at least communicated with me throughout my fieldwork. They are not responsible for anything I say, but in so far as this book reflects workers' everyday concerns, it began in the talks I had with them. Two tomato entrepreneurs (Eusebio Jiménez and Alfonso Aréchiga) tolerated my questions and accepted my presence in their companies and for that reason merit my acknowledgment. I am also indebted to the chemical engineer Víctor Quintero, the group of student workers and the squad from Teutlán.

There were also many friends who made me feel at home during fieldwork. Among them were Pedro Silva and Mily Figueroa, Gregorio Rivera, Nacho and Andrés Gómez Zepeda and Rosy Franco, Doña Chayo and Dr Andrés Gómez, the beekeepers of Ayuquila, the teachers Miguel Delgado, Augusto Suárez and Ofelia Peña, Pedro and Miguel León, the mill worker Roberto Vargas and Don Ernesto Medina Lima.

Thanks to the members of the Colegio de Jalisco-Wageningen University (WAU) project: Dorien Brunt, Elsa Guzmán, Monique Nuijten, Magda Villarreal, Humberto González, Pieter van der Zaag and Marlou, Gerard Verschoor and Margreit, and especially Alberto Arce, who introduced me to the team. I appreciate the

vii

discussions with Horacia Fajardo, Joel Cuevas and Gabriel López, which played an important role, above all in Chapter 2. I thank the Ford foundation and the WAU for the financial support they provided to finish this book. At WAU I am especially indebted to Mr van der Heijst, Mr de Raniitz and Jan den Ouden of the Department of Rural Development Sociology. There is a long list of people from Wageningen that I will always remember: Jan Douwe van der Ploeg, Jos Michel and Nanny van de Brink, Pieter de Vries, Kees Leuwis, Doortje Wartena, the Zimwesi prep team, the Osterkamp family, Mara Miele, Pieter Gerritsen, Paul Engel and Maria, Andre Bon, María and Dolores Fernández and Rafael Cabrera.

Jane Hindley and Paul Wheeler were the Samaritans who offered hospitality to a strange Mexican in London for the first time. They put me in contact with David and Ann Marie Wheeler, who showed me the British way of life for a month. Elizabeth van Aller did a great job of teaching me not only English writing but also the Dutch way of life and universal human kindness.

A special acknowledgment is for my supervisor Norman Long and his wife Ann Long. I admire Norman's ability to deal with a difficult subject and a difficult researcher, and above all his tenacity in searching for new ways of thinking. Ann went far beyond editing; she discussed this book with me bit by bit and made my peculiar Spanglish comprehensible.

Thanks to my father, brothers and sisters, who were very supportive when we came back to Mexico. I also say thanks to my colleagues at the *Centro de Investigaciones y Estudios Superiores en Antropología Social*, especially Guillermo de la Peña, Luisa Gabayet and Jorge Alonso. I have to express my special gratitude to John Gledhill and Kathryn Earle for their encouragement in preparing this book and to Paul Liffman for his editorial suggestions and enormous support. Thanks to Karl McCullough, Elena and Olivia Mulcahy and Carlos Heredia from Chicago.

My daughters Ana and Sara continue to be my main reasons for happiness and inspiration. I appreciate very much their love and many forms of solidarity. Last but not least, I would like to say *muchas gracias* to my partner Magda for her constant stimulation and contribution to my academic career.

Foreword

Farmworkers have seldom attracted the interest of social scientists. Even those anthropologists and sociologists who have focused their attention on rural societies have tended to focus on peasant farming and its prospects for survival rather than on rural proletarians, substantial numbers of whom, it should be noted, are women and children. Although this bias reflects both the continuing legacy of the old debates on the 'agrarian question' and more recent preoccupations with 'sustainable development', it is not easy to justify. A majority of peasant families cannot survive from the income generated by cultivating their own land under contemporary global conditions: the peasant farmer is frequently a part-time proletarian, and at least some of his (or her) children will almost certainly be working for capital, alongside the children of the many rural people who will lack access to land even in a country like Mexico which has experienced a significant land reform. *Where* this work will be performed within an increasingly globalized economy is, however, an even more interesting question today than in the past, given the footloose nature of modern capitalism as well as the pull of Northern metropolitan centres in the world labour market.

Gabriel Torres's study is set in Autlán-El Grullo, in the southern part of the western Mexican state of Jalisco, a region of the country which was already supplying migrant labour to the factories and farms of the United States in significant quantities before the Great Depression of 1929. The movement of labour to the North as well as to the cities has continued over the years, and, indeed, accelerated as first structural adjustment and then a peculiarly traumatic experience of neoliberal economic 'reform' added to the woes of middle-class as well as working-class and peasant households. Yet transnational capital has moved in the converse direction, promoting new patterns of agribusiness development in the South. These are invariably justified by businessmen and governments alike in terms of their capacity to create new jobs for the rural poor, stemming the tide of abandonment of rural regions for the cities (which in the case of modern Jalisco may be US cities such as Los Angeles, Houston or Atlanta or even a small Mid-West town with a meat-packing plant, rather the regional metropolis of Guadalajara or the national capital). Yet, as is also sadly the case in Autlán, dreams of local 'development' premised on new products, technologies and relations with the global market may prove elusive, as mobile capital moves on to greener fields and even the worst of jobs in terms of pay and conditions becomes unobtainable.

The world's poorest people live in rural areas, and most of them are farmworkers. In terms of numbers alone, they hardly merit the indifference mainstream social science displays towards them, but their invisibility on the political agenda is equally interesting. Historically farmworkers have always been at the bottom of the ladder in terms of pay and conditions (a matter which even the somewhat 'urban-biased' Marx felt deserved special theoretical consideration, offered in Volume Three of *Capital*). As time has gone by, they have become increasingly invisible to urbanized societies which have re-imagined the 'countryside' as a landscape beyond the asphalt. Globalization has, however, added new twists to the problem: increasingly radical technological transformations of farming and food-processing systems seem to do nothing to improve the conditions of agricultural labour, as witnessed not merely in the situation in the United States but recent scandals in England and other European countries involving the recruitment of migrant workers from Eastern Europe. Yet, as Gabriel Torres argues, a one-track focus on the rural worker as merely a victim of poverty and exploitation, backed by the statistical measures that feed the social-policy industry, contributes to a pervasive tendency to deny agency to the men and women who produce the food the rest of us eat. Even (or perhaps especially?) those on the classical Left of the political spectrum tend to despair at the apparent powerlessness and lack of organizational potential of farmworkers. What this book suggests is that we need to look at the question again, suspending our preconceptions.

In undertaking this project, Gabriel Torres has written a book that has wide relevance for the study of workers in general and for

the study of power and everyday 'resistance', a topic which has
become increasingly fashionable in a variety of fields, ranging from
James Scott's now long-established contributions in political
science and E.P. Thompson's reworkings of class analysis in social
history, through to the more recent flowering of the 'post-
coloniality' literature that provides a 'Third World' focus in cultural
studies. Given that the book repeatedly highlights that its results
are essentially *local* and stresses the dangers of abstracting from
heterogeneity in assessing relationships between the local and the
global, this claim may seem paradoxical. That it is not is a
consequence of the way ethnographic enquiry has, in this case,
been the basis for theoretical development. For the author, the
ethnographic encounter with his subjects – a wide variety of men
and women from different communities and backgrounds – led to
a radical questioning of his own political assumptions and his
social positioning as a researcher and more comfortable member
of Mexican society. By reflecting on his own and his co-workers'
interactions with the men and women working in the fields and
greenhouses, the author found himself able to understand more
about how his subjects related to each other and to the foremen,
managers and bosses who appeared to enjoy such overwhelming
power over them.

As the ethnographic process unfolded, he developed a growing
appreciation of the way the workers deployed irony in facing the
more powerful, to substantial practical effect, and began to glimpse
the 'contingent utopias' which belied the idea that they could not
articulate their own power strategies in a systematic way because
of the alienating conditions under which they lived. He paid
attention to their understandings of the workings of the regional
political system and of the way the *cacicazgo a la alta escuela* of the
notorious General García Barragán had influenced the development of the local economy. Encounters with new groups of
workers, such as those from the village of Teutlán, revealed
distinctive and unexpected forms of historical consciousness being
brought into play in the politics of tomato work and provided the
empirical grounding for reflection on the possibilities of social
change embedded in the interconnected situations of everyday life.
Analysis of social situations and the place of the actors in social
networks and status orders indicated that apparently passive and
subordinated agents could be more active than they appeared at
first sight, if the researcher was prepared to think about what was

going on without prejudging what form 'action' should take from the vantage point of his or her own life-world.

This, then, is a book which demonstrates what ethnography should be: a process which disrupts what we think we know and teaches us things that we did not know and could not have imagined without going to the field and learning from our subjects. It is ethnography of a sensitive and humane kind and it is theoretically informed ethnography: in developing his analysis, the author ranges very widely over the terrain of contemporary social theory and over a good deal of more specialist argument in the sociology of labour. Yet most important of all, it is theoretically *informing* ethnography, opening up spaces to critique the arguments of figures of the stature of Habermas and Bourdieu, for example, that also leads to an evaluation of ethical and political arguments about ways of ameliorating the conditions of farm work which, for once, resonate with the world-views and life-worlds of the workers themselves.

Gabriel Torres's work formed part of a larger research programme on the South of Jalisco, directed by Professor Norman Long of the Wageningen Agricultural University in Holland, in partnership with the Colegio de Jalisco. It is a fine example of what can be achieved by pursuing the 'actor-orientated approach' which Norman Long has advocated. It is a real pleasure to welcome this up-to-date work on rural Mexico by a Mexican author in which the everyday lives of rural workers of whom the rest of the world is largely ignorant can resonate with the more familiar images of the Zapatista rebellion in Chiapas and the ebbs and flows of transnational capital. In Gabriel Torres's case, the ethnographic study of the local does indeed speak to global issues.

John Gledhill
Professor of Social Anthropology
The University of Manchester

Introduction

This is a book, about tomato workers and power, based on intensive research and reflection since 1987. Two issues have intrigued me. The first is workers' heterogeneous responses to exploitative practices and the deterioration of their family living conditions. These responses ranged from resistance to avoidance and consent. The second is the unstable organizing routines developed by local and foreign entrepreneurs to contend with workers' uneven commitment to the tomato industry. To deal with these issues, this book takes domination and subordination to be problematic realities that emerge from ethnographic narratives constructed in everyday life. These realities rarely repeat themselves in the same way.

Therefore explanations of the rural workers' social world that assume that relations of power/knowledge are always simply unfavourable to them are not worth much. Such explanations fail to account for the intricate relations between the home and the workplace, as well as for insubordinate behaviour, however momentary. The challenge is to understand the social world as admittedly highly conflictual and routinized, but also as ever-changing. My task will be to look at tomato workers in concrete situations, and especially to see to what extent they could delegitimize the plans and policies of those apparently in power. Hence, this book seeks to explain three major problems: (1) the workers and their capacity for transforming their social standing; (2) the global/local nexus reflected in the diverse productive contexts that form part of local society's cultural repertoires; and (3) the planned and unplanned strategies that tomato entrepreneurs develop to control workers politically. Two events influenced me during the writing of this introduction: the 1994 indigenous rebellion in Chiapas and the collapse of the tomato industry. I will briefly discuss the concerns these situations brought up for me.

1

The Extraordinary/Ordinary in the Rebelión de Los Indios

The unresolved uprising of Chiapas is very much part of my reflections on Jalisco tomato workers. The Zapatista uprising recalled the extraordinary changes discussed in Chapter 7 of this book. Consequently I asked about the emergence of subaltern classes, the development of their transformative capacities and how change is forged in people's everyday lives. The Zapatistas' *ya basta!* (the title of their first communiqué) broke with the everyday life of deaths, jailings, repression, injustice, the destruction of harvests, and lack of democracy that the Indians experienced until 31 December 1993.

In his discussion of the conflict, Carlos Monsiváis considered that 'Mexicans cannot approach dramatic situations without irony and sarcasm' (*Siglo 21*, 13 February 1994:2). He celebrated political cartoonists' ingenuity in portraying the revolt as a sharp alternative voice that subverted the official truths of the Mexican government and mainstream media. Even if cartoonists could not overthrow the Mexican government, they undermined politicians' legitimacy. In this sense the rebellion had a postmodern character derived from the global and local effects present in the conflict. Monsiváis interpreted the humorous rhetoric that Subcomandante Marcos, the revolt's non-indigenous leader, employs even for war as a trope that helps a wide Mexican audience identify with Zapatistas[1] from the poorest and most remote region of Mexico: the Lacandón rain forest.

The rebellion began on the day that the North American Free Trade Agreement (NAFTA) among Mexico, the United States and Canada entered into effect. Thus, in the aftermath of New Year's Eve, Mexicans awoke to a widely publicized and very surprising revolt in which over 2,000 armed Indians took control of four county seats in the state of Chiapas. It was an ironic comment on Mexican President Carlos Salinas de Gortari's promise to transform all Mexicans into citizens of the First World beginning in 1994. Suddenly, the people ignored by NAFTA had acquired a belligerent voice heard nationwide. In fact, the Zapatistas' demands for work, land, housing, food, health, electricity, education, autonomy, freedom, democracy and peace became a catalyst for other indigenous groups, workers and peasants from practically all regions of Mexico to reformulate forgotten claims.

It is worth asking why Indians ignored for over 500 years were suddenly seen sympathetically not only in Mexico but many other countries. The novelty was not in the demands, since twenty years earlier an indigenous congress had formulated four points that included the Zapatistas' demands. That congress ended with the idea expressed by an Indian from Morelos that 'Indians will count when they organize, when they have the courage to demand their rights' (Mestries 1991:489). The novelty was precisely in the organization of Indians in the midst of a Mexican political crisis.

Neil Harvey (1994) mentions a host of structural causes for the conflict: the fall of world coffee, livestock and corn prices and the resulting decapitalization of most agricultural enterprises; the opening of the capitalist market, which meant ending land reform as well as greater competition with producers from other countries; the government's authoritarianism and inflexible political manage-ment; the lack of resources to do away with poverty; increasing migration; church activism; the shrinking of the state; the impunity of landowners' personal armies; and their great power. One could add further factors, but the interesting feature of the debate that has developed in parallel between intellectuals, bureaucrats, Indians, clerics and other interested parties is the insistence that the problem is not so much the volume of available resources, but the way they are distributed. In this sense, the problems of Chiapas have become current national problems related to the bankruptcy of the countryside, the ecological question and the recurrent need for greater democracy.

As Hernández (1994:51) argues, 'thousands of campesinos have decided to take the path of armed struggle as a means for resolving longstanding needs and for constructing a future in which they would have a place'. More than a rebellion for power, we are deal-ing with a war of positions that proposes installing a 'democracy with options' (González Casanova, quoted in Harvey 1994:36). Thus the most significant aspects of the Zapatista message is its insistence on constructing a national and international force for Mexican democracy. This was the purpose of the most lucid and decisive Zapatista actions, such as the *Convención Nacional Demo-crática*, national referendum and encounter against neoliberalism: they were directed to having civil society bridge between the local and national. The decisiveness of the Zapatista argument is to put development for everyone on the same footing as alternative improvements for the country. This is effective despite all the doubts about the EZLN's militarist leanings and the accusations against Marcos. As long as they remain undefeated, the Zapatistas will maintain that, for warfare not to prevail, politics must be more effective and just.

In Jalisco, which is as far from Chiapas as Holland is from Spain, many people were involved in the protests and debates. Wixárika (Huichol) Indian political actors, including members of the UCIH-J (Unión de Comunidades Indigenas Huicholas de Jalisco) have made public analogies between themselves and the Mayas of the Lacandón rain forest in Chiapas in terms of the centuries-old invasion of their territory by cattle ranchers, in this case from the neighbouring state of Nayarit. To indicate the seriousness of their claims, these combative *wixáritari* warned that the potential for violence is logical in both cases (Liffman 1996:60).

Also, at the University of Guadalajara there was a well-attended academic forum that included Indians, Bishop Samuel Ruiz (the principal mediator between Zapatistas and the government), and two members of a special government commission, intellectuals and representatives of the political parties. But the significance of the event did not rest exclusively on the participants' credentials. The emergent properties of the actors and the context were evidenced by the fact that ordinary people also participated. Students and members of Christian lay communities went to Chiapas to bring food and other aid to people uprooted by the army and rich ranchers.

It is still too early to arrive at conclusions about the transformative effects of the conflicts in Chiapas and other parts of Mexico; but clearly simplistic, romantic revolutionary images or those that justify the status quo have become totally discredited. After three years, no one believes that Chiapas is an isolated conflict between the government and Indians led by radicals: there are diverse interests, including soldiers, politicians, clergymen, landowners, small farmers, landless peasants and indigenous organizations. Even though the problems may be complicated and not all the fault of the current government, no one believes that just, lasting solutions for the conflict cannot be found.

During the 1988 presidential campaign, at the end of my fieldwork, I spoke with an Indian from Chiapas who worked in the Autlán-El Grullo tomato industry. I was struck by the racism and negative stereotypes that confronted Indians in Jalisco as well as by their ability to turn racist satire against its perpetrators. At that time it was widely held that the PRI candidate, Carlos Salinas de Gortari, could be defeated. To deal with that eventuality, some local PRI politicians and tomato entrepreneurs agreed to employ the workers as voters.

On election day (6 July) tomato company personnel directors gathered the workers to give them instructions for a special day of 'work' on which their main task would be to vote for the PRI. If they agreed they would receive an extra day's pay, a free lunch, a day off and a party. The entrepreneurs had arranged special transportation to bring discreetly groups of workers to the polling places throughout the day. Later I remarked to the Chiapas worker that opposition protests seemed to be in vain, and the bosses' manipulation of their votes blackened their reputations. He laughed:

> if the bosses think they can buy us, they're wrong. I know for sure that several workers did everything. They ate lunch, skipped work the next day, took the extra money and enjoyed the party. The problem for the bosses is that nobody can be sure if they got the votes they paid for because the vote is secret. So, when they voted, they did so for whoever they wanted.

The Collapse of the Autlan-El Grullo Tomato Industry

In late January 1994 the Autlán-El Grullo local tomato industry was close to disappearing. Of the 1,367 hectares cultivated in 1988, only 150 hectares were now planted with tomatoes. A mere 30 per cent of the 4,735 workers employed in the tomato industry in 1988 were still so employed six years later (cf. Chapter 3). Most of these workers lived in nearby communities. Most migrant tomato cutters from other regions had disappeared from the local scene after two years. Among the local workers still in the tomato industry were some of the principal characters in this book: Chimino, Rogelio, Ricardo, Alejandro, the women of the greenhouses and part of the Teutlán group. But Jeanette, Polo, the jokers, the semi-engineers and even more students and children workers were no longer there (cf. Chapters 2, 5 and 6). Local workers now had to migrate for at least three months a year to other regions where the companies are still in production. Ironically, the company holding up best was the Aréchiga confederation; it was producing almost 60 per cent of the current harvest, despite the fact that it previously appeared to be more conservative and slow to introduce technological packages (cf. Chapter 3).

It is not easy to explain the collapse of the Autlán tomato industry. The entrepreneurs, government officials, producers and workers that I interviewed offered various different explanations. Entrepreneurs and government officials commented on uncontrollable viruses and other diseases, a changing climate, declining water levels and the restricted area available for cultivation. Other producers and workers recounted rumours of entrepreneurs involved in drug trafficking and subsequent criminal prosecutions. But mostly people pointed to falling profits as the main factor. This is not unique to the tomato industry, because bankruptcy is generalized in Mexican agribusiness. Producers place most of the blame for lower profits on the Salinas regime's erratic policies, such as ending subsidies, organizational changes, uncontrolled imports of products and inputs, and, above all, new credit standards.

Most Autlán tomato producers have accumulated huge debts. Some producers faced monetary losses, foreclosure and criminal prosecution by reprivatized banks and government agencies. It is no surprise that these bankrupt tomato producers joined the El Barzón debtors' union.[2] The concerns and sympathies of this emergent agricultural producers' organization have changed through successive conflicts. The majority supported the PRI in 1988, and at least one entrepreneur directly organized indigenous workers to vote for Salinas, as described above. Some of these producers avoided bankruptcy with massive financial support from the National Solidarity Programme (Programa Nacional de Solidaridad, ProNaSol), which ostensibly allocated resources to the poor. Guillermo Cosío Vidaurri, the governor of Jalisco at the time, was later caught in a corruption scandal and deposed. He carried through this vain attempt to avoid bankruptcy on the grounds it would save jobs and provide benefits to the region; but it was not enough.

The Barzonistas' protests started when foreclosures began in April 1993. Twenty producers organized a tractor procession to the Autlán plaza to demand solutions for the debt problem, and stayed there for a month. This was paralleled by similar protests elsewhere in Jalisco. In Autlán they won sympathy from other large producers and a few small producers, but not from workers. They also maintained the support of the PRI mayor and municipal representatives. When federal government ignored them, they shifted the protest to the main plaza of Guadalajara. There they joined with other tractor protests and quickly won support from practically all sectors of Guadalajara society: the city was taken by the image of an abandoned rural sector in need of support.

During this phase, at least 3,000 small producers and a considerable number of workers (tractor drivers, truck drivers, mechanics and union members) actively supported the protest. At the same time, it gradually lost support from the PRI's corporate organizations and distanced itself from the Jalisco state government, but kept open some direct lines of communication with the President. Nevertheless, when they kept the tractor demonstration going for over fifty days, the President got angry. When El Barzón tried to move the protest to Mexico City on the same day that the President was to name his successor (one of the PRI's supreme rituals), the leaders were imprisoned and the tractors seized.

A paradoxical feature of El Barzón was that the only people from Autlán who publicly expressed solidarity with the Zapatistas and openly distanced themselves from the President and his announced successor were two large tomato producers and El Barzón leaders. Considering that Chiapas Indians' living conditions are more like those of Autlán tomato workers than those of Autlán tomato producers and entrepreneurs, it would seem more logical to expect solidarity from the workers than from the entrepreneurs. However, the event was just the reverse. This shows how a deterministic argument can create more analytical problems than it solves. Similar situations are described in nearly every chapter of this book. Hence, my effort is to understand the multiple logics connecting workers' behaviour to their transformative capacities. Moreover, it is nonsense to conclude that simply because tomato workers did not express open solidarity with the Zapatistas they are backward and politically apathetic. In the same vein, we have to interpret the public expression of support by rich farmers as a political posturing to get attention from the state. This book shows that behind apparent subordination and backwardness is the potential for action and transformation. In the following chapters I offer an open theoretical framework for analysing this potential.

Structure of the book

The empirical foundations of this book are the ethnographic situations described in Chapters 2 to 6. Contrary to the opinion that ethnography is theoretically weak, I believe that the ethnographic situations presented in these chapters are inextricable from my theoretical efforts. There are two overriding themes: the theoretical and methodological reflections (Chapters 1, 2, 7 and the Epilogue) and the political analysis of tomato work (Chapters 3, 4, 5 and 6).

The chapters are organized as sequential pairs. Chapters 1 and 2 interweave methodological and theoretical reflections. Chapters 3 and 4 concentrate on the effects of globalization and re-localization on specific working situations. These chapters also analyse work situations and the tomato companies' broader context in more detail. Chapters 5 and 6 focus on inequalities in power/ knowledge and on workers' everyday strategies as ironic practices. Chapter 7 discusses social change, summarizes the results of the study and briefly reviews other worker studies and theories of labour. Rather than a conclusion, The Epilogue reconsiders these problematic tomato workers' human agency.

Notes

1. The guerrilla movement took the name Zapatista National Liberation Army (Ejército Zapatista de Liberación Nacional, EZLN) in honour of Emiliano Zapata, the famous early-twentieth-century revolutionary.
2. The name comes from a revolutionary era ballad. For a more comprehensive account of this movement see Torres and Rodríguez Gómez (1996) and Torres (1997).

CHAPTER ONE

Searching for New Ways of Understanding Farmworkers

> Things deprived suddenly of their putative meaning, the place assigned to them in the ostensible order of things (a Moscow-trained Marxist who believes in horoscopes), make us laugh. Initially, therefore, laughter is the province of the Devil. It has a certain malice to it (things have turned out different from the way they tried to seem), but a certain beneficent relief as well (things are looser than they seemed, we have greater latitude in living with them, their gravity does not oppress us).
>
> Milan Kundera, *The Book of Laughter and Forgetting*, 1980:61.

The Research Problem

The postmodern imagination does not like prophets. Postmodern writers therefore rarely make forecasts, but they do play language games (Bauman 1992). These can tell us the same kind of truths that shamans, astrologers and novelists provide. But neither shaman nor scientific expert has the language to predict accurately how researchers will change their focus of investigation, face failure or abandon what cannot be explained.

This may be an uncommon way to start a book, but perhaps it is better to introduce the reader from the outset to the uncertainties of doing sociology. All I can promise is to make some of the difficulties and uncertainties involved more explicit. As my Wageningen colleague Ronnie Vernooy (1992) has shown, sociology is full of surprises that transform the course of inquiry. In addition to being an analytical challenge, the indeterminacy and relativism of the research process cause uneasiness and generally transform the sociologist's sense of being. If someone asked me whether fieldwork and writing had provoked unease, I would say yes, because we play the special game of forever changing our

9

minds. Playing such a game is part of how daily interaction is reshaped and analytic questions are reformulated in fieldwork.[1]

Let me describe here how this took place. I started with a research proposal about tomato workers in the irrigated area of Autlán-El Grullo, Jalisco, Mexico.[2] Inspired by Marxist beliefs, I delineated a framework concerned with reinforcing workers' class consciousness, which entailed theoretical assumptions about false consciousness. My agenda also included manifesting solidarity with farmworkers and combining theory with practice. Thus, I was concerned with examining workers' living conditions along two axes: (1) forms of autonomy and self-organization oriented toward developing worker consciousness (the subjective aspect); and (2) the construction of social contexts (the objective aspect). This entailed describing the constraints, influences, instructions and planning of the companies in general and of specific personnel at different levels. I aimed to identify globally labour contracting conditions, forms of subordination and 'the undesirable routinization of work'. Basically I wanted to emphasize that workers were living under conditions of subordination and exploitation. So a central question was why workers do not rebel.

When I presented the findings from my first three months of fieldwork to the other Mexican and Dutch researchers on the team,[3] I realized that my central questions and concerns with worker consciousness had not worked at all. My supervisor, Norman Long, encouraged me to take a more innovative route by using people's working conditions for theoretical analysis and comparison. Dr Long pointed out that dynamic situations in the workplace were interesting to study. This challenge prompted me to imagine what a theoretically informed ethnography of work might consist of. I reformulated the research question by looking into resistance instead of rebellion, and how it combined with collaboration in emergent workplace situations. But my picture of the field situation was still coloured by the selectivity of my data, which stressed labour organization. The inexplicable gap separating powerful bosses from powerless workers, and the untenable dichotomy between systematic company control and uncontrolled worker behaviour, became central concerns.

A second reformulation occurred when I had almost finished my fieldwork and became more aware of the complexities involved. This reformulation was based on the internal variation in workplace conditions and differences between the workplace and workers' living conditions in the household and labour camp. My focus turned to examining how workers survived in different circumstances, internalized values and used the resources that they took from and brought to the workplace. Variable work routines, numbers of consecutive shifts worked, gender, age, ethnicity and technology in different companies now drew my attention.

Still, I abandoned neither my concern with workers' group behaviour nor the effects of power differentials; but I did discover new ways of interacting with workers and understanding work practices.[4] By using an actor-oriented perspective (Long 1992), I reshaped these concerns and built a theoretically informed ethnography (cf. de Vries 1992a). By renewing questions and remaking texts, I gradually became more aware of the complexities of everyday workplace situations. I also analysed issues of asymmetrical power/knowledge relationships that emerged in working and domestic contexts. Readers can judge for themselves how far I got with this perspective.

A Shift in Worker Studies

For many years worker studies had focused on workers' knowledge about the extraction of surplus value. Sociological studies of workers became less attractive to wide audiences and more confined to the subdisciplines of rural and industrial sociology. Marxist studies of the 1960s and 1970s failed to demonstrate whether and how workers' consciousness was determined by exploitative practices. Their focus on collective class behaviour and search for alternative ways of interrelating theory and practice failed to take account of other forms of solidarity in the household, neighbourhood and community. Hence the diverse histories and organizational patterns that constituted social networks, family ties and cultural identities were often not included in the analyses.[5]

Burawoy's *Manufacturing Consent* (1979) made it clear that a shift in theoretical orientation was necessary. This shift could be linked to global changes like the decline of the labour movement and the failure of Communism, which was foreseen in André Gorz' *Adieu aux Proletariat* (1980). Gorz showed that the collective appropriation of the means of production and the command of society by proletarians did not work.

Bourdieu (1981) also expressed his disenchantment with 'descriptions of the most alienating working conditions and the most alienated workers'. He found them

> so unconvincing – not least because they do not help to explain why things are as they are and why they remain as they are – that is . . . they fail to take account of the tacit agreement between the most inhuman working conditions and men who have been prepared to accept them by inhuman living conditions (1981:314).

To come to terms with this 'tacit agreement' we must take into account what Giddens calls 'the pragmatic/ironic/humorous behaviour of distanced workers participating in the routines of alienated labour'(1979:xx). Giddens also suggests that when studying power relations in the workplace, we have to consider them to be 'two-way . . . all human relations manifest autonomy and dependence in both directions . . . however wide the asymmetrical distribution of resources involved' (1979:148–9).

This is Burawoy's point of departure for bringing together an ethnographic and theoretical analysis of the 'politics of production'. He stresses how workers spontaneously consent to coercive situations in the productive process. Workers' ways of making a life for themselves under the 'alienated conditions' of work demonstrate how cultural repertoires are locked into the home and workplace. These concerns epitomize new ways of looking at workers' everyday lives and reject from the outset 'the view that workers are somehow irrational in their responses to work' and 'a narrow emphasis that insists that workers only lean toward economic rationality' (Burawoy 1979:4). In other words, we cannot hope to get a fresh sociological focus on workers by repackaging old problems or resuscitating fossilized concepts. The way out is to learn how to deal with the complexities of workers' everyday lives.

Contending with Ethnocentrism

Foucault (1977) suggested that the worldwide upheavals of 1968 taught the masses that they no longer needed intellectuals, that they knew and could express things for themselves. Later Baudrillard (1988) took up this argument from another angle and argued that the enforced silence of the masses in the media makes them seem ignorant or passive, but this is only an 'obscene appearance', because no one can predict its final form. He further argued that it is easy to see when power is lacking or has been abandoned, but it is hard to observe hidden power, predict when it will emerge, or find ways of compromising with it. This also implies that the search for a single context for all human lives should be abandoned (Rorty 1989). Thus, our approach to analysing the mysteries, ambiguities, contingencies and trivia that Baudrillard observed as the behaviour of the masses has to change. Scott (1990) calls such behaviour the 'often fugitive political conduct of subordinate groups'. He identifies rumours, gossip, folktales, songs, gestures and jokes as apparently innocuous verbal genres through which the masses anonymously insinuate a critique of power. In fact, the enormous potential power of mass anonymity worries or at least attracts the attention of rulers everywhere.

This conceptualization of 'the masses' as a problem is the basis of recent discussions about ethnocentrism. Derrida argues that knowingly or not, ethnographers are ethnocentric because they take the supremacy of the expert over lay people for granted (quoted in R. Turner 1989:15). Ethnographic ethnocentricism may seem desirable because of the belief that knowledge and scientific skills contribute understanding about or at least offer novel accounts of research topics. However, Turner portrays the ethnocentric researcher as a 'kind of inquirer acting as social physician diagnosing troubles and inventing remedies' (1989:28).

In the study of tomato workers, ethnocentrism is of great concern. A subsequent question is whether research findings can change political situations or be transplanted (from Europe to Mexico, for example) to ameliorate poor living conditions. Orwell once said that 'human equality is technically possible but practically infeasible'. Rorty (1989) considers that this characterizes modern science's ambivalent achievements very well. Orwell's ironic perspective is still useful for criticizing scientific rationalities that stress maximizing goals and ignore 'trivia' like farmworkers' everyday lives.

In fact, issues like adequate food supplies, sustainable development, global ecology, profitability, automation, efficiency and expertise are at the top of most expert circles' agendas. In this perspective, projections of more comfortable working conditions depend on designing more sophisticated greenhouses in which computerized systems will help starving people and where workers will push buttons in new international production centres.

Although the robotization of agricultural labour is still in its preliminary stages, future productive processes will depend on farmworkers' becoming familiar with increasing mechanization. This also implies that they will no longer be willing to do the hard tasks taken over by machines. In Germany and Holland the greenhouse is becoming a common way to produce tomatoes. This is a successful technological development in which technicians and farmers achieve an admirable degree of control over nature. Bad weather, blights and changing markets are no longer considered problems; but agricultural labour *is* still onerous and at times dangerous, if not for everybody then at least for many unskilled workers.[6]

The failure to abolish agricultural labour's inherent harshness is due to a misplaced insistence on automation, efficiency and standardization. This is an ironic aspect of technological and social progress that makes better living conditions for the mass of workers problematic and unlikely. Even more ironically, social engineering is trapped in dilemmas created by the very social engineers. Designing universally better human conditions is a profitable business that largely ignores the poor.

If we cannot be very optimistic about the likelihood of technological and social progress abolishing exploitation in agricultural labour, perhaps we can learn from similar situations in the past. Looking back to the eighteenth century, British farmworkers interpreted the invention of new cultivating machines as an enemy that had to be destroyed (Hobsbawn and Rudé 1969). One cannot predict that similar things will never happen again; and, for countries like Mexico, building complex greenhouses is not immediately generalizable.

To illustrate the ambiguities inherent in the most developed greenhouses of Holland and their implications in terms of values, legal frameworks and equality, in areas surrounding The Hague, there are 15,000 to 30,000 illegal migrant workers. These workers receive 80 per cent lower wages than their Dutch counterparts, and have practically no rights. Moreover, 'illegal immigration put many legal immigrants out of work' (*NUFFIC Bulletin Newsletter* NL 6/92, 13 February 1992). Thus the asymmetrical economic and power relationships between legal and illegal migrants are exploited unscrupulously in the most technologically advanced agriculture. Despite this report's 'objective' language, it supports a partisan solution (cf. Appendix 1), puts most of the blame on illegal immigrants and employers who do not comply with regulations, and only implicitly criticizes the complacent police. The report ignored the role of legal migrants and the lax enforcement of immigration and labour regulations. By not acknowledging the complexities of Holland's multiracial society, the report's condemnation of greenhouse owners conceals unequal practices and privileges theoretical equality under a law that seeks full employment for legal migrants. The report also says nothing about how migrant workers need to evade Dutch legal regulations and find work in the greenhouses in order to survive.

This complex situation highlights the need to abandon simplistic explanations and raises doubts about the general application of legal solutions. The abstract legal equality promoted in the *Bulletin* refers to Western conceptualizations of equality and alienation that are also part of the problem. For Marilyn Strathern (1988:142), equality denotes people 'owning' the work they perform, and alienation is the separation of a person from her/his work. However, Strathern argues that these are not universal dogmas; they are ambiguous social constructs that vary according to context. Most ethical discussions of equality and inequality have unexamined assumptions. Hence relationships such as property and exploitation, social structures and standards of living are taken for granted and linked to the process of evaluation. An odd outcome of this discussion in the literature on workers is that the romantic hope for revolutionary change, scientistic belief in abstract technical solutions and relativism may actively conceal persistent inequalities.

There are big differences between bosses and tomato workers in terms of income and living conditions. This, however, does not necessarily justify predefined categories of desirable vs. undesirable living standards; neither should we become complacent and ignore evident disadvantages. One should not view workers as helplessly under totalitarian conditions in company-owned migrant camps reminiscent of Goffman's (1961) total institutions. Thus, without ignoring cruelty or exploitation, one has to acknowledge that working situations can be flexible and spontaneous environments (cf. Newby 1977:289). All this suggests that it may be more useful to analyse what workers do and how they attribute meaning to their lives and work than merely to focus on income, externally defined status differentials, or whether workers should own the means of production. It is necessary to unmask how the idea that all human beings are autonomous and free is reproduced.

Building a Local Theory

Farmworkers are often reified in both common sense and sociological theory. This happens in part because farmworkers' subordinate and stigmatized social standing tends to make them invisible (Newby 1977:11; Paré 1980:7; Grammont 1986:7). This is the case in Autlán-El Grullo. Tomato company managers, large-scale farmers and sugar-mill executives consider agricultural workers to be genetically handicapped or at least incapable of organizing production themselves. Another paternalistic view considers workers to be starving wretches who can be redeemed through the jobs that entrepreneurs create (González 1994). A third, more pragmatic view treats workers as a commodity reducible to the number of 'hands', without rights to minimally acceptable living conditions.

Despite these degrading attitudes, the scarcity of such 'hands' is sometimes so severe that production can only be assured by involving workers in managerial tasks. In order to attract a privileged minority of employees, entrepreneurs offer wage, housing, transportation, food and credit incentives. The entrepreneurs and managers develop close relationships with this élite workforce, reminiscent of the *peones acasillados* of the prerevolutionary era. In contrast, when conflicts arise over wages, working conditions, or other issues, employers circulate derogatory comments about workers' loyalties, the validity of their claims and the legitimacy of their leadership. This tactic is often used to justify firing workers labelled as a small minority, rebellious, agitators, corrupt or communists.

There are also so-called progressive groups (often affiliated to the Catholic Church) in the region. They depict agricultural workers, especially Indians from other regions, as the poorest of the poor. In addition, students and members of élite families related to the industry disapprove of workers' sanitary habits and claim that they act like animals because they do not cooperate in public health campaigns to clean up the barracks where they live. Other students, farmers and workers who want more freedom for agricultural workers see their living conditions as slave-like and believe that only by changing the whole political system can those conditions be changed.

Of course workers also have their own consciousness of their situation. For instance, they give themselves derogatory labels with an ironic twist in order simultaneously to convey acceptance of their status and challenge its premises (cf. Villarreal 1992:253). Other workers criticize their workmates' backwardness and cowardice. They point to other political struggles that ended in the repression of the minority and the disorganization of the majority. Still other workers appear resigned and desperate because they feel they are *jodidos* (condemned to their fate) and have no future without these jobs. Workers almost unanimously view the official trade unions as bureaucratic, corrupt and having little clout.

There are few sociological studies of agricultural workers, and most of them fall into a kind of 'politically committed sociology'.[7] They frequently make ethical condemnations, denounce existing situations and raise new issues for academic and political discussion as well as social action. These studies range from revolutionary perspectives on the rural proletariat's political role (Paré 1980) to pessimistic depictions of rural workers as 'human commodities that cannot think' (Astorga Lira 1985:118), 'politically powerless' (Danzinger 1988) and 'deferential' (Newby 1977). To quote Genovese (1974), most of these studies fail to take account of 'the world the slaves made'. Instead their predominant focus is on the world that made workers into slaves.

Although various concepts and caricatures interpret the world agricultural workers inhabit, partial accounts are insufficient for comprehensive theory. Deleuze's dialogue with Foucault proposes new relationships between theory and practice: 'Who speaks and acts? It is always a multiplicity even within the person who speaks and acts. All of us are "groupuscules". Representations no longer exist; there is only action – theoretical action and practical action which serve as relays and form networks. We have no choice but to make new theories' (Deleuze and Foucault 1977:205-7). Foucault concludes that 'theory does not express, translate, or serve the application of practice: it is practice. But it is local, regional and non-totalizing. This is a struggle against power where it is most invisible and insidious' (1977:208).

In other words, to define a society or a social group, theory should never be restricted to the dominating facet of power. The analysis of mechanisms and positions of power will always be insufficient. Theory must work with more fluid ways of understanding power/knowledge in dialogical contexts where cultural repertoires overlap (cf. Villarreal 1994). Moreover, theory should avoid speaking for others in a practical way, because only those directly concerned can speak for themselves.[8] Therefore, my main objective in this book is to explore the practicalities of tomato workers' everyday social situations and their dialogues with researchers.

Practices of Irony

In order to build a local theory as outlined above, it is important to show how theory and practice shape each other in social networks. In the chapters that follow I explore how this principle relates to other concepts and situations: tomato work politics, the politics of fieldwork and the effects of power/knowledge. This means coming to terms with the 'groupuscular and interlocking nature' (Deleuze and Foucault 1977) of social interactions, what people do and how they reflect on it. One way of doing this is to examine what I call 'practices of irony'. I start with Bourdieu's (1977) definition of practice as a cognitive operation combined with the performance of tasks and implementation of plans.[9] Know-how is revealed through people's actions. Actors' thoughts, gestures, emotions, perceptions and actions reflect different practical logics; these allow us to deepen our understanding of actors' interventions in everyday life. In sociological texts human agents appear as objects for observation, categorization – data and discourses related to specific situations; but these become meaningless when disconnected from the human agency that lies behind them.

Knowledge is thus a shared enterprise present in all practice. In his study of an irrigation system, van der Zaag describes how social interaction reveals the pattern of relationships. He argues that

> by the concept of "social interaction" we mean the processes which ensue when people come together and exchange goods, words or shared experiences. Social interaction, more than practice, is a dynamic concept since it acknowledges that when people come together a middle-ground emerges which cannot be wholly reduced to the

constituent parts of the interaction. Social interactions thus have an emergent nature (Long 1989 quoted in Van der Zaag 1992; cf. Sayer 1984: 113).

Outcomes of interactions consequently may be unexpected because knowledge resulting from interaction is dynamic and reflects the heterogeneity of the people involved (Van der Zaag 1992:5). Newby (1977:289) recognizes the dynamic variability of social practice when he characterizes English farmworkers' practices 'as never the same two days running'. He goes on to explain that those workers 'lacked any single abstract model of society which constituted their entire social consciousness. Instead many seemed to operate with a multiplicity of images . . . beliefs and opinions which did not add up to any simple coherent image' (ibid.:387). The same applies to Mexican farmworkers, and I use their deployment of irony to demonstrate this. Although I adhere to specific philosophical conceptions of irony,[10] I prefer to study how diverse practices embody them in specific contexts.

Thus, I use an analytical perspective on irony to grasp what Kundera calls the devil in laughter and to look differently at the prevailing order of things in the region studied. This entails extending the search for meanings beyond those that workers openly express, scrutinizing their hopes and visions of the future and considering other people's descriptions of them. As we saw in the previous section, these descriptions include stereotypes of tomato workers as backward. I suggest that these stereotypes reflect a dichotomy between 'native' and 'Western' standards of living and equality as well as an ideological bias in favour of experts.

I address ironic conditions and practices like the figures of speech that actors employ in everyday life to embody states of mind. Ironic conditions embrace both researchers' constructs and workers' everyday images of the history that weighs upon them: the set of conditions beyond their control. Of course, ironic conditions are not the same for everyone. This contrasts with a notion like structural constraints, which are assumed to determine the same outcomes for everyone. Ironic practices include ways of dealing with the prospect of living without radical alternatives and coping with only partially improved conditions.[11]

Although work situations may reflect power imbalances, these should not be taken to be definitive. Moreover, despite company promises and their own dreams, most agricultural workers cannot easily avoid dangerous work. However, irony allows workers to entertain the idea that even though apparently nothing changes, there is room for free action, joy, resistance or at least fugitive behaviour (cf. Scott 1990:xi). Such demoralizing appearances (cf. Baudrillard 1988) are endlessly ironic, not because they are mysterious, but because changes in such situations are virtually imperceptible. Furthermore, change sometimes takes the form of words or feelings that give hope without really improving material conditions. Despite these limits, emergent work arrangements point to new forms of consensus, labour organization, compliance, and ways of dealing with the unintended consequences of actions. These emergent forms are not fantasies, but implicit assumptions and concepts in a social process that includes fieldwork itself. Of course such forms could also be mere theoretical effects of research in which researchers see the objects of analysis as being more ingenious and cynical than they themselves are (Baudrillard 1988). I will develop this point in Chapter 2. There may also be ironic limitations on researchers themselves. The inequality between them and their objects of study circumscribes their understanding. Thus the sociology of ironic conditions becomes an interconnected, multilayered study of workers, management and researchers.

It may be impossible to list all ironic practices because of their enormous variation and the difficulty in defining them precisely. However, it is interesting to examine different ironic practices and their critical potential. In Kierkegaard's terms, ironic practices 'seek to balance the accounts' (1965:340) and in Woolgar's constructivist approach they are useful for maintaining the ambivalence of things that can never be known for sure (Woolgar 1983:260). This leads us to states of mind and figures of speech in different ironic practices.

Rorty (1989) regards irony as continuous doubt about people's final vocabularies (the words they use to justify actions, beliefs and lives). This offers a methodological jumping-off point for exploring variations in ethnographic accounts as contextually grounded. The difficulty with ironic practices is that they are mainly expressed in words, gestures, circumstantial attitudes and contextualizations that may not convey the same meaning to everyone. One can hear all the words or see all the actions, but both actions and words are fleeting, so presenting situations that embody ironic conditions give us more concreteness and thus help us avoid the risk of arbitrariness. Arbitrariness in the interpretation of irony is especially problematic in literary criticism because it has become an umbrella concept for such an enormous range of perspectives that it has largely lost its meaning. Woolgar (1983:248) criticizes the theoretical weakness of what he calls the blandest formulation of irony, denoting 'a figure of speech in which the intended meaning is the opposite of that expressed' by an individual.

However, this does not mean that we have to opt for fixed schemes of interpretation. Ironic conditions can be grasped by observing recurrent circumstances over a long time, as I was able to do in my research. I observed specific aspects of ironic conditions and linked group situations so that a series of practices began to cohere. Still, we have to remain sceptical about equating the ironies of life with structural constraints. Further, we must deny the power of irony as an explanatory principle even as we recognize the context and dynamism that it provides for understanding action.

In the following chapters I build a picture of the implicit and explicit contexts for various ironic practices by focusing on the meanings of fleeting states of mind and figures of speech. What I show is people interpreting contexts and speaking about their ways of thinking in momentary and recurrent practices. This is what I take from Kierkegaard's (1965) description of ironic practices. He argues that through contextualities we can build up different states of mind. These contextualities include conflictive or hierarchical relationships, how people define and behave with different audiences, and social categories like witnesses, collaborators, proselytizers, converts and intellectuals. In relation to the meaning of figures of speech, Kierkegaard mentions linguistic indices of politeness, attack or conspiracy. He shows that states of mind and figures of speech combine in negative gestures, mockery, dissimulation, feigned acceptance and defensive refusal. Thus, subtle uses of irony reveal complex combinations of the thought and speech, such as when questioning is used to humiliate, answering to infuriate, obnoxiousness to repulse and diagnoses to reveal weaknesses. States of mind can be more fixed than the fleeting moments of ironic behaviour or language.

Although Kierkegaard's approach to ironic practices is lucid, it is not free of ambiguity. It is almost impossible to avoid some of the confusions in contemporary sociological discussions concerning structure and action.[12] By linking practices of irony with people in context, I explore how contextualities are prompted by actors in ethnographic scenarios. My challenge is to offer a sounder reflexive understanding of the theoretical issues involved in the workplace. Of course, a focus on irony cannot solve all theoretical problems; but we can do what Kundera calls making things 'less heavy and oppressive than they appear'. At least by junking heavy conceptual frameworks, we can achieve a more lively dialogue with flesh-and-blood workers.

Research Setting and Methods

The Autlán-El Grullo valley is located 200 kilometres from Guadalajara, the capital of Jalisco, and 100 kilometres from the Pacific coast (see Map 1). The panorama as seen from the three roads connecting the valley with other regions shows an irregular pattern of villages and towns snuggled into the mountains and vying with agricultural land. A local poet suggested that anyone who dies of starvation in this lush land does not deserve to be buried because of the abundant fruits and other crops (Rubín 1987:131–2). In fact, the 200-square-kilometre valley's impressive setting at 1,000 metres' elevation amid the Sierra Madre Occidental has endowed it with a warm climate that local residents claim is the best in the world (Rubín 1987:14). The valley is privileged with enormous water resources in rivers and streams.[13] There are over twenty villages with populations ranging from 500 to 3,000 spread throughout the valley, which is divided into two municipalities whose seats are located in the towns of Autlán (with over 30,000 inhabitants) and El Grullo (with over 15,000). The region's fragile domestic architecture reflects the history of political, agrarian and technological developments as well as adaptation to geological and hydrological conditions.

In a Dutch researcher's impressionistic description of the region (Van der Zaag 1992:10), the huge black columns of smoke from scorching 50,000 tons of sugarcane before harvest are juxtaposed with the traditional image of the privileged and balanced nature of the region. In fact, since the introduction of irrigation infrastructure in 1970, cultivated land steadily increased to 8,700

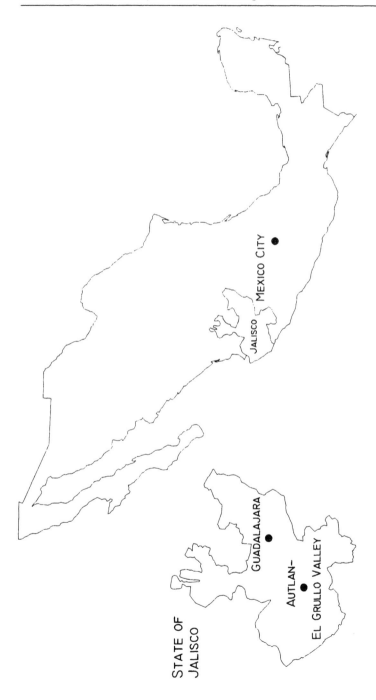

Map 1. Research Setting.

hectares in 1988. Of these, 1,200 were sown with cereals (maize and sorghum), 6,030 with sugarcane and 1,387 with tomatoes. The massive presence of day-labourers (an estimated 4,500 in the tomato industry and 3,000 in sugar) is linked to this irrigation system. However, most tomato farms in the western part of the valley still do not benefit from irrigation infrastructure.

For the American pioneers of tomato cultivation in the region, Autlán's first advantage was the excellent weather, with warm conditions throughout the year and fresh night winds to favour plant growth. However, since 1985 tomato cultivation has suffered from viral plagues (Verhulst 1988:4). This has led some companies to abandon the region. The romantic image of the valley must now contend with the paradoxical effects of modern development: thousands of tons of tomatoes rot because of market uncertainties, at the same time that local consumers pay more for tomatoes trucked in from Guadalajara, and those who want to use water for human consumption compete with those who want to extend irrigation.

Most of my field research took place over 18 months in 1987 and 1988. My principal activity was to observe and document the contexts in which six groups of local and migrant workers employed by two different tomato companies worked and lived. Two of these groups consisted of senior labourers who had been working in the tomato industry for 15 years. Their situations are analysed in Chapters 2, 3 and 5. Two other groups of workers came from small villages in the region (see Chapters 2, 3 and 6), and the last two had recently arrived in the valley from villages outside the region (Chapter 3).

During fieldwork I interacted with workers in diverse situations without preconceived guidelines, and used various means of collecting information. My most common procedure was to combine participant observation, situational analysis and discourse analysis. I conducted many extended interviews and collected life histories, which were complemented by accounts drawn from oral traditions and documentary sources to provide a historical and political background. Similar procedures were used to investigate social conflicts and events important for understanding specific contexts. Most of the situations and activities analysed took place on company farms and in greenhouses; but some also in laboratories, administrative offices, machinery depots, packing plants and warehouses (see Figure 1 for the layout of one of the companies).

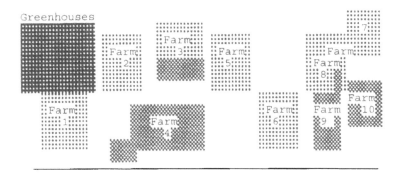

GUADALAJARA-AUTLAN HIGHWAY

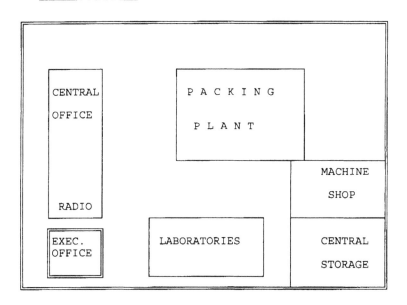

Figure 1. Plan of a tomato packing plant and farms

Notes

1. I use the notion of game to refer to actions and discursive strategies
    employed in reflexive performances mutually constructed by workers
    and their interlocutors (including myself and company management).
    My understanding of 'game' connects with practices of irony (see this
    chapter and Chapter 6). This embraces two meanings. Firstly, the
    game may indeed interrupt normalcy. Secondly, during the games
    the players have to change the roles and positions, i.e. they have to
    play for others and others have to play for them, which implies a
    constant mutation of characters. Thus, my aim is not to construct
    a regulating model for games, but to search for their emergent
    properties. That is, I am interested in identifying the possibilities for
    change inherent in games, in interpreting strategies and payoffs, in
    asking questions, and in interrelating and delimiting topics. For an
    exploration on the anthropological pedigrees of this notion see Gled-
    hill (1973) Chapter 2.
2. I entitled this proposal '*Vendemanos* or *prestamanos*: a study of the life-
    worlds of agricultural workers' (September 1987).
3. This study was linked with a collaborative research programme called
    'Contrasting Patterns of Irrigation Organization: Peasant Strategies
    and Planned Intervention'. It had been developed jointly by the Wag-
    eningen Agricultural University and the Colegio de Jalisco, Mexico,
    and was coordinated by Professor Norman Long of Wageningen.
    The programme included comparative studies of households, local
    women's organizations, sugar cultivators, tomato companies, small
    farmers and government agents. An interdisciplinary team of six Ph.D.
    students (Magdalena Villarreal, Elsa Guzmán, Humberto González,
    Dorien Brunt, Pieter van der Zaag and I) supported by Dr Alberto
    Arce carried out over 20 months of fieldwork. The programme was
    financed by the Netherlands Foundation for the Advancement of
    Tropical Research (WOTRO) and the Ford Foundation.
4. This is a reformulation of the relationship between theory and prac-
    tice that I touch upon in the next section. For a more comprehensive
    appraisal of this topic, cf. Norman Long's Introduction to *Battlefields
    of Knowledge* (Long and Long 1992:3–8).
5. For an exception, see Bulmer's (1975) collection, which offers a
    critical assessment of Lockwood's earlier industrial workplace studies
    and highlights the wider social contexts of workers' lives.
6. Tomato workers can die from pesticide poisoning. During my field-
    work I knew of three workers dying this way.
7. Apart from those discussed in the text, see Roldán (1980) and Lara
    (forthcoming) for Mexico and Lycklama (1980) for the US. Ghai, Kay
    and Peek (1988) use an economic approach to present the Cuban state

as the redeemer of rural workers (see also the critical comment by Redclift 1990:315).

8. Anyone who claims the right to change society for others is wrong if they assume that they have more talent or knowledge than those they presume to help (Brown 1987:6).

9. Bourdieu (1977) defines practices as performances through which objects of knowledge are constructed. This means that knowledge is implicit in all practice.

10. The concept of irony goes back to the Socratics. Kierkegaard reintroduced the concept more imaginatively in modern times and used it to criticize the incongruencies of modern life. Later Orwell (1965), Arendt (1958), Baudrillard (1988) and Rorty (1989) have offered variations on irony. Brown (1977; 1987) suggests that the concept provides a programme for sociology. Woolgar (1983) has employed the concept to study science from a perspective of sociological constructivism and epistemological relativism.

11. Giddens (1979:148-9) defines living without alternatives as the lack of solutions to social problems or of other conceptions of society, not as the lack of horizontal occupational mobility.

12. For a more comprehensive assessment of this issue, see Long (1992: 24-8,38) and Giddens (1979; 1990:310-15).

13. It is no accident that the main town of the region is called Autlán, a Nahuatl name meaning 'in the water'.

CHAPTER TWO

Plunging into the Garlic: Methodological Issues and Challenges

This chapter continues the methodological reflections initiated in Chapter 1 by focusing on the critical dialogue[1] between researchers and informants as social actors. It concentrates on the politics of fieldwork, in which actions and contexts shape each other through dynamic power relationships. The underpinnings of this fabric are the participants' and researchers' multiple discourses and practices. I analyse how theoretical preoccupations inform the construction of ethnographies during fieldwork. My purpose is also to transcend the methodological dualism that arises when the ethnographic moment is disconnected from analysis and theorization.

This chapter deconstructs an earlier article on encounters between researchers and farmworkers (Torres 1992). In so doing, I move beyond the standard meaning of the Mexican metaphor 'plunging into the garlic' (*metiéndose al ajo*) to probe into the politics of fieldwork and sociological analysis. In this endeavour, I have benefitted greatly from the insights of my Wageningen colleagues (de Vries 1992a and Seur 1992 in Long and Long 1992) and other writers (Polier and Roseberry 1989; Silverman and Gubrium 1989; R. Collins 1992).

The chapter is organized in four parts. The first offers a sociological exploration of the garlic metaphor. The second introduces the politics of fieldwork. The third discusses the issue of methodological accessibility, and the fourth summarizes the political implications of doing fieldwork and analysis. Finally, I offer some insights into the sociological significance of the research encounters I describe.

How Sociologists Take Up Particular Challenges in Research

The Mexican expression *metiéndose al ajo* ('plunging into the garlic') refers to how one leaps in at the deep end of the pool in order to understand complex human activities. It implies a long-term commitment, which is why it often refers to sports or political careers. The metaphor's richness is based on the difficulty of peeling garlic by removing the husks of the closely joined segments and the pungent, lingering smell. We might extend the metaphor to the challenge sociologists confront when they get involved in complex social situations and analyses.

The sociologist's passion for intellectual adventure entails exploring new forms of research and interpretation. The metaphor is a localized equivalent of Giddens' notion of 'double hermeneutics' (1987:18):[2] the mutual determination of sociological analysis and social interaction. As Seur (1992:116) suggests, 'since we do not have direct access to the personal life-worlds of others, the meanings that individuals assign to the natural and social world around them can only be elicited from their actions, which include their verbal expressions. This is so whether the actor is an individual or a corporate entity.'[3]

Thus, knowledge is a shared enterprise affected by people's interpretations of events and negotiated meanings, which may not correspond to the programmed research process. The analytical challenges facing the sociologist are associated with words like 'contradiction', 'indeterminacy', 'changing situations' and 'ambiguity', whose nature cannot be predicted from the outset. These generally arise from the informal circumstances in which researchers are involved. A case in point is a discussion I had with an American academic in the last phase of his doctoral fieldwork, which also focused on rural workers, when I was just making my first visits to the field to talk with tomato workers. He shared his negative impressions of the workers:

> I leave disappointed because of the impossibility of articulating a discourse of class formation in terms of the proletariat. The only thing that is clear for me is that even at a discursive level we cannot find a counter-hegemonic statement. In the end, what remains is pure realism, isolated expressions and hardly any organizational consolidation . . . it was only in the last few days that I have managed to speak with some of

those brave ones from San Juan, who even turned out to be relatives of a guerrilla fighter . . . With them I have been able to speak in a frank atmosphere and open up deep issues concerning politics. If it weren't for this, I would leave completely frustrated. The people of San Juan complain that Jaliscans are feeble and apprehensive (6 November 1987).

The American's disappointment lay in the fact that he had only barely met his analytical expectations. His view that workers cannot articulate a 'counter-hegemonic discourse', are confined to 'pure realism' and generally avoid 'deep issues' reflects his difficulties in grasping the subject-matter, and as such forms part of the context of workers' lives. Looking at this context opens up the complexities and ambiguities of fieldwork. This leads me to examine some of the biases underlying fieldwork and to place politics at the centre of ethnographic narratives.

The Politics of Fieldwork

Fieldwork data are neither neutral nor self-evident, but problematic and politically skewed. Silverman and Gubrium (1989) suggest that the field data's political character and effects must be spelled out. This politics of fieldwork and its results should examine the construction of research networks and the consequences of alliances and confrontations. This contradicts the idea that sociological texts do not embody conflict and that they produce new, progressive discourses and solutions to social problems. Moreover, as Latour (1988) emphasizes, 'the whole business of explanation' must be abandoned. This means considering the reflexivity of the text and avoiding the contradictions produced by the author's reducing the audience to faithful, captive readers.[4]

As we saw in the last chapter, researchers cannot evade ethnocentrism in ethnographic accounts. This places them in an ambiguous situation. On the one hand, they have the privilege of creating convincing ethnographies that are understandable to certain audiences. Foucault assumes that power projects an image that is 'all pervasive, unavoidable and inscribed in the very heart of all ventures of knowledge'. Even if this is true, it remains necessary to explore those power relationships, because the researcher's accounts have different kinds of complicity with the status quos in ethnographic interactions.[5] Ethnocentrism is not only a moral or epistemological issue; it is also political, in so far as it questions the authority of the analyst[6] and his/her account.[7]

My analysis of the politics of fieldwork implies not confining politics to state practices or great transformations. Instead, I examine how power inequalities vary according to context and audience and how methodological approaches to social interaction are not neutral. In other words, whether they know it or not, researchers and informants disturb the taken-for-granted nature of power relations and political understandings. Like Turner (R. Turner 1989), I do not believe that researchers can freely decide to detach themselves from the life-worlds of others, comment without bias or avoid over-criticizing those who intervene in local interaction. But we can attempt to reveal some of the assumptions implicit in sociological analysis and show how bias is intrinsic to knowledge. This coincides with Woolgar's idea of ironical conditions in which 'things can never be known for sure', as developed in the last chapter.

Collins (R. Collins 1992) offers an example of how ideologies incline people towards particular analytical outcomes. He criticizes the 'predefined conservative cognitive practice' of micro-sociologists like Goffman and Garfinkel, who present a miniature social order that 'is obdurate and extremely hard to overthrow'. This 'ethnomethodology shows actors have a preference for normalcy, and resist having to rearrange their practical actions in a way that disturbs the working consensus of everyday life' (1992:85). As we saw with the American researcher in Autlán, not only conservative but also 'revolutionary' bias produces teleo-logical arguments. Researchers' preoccupations and analytical perspectives mask specific assessments of power relationships.

To summarize, the politics of fieldwork is about the relationship between ideological bias, political strategy and common sense. I seek to find the political biases in fieldwork and use these to determine the political implications of ethnographic interactions. However, the same bias does not occur in every context or correspond neatly to the researcher or people researched. Instead, some biases become part of the production of ethnography itself. In the account that follows I use a vignette from my own role as a researcher to show how bias operates in context and points to interesting problems.

Rogelio and his Lecture on cacicazgo a la alta escuela[8]

Rogelio is a tomato company foreman whose job is to coordinate the tasks of twenty to fifty pickers. Mely, an always-smiling woman who was working for the same company, finishing high school and cleaning the research project house, first brought these local tomato pickers to my attention. She had been in charge of registering absenteeism for the company for ten years, and thus knew many of the workers. She caught on quickly to my research and suggested that I meet Rogelio. His house was nearby and she considered his career to be very interesting. What impressed me most was her comment that 'He gets the salary he wants from the company because he knows everything to do with the law.'[9]

Mely introduced Rogelio to me during one of my first visits to the tomato fields. The head of the tomato farm – whom I also met through Mely – asked Rogelio and his brother to accompany me. I interpreted this as standard procedure with visitors. They asked me what I wanted to do, and I explained my plan to write a sociological study of farmworkers and learn their points of view directly from them. From the first moment, Rogelio appeared keenly interested; but before explaining anything he tried to make sure he knew who he was talking to. He wanted to know concretely how I planned to carry out the research, as if my first explanation had not convinced him. I told him I intended to be present in the tomato fields, observe the working day and understand specifically how workers carried out their tasks and identified themselves as workers. He still appeared unsatisfied:

> The issue is very clear and doesn't need so many twists and turns. There's no need to go pecking around so much. If you want to, it'll surely end up amusing you, since you'll find a lot of different mentalities, but it's not necessary to take so many detours. Let's concentrate on one theme. For instance let's tackle the economic or political aspect.

When I persisted with specific questions, Rogelio responded in registers ranging from philosophical comments to subtle jokes. For example I asked why he instructed women pickers to cut the fruit with both hands. He explained,

> We have to learn to train the body and know how to move it, because movement is life. If you carry your weight on only one side of your body,

it'll bend and hurt. Your body can only maintain equilibrium if you move it both ways. It's necessary to keep the body in shape because as the saying goes, it's the only way to earn your bread with the sweat of your *frente* [brow] and sometimes also from your 'second *frente*' [second front; i.e., lover's house].

He was also frequently testing me, as when he said in a hushed voice,

What has not been eradicated here is the *cacicazgo* because we experience it in its sophisticated form. El General[10] inherited this tradition from several landowners and politicians, although economic resources had a lot to do with it. But now it's not only an individual, they've become a gang that can't be finished off so easily. What do you think? What do we need in this region for the peasants to produce better? Do we need capital, or is it opportunities and motivation that we lack?

He pointed to the bare hills and uncultivated land. I thought it over a bit and then answered that maybe the problem lay in what he had mentioned about the *cacicazgo*. Rogelio was pleased with my response and continued,

Exactly! The problem is that those hills could produce guavas or medicinal plants and those uncultivated lands could feed many more families, but since they're in the hands of those lazy rich people, they don't produce and they don't let others produce either.

On another occasion, I asked if he had ever owned land. He said that it was his lifelong dream but that 'things are hard'.[11] The land his father had acquired (seven hectares) was insufficient for the fifteen brothers and sisters. Several times, Rogelio proudly invited me to his 'experimental plot', as he called the half hectare his father had passed on to him. He had approximately 100 fruit trees, which he constantly grafted and experimented with.

From then on we became friends: we saw each other at least once a week during my eighteen months of fieldwork. He liked to comment on his everyday problems in the company and interpret other situations we encountered, and would wait for me to write them down. Once he confided that he had had to persuade other workers to open up to me, because they were afraid they would face problems with their superiors if I divulged information I had written down. He claimed to have said to them, 'Don't worry, let yourselves confess (*déjense confesar*), there's no problem.' He explained that peasants' reluctance to talk reflects the days when, after hearing *agraristas'* confessions, Catholic priests fingered them to the landowners and bosses. One must wonder if in his account of supposedly persuading these peasants as a group to open up to a Guadalajara sociologist, he was aware of the irony in using the verb 'to confess'. Another day he mentioned that he was enthusiastic about being an actor in my sociological study, and challenged me to reconstruct his life history systematically. He insisted on revising and adding things to what I had written. Rogelio suggested workers for me to interview when he thought their careers were interesting.

In his guest lecture to the research team 'on the *cacicazgo a la alta escuela* and the two-faced nature of the powerful', he described El General as

> something special. Deep inside, he distrusted everyone and was always afraid. For example, in the main house of Sea Turtle Ranch, there was a large rectangular table which he used to screen new workers. El General liked to visit this ranch, and when he arrived and noticed an unfamiliar worker he would immediately ask his military assistants and close relatives about the man. He would not settle for simple answers, and would ask several times in a loud voice, 'Who is that bastard'? Still unsatisfied with the explanations, he would sit at one end of the table in front of the door with his Colt 45 near his right hand and make the worker sit at the other end. Only when he was convinced that there was no risk would he give his approval, afraid that his enemies would send an assassin.

However, Rogelio also credited El General with another side: he was considerate to his workers and identified with them:

> El General liked to recall that he was the son of a poor mother and so he knew what it was like to be abused by the rich. He even suggested that we should not let ourselves be exploited, since the boss (referring to his own son, Osvaldo) was the son of rich people and did not know what it was like to suffer.

Rogelio also gave an account of El General's style of exercising power and the special role he assigned his workers when there were conflicts with *ejidatarios*[12] bordering his land:

Those lands of Sea Turtle Ranch were the best on the coast and much disputed. There were several *ejidos* claiming them. We were taken there as workers and advised to be ready in case of confrontations. We were seen in the region as El General's gunmen, but there were also soldiers working there. The soldiers built the road leading to the ranch. They paved it, using equipment belonging to several government institutions. There was even the rumour that Liz Taylor had given him a piece of land.

This vignette contains a response to the question of the 'pure realism of workers' raised by the American researcher. Other important elements are how workers distance themselves from the researcher; their explanations of how economic and political manoeuvres create inequalities in power and living conditions; and their description of the weakness of power. These elements question the assumption that workers lack a counter-hegemonic discourse. However, I want to concentrate on the methodological implications of researchers' and researched people's biases for coming to terms with political contexts. I also want to reflect on the making of sociological knowledge and the analytical challenges in complex everyday interactions.

The reasons for the sociologist's presence in the tomato fields are not obvious and even ambiguous for others. My self-definition as 'writing a sociological study of farmworkers' evoked attitudes that might either tolerate or undermine my authority. The attitudes expressed ranged from curiosity about my intentions to politically based suspicions of me as a collaborator with the bosses. Eventually I won workers' collaboration in constructing a picture of their views; but not because of some predetermined and systematic research strategy. It was achieved implicitly through negotiated meanings and adaptations. The moments of convergence came when we agreed on the implications of the *cacicazgo a la alta escuela* and when the research team accepted the workers' participation in our meetings. This was not only a tactical measure, but a prerequisite for dialogue that shows how a shared political approach develops and interprets contexts to understand future situations.

Behind the notion of the *cacicazgo a la alta escuela* are issues like violence, political factionalism, restricted economic resources (especially land), exploitation and manipulation. These issues show why workers cannot easily hold radical positions: there is no point in endangering one's livelihood or even physical survival. In short:

for the researcher, Rogelio's description of the *cacicazgo* is a specific instance of a general sociological problem; but for workers it is a traditional description of a local power structure, which is not necessarily generalizable to all circumstances. Even though I adapted my line to the workers' discourse on the *cacicazgo*, I was still not immediately able to grasp all the political issues involved. That is, the workers had not yet undermined my rigidly deterministic explanation of the *cacicazgo* as a general framework for specific practices. They do not conceive of the *cacicazgo* as a deductive theoretical framework that uniformly predicts all practices. Instead, they focus on concrete issues and challenges enacted, involving people deploying concepts in specific contexts. In Chapter 4 I explore what the *cacicazgo* means in the historical regional context.

My American colleague considered that these workers were less politicized, weaker and more apprehensive than in other regions, but this only means that he could not grasp their political insights and that his political concerns had implicit ideological biases: a positivistic belief in the authority of the researcher evidenced in the kind and quality of data collected. This implies that the researcher's access to information is determinant for the analysis. I address this question of methodological accessibility in the following section.

Methodological Accessibility

As we will see in Chapters 3 and 4, tomato work is based on flexible verbal and written subcontracting arrangements and new forms of labour recruitment, particularly of cheap casual labour by women and children (cf. J. Collins 1993:56–60), associated with flexible industrial or marketing strategies. Such forms of labour organization still employ traditional images of centralized organization from historical accounts of *hacendados'* hierarchical power structures. The problem with employing this historical image as an analytical model is that it does not pay attention to the changing dynamics of everyday working situations. Also, ethnographic studies of power are fraught with problems of accessibility (Long 1992:277), which are not confined to the pinnacles of power and decision-making. Moreover, the researcher's theoretical choices shape the sociological narrative.

The Positivistic Padlock

Tom Brass (1989; 1990) argues that there is a barrier of methodological inaccessibility between the researcher and the researched. This barrier prevents the researcher from directly verifying unfree conditions, in Brass' case the *enganche* system (a form of debt-bondage). For Brass, landowner coercion and repression prevent the observer from gaining access to the world of the bonded labourer. Achieving complete understanding is also unlikely if the researcher is confined to a compartment with a positivistic padlock, as Brass seems to be. He argues that the researcher should understand the *modus operandi* of bonded labour relations, witness the labour transaction or at least know the terms of the written 'unfree contract' (Brass 1989:54–5). But this does not go far enough. By giving primacy to the mechanisms of exploitation, he fails to explore labourers' life-worlds and self-understandings. Thus he is blinded by teleological arguments constructed far from the actors involved.

Methodological access does not rest on the simplistic assumption that interacting with informants automatically solves theoretical questions, reveals real-life circumstances and makes it possible to identify with informants (cf. Newby 1977:122). Access means trying to adopt the informants' point of view through a pervasive dialogue that includes both acceptance and criticism of the status quo. Methodological access thus refers to the boundaries of the interaction. This interaction is not limited to gaining access to the world of the researched with a theoretical and methodological apparatus that imports explanatory constructs like gender, ethnicity or class. Nor is it limited to how local conceptions and practical strategies structure access. Neither is it enough to look at the institutional context and the big interventions that achieve dominance or are resisted.

It is also necessary to include the simultaneous interpenetrations in everyday situations. For instance, how do people simultaneously internalize and externalize the issues facing them? What is the communicative interplay in which people both learn from and influence each other? These issues are pertinent for both general social encounters and sociological research in particular. With this perspective one can analyse how people break down barriers in different interactions and take positions in constrained encounters. Although I limit the analysis to structural locations (farmworkers, foremen and researcher), they all exhibit variable, flexible responses to the vicissitudes of everyday life, including sociological intervention.

Theoretical Focus and Methodological Access in Studies of Farmworkers

Before documenting how researchers and informants-as-actors develop strategies for breaking down barriers and constructing *modi operandi* to deal with each other, I wish to sketch some similar problematic situations faced by other social scientists who have studied farmworkers. First, Newby's well-known study of English farmworkers (1977) is pervaded by an unresolved problem: his contrasting interpretations of social constraints. That is, his systemic approach suggests that constraints are imposed uniformly on farmworkers, at the very same time as he is providing empirical evidence of how these workers experience and respond to them differentially. More specifically, he considers that the political economy of British agriculture imposes structural conditions that equally affect farm enterprise and farmworkers (Newby 1977:141). Yet at the same time, he confesses his difficulty in generalizing about farm labour, because workers' social positions in labour hierarchies and productive regimes vary from farm to farm (ibid.:371). Indeed, every constraint (for example, the rural labour market, housing, wages and working conditions) presented many variations. Hence although the rural labour markets were 'nationally determined in certain aspects', they were markedly different according to the region, locality and type of worker involved (ibid.:151).

Danzinger's (1988) account of British farmworkers has similar theoretical problems in attempting to match farmworkers' objective conditions (wages, living conditions, etc.) with contextual features. He ends up restricting his analysis to the capitalist economy without discussing how workers themselves develop understandings and strategies *vis-à-vis* their constraints and opportunities. His analysis of farmworkers' life-worlds treats their work in the capitalist enterprise as separate from the household, religion and recreation.

Turning to Mexican studies of farmworkers, Astorga Lira (1985) seeks a global interpretation of Mexican farm labour, but expresses his disappointment with the contribution of the social sciences to capturing the reality of rural workers:

> Social science does not possess the means to capture in all their importance the situations that men find themselves in: the *peon* who comes to these lands from a distant place, the day labourers who descend from the Sierra de Sonora to the irrigated valleys in the middle of the desert. Social science does not register in its categories the whole range of richness that these human beings experience in real life (1985:27; author's translation).

However, Astorga then reduces sociology to positivist methodology with his dependence on statistical data to characterize shifting labour markets in terms of technological changes, foreign capital flows, the reproduction of the agricultural workforce, and political and institutional factors. He completely fails to address farmworkers' experience or the dialogical relations between them and researchers or other actors. Astorga's caricature of rural workers as 'human commodities . . . condemned to a lack of consciousness' (1985:117–22) is the result of working with the blunt instruments of positivism and interacting with managers instead of the workers he describes.

Other Mexican studies conducted by Paré (1980) and Grammont (1986) in central Mexico recognize the difficulties in elaborating typologies because of farmworkers' heterogeneity. After examining a number of regional and comparative studies, Paré remains doubtful as to the usefulness of case study data for generalizing about Mexican farmworkers. Along with similar works, the studies of Paré and Grammont underscore the need to understand farmworkers' subjective experiences and everyday practices as well as how researchers can draw upon their dialogical experiences with them.

To conclude this section, let me emphasize once more the need for a methodological flexibility that recognizes the essentially local character of the research process. This frees us, initially anyway, from the obligation to produce big inferences. This viewpoint is congruent with Knorr-Cetina's call for methodological situationalism, which she describes as 'the principle which demands that descriptively adequate accounts of large scale social phenomena be grounded in statements about social behaviour in concrete situations' (1988:22; also see Fielding 1988:12). The foregoing discussion of methodological accessibility and the brief literature review concurs with Knorr-Cetina's plea for a more micro-level, reflexive approach to ethnography as broadly described in the last chapter.

Interactive Dynamics

As has been suggested above, fieldwork is everyday politics. Concrete political struggles between researchers and those they research define important research priorities. It is distressing to see that the political relevance of sociological analysis is very often addressed mechanistically in the literature on workers. Indeed much of the literature equates penetrating power centres, labour control mechanisms and their decision-making processes with analytical achievements and political transformations. This book seeks to demonstrate that such a view is simplistic and naive.

Researchers and workers alike shape the multiple realities they address through the bias and distrust depicted in the ethnographic narrative. For both me and the American the disturbing appearance of farmworkers' political backwardness was a conundrum. The politics of fieldwork occurs in complex and variegated situations where unresolvable dilemmas abound. Still, pointing to complexity is no way of escaping difficult questions. Dichotomies like freedom/slavery and progress/backwardness cannot decipher concrete work situations. Nor does it help to ask whether the researcher is coerced or free to save people and stop exploitation or guilty of colluding with exploitative practices for not actively intervening. What does help is to describe how workers manage these situations themselves. This is my aim in presenting the following two ethnographic vignettes.[13] These incidents show the overt and covert political agendas behind everyday interactions between researchers and those being researched. They also allow me to comment further on methodological issues and the theoretical implications from an actor-oriented perspective.

Vignette 1: Lessons for Luis the Teacher from his Students

Luis had been a rural schoolteacher for eight years, and was well known in the state of Jalisco for his political activism. Over a week the following exchange developed between him and a squad of tomato workers, many of whom came from the village where he lives. I had met him four years earlier in another part of Jalisco. He was very committed to peasant struggles, and participated in a group trying to obtain land. Because of his sympathy with workers and interest in the research project, I invited him to work with us as an assistant researcher. He believed workers were a potential force for change, but were at the moment dormant. In any case, he did not rule out the possibility of encouraging some organization among them.

I suggested to Luis that he become a paid member on a squad of thirty-three workers from the village where he lived and worked in order to follow their workday. He liked this idea of doing farm work to understand workers from the inside, and in any case was not afraid of working in the fields because he had often helped his father, a peasant in another region of Jalisco. Some of the workers between nine and fourteen years old were his students or ex-students, and others parents of students. We decided that he would later follow their careers in depth and find out more about their domestic lives. At the end of each day, I would make detailed notes on the basis of his oral report and define issues for further exploration. Luis suggested this procedure because he would not have time to draw up written reports. He was confident that he had earned the workers' trust and respect because he knew many of them from meetings and other activities he organized in the primary school or from his child's kindergarten, where he was president of the Parents' Association.

On his first day at work, Luis was aware of everyone's surprise at seeing a teacher working on the tomatoes. In the truck that was to take them to the fields, the foreman invited him to sit next to the driver. Luis had to manoeuvre to be allowed to climb in the back with the rest who rode standing and or leaning on the rails, the chilly morning air stinging their faces. One of his students asked with both sarcasm and curiosity, 'Are you really going to work, sir?' Others told him they thought it was strange that their teacher should have to work like this. He answered, 'Well, in order to eat one must work.' This stopped the questions, but Luis noticed that his presence had taken them by surprise and provoked a variety of responses. Some prodded others to behave well, nodding towards him as a symbol of correctness and authority. Others tried to get lessons on various subjects. For example, the squad was using special Japanese irrigation pipes, and one worker asked him to explain why the Japanese were so competent. Other people would come to him and disclose personal problems. The illiterate parent of one of his students told him how it was a great feat for him to measure lengths and work with numbers in construction work. He asked for support to learn maths in a more systematic way. The foreman assured Luis that he would not let him get into any of the heavy jobs; but Luis ignored this protective attitude. His aim was to observe closely the details of the workday at first hand, so he did not want any privilege that would keep him from doing so.

The respectful atmosphere only lasted three days, however. To begin with, Luis used the workers' questions to promote his own interests. For instance, when asked about the Japanese, he changed the subject to the recent presidential elections and told them that Cuauhtémoc Cárdenas was the candidate of the poor (*de los jodidos*). They appeared uninterested, and when he pressed further he learned that they had not voted because they had not registered.

One day an ex-student now in secondary school mentioned that her sixth grade teacher had recommended that the class vote for the PRI when they were old enough, because the ruling party was for democracy. Luis retorted that the party was composed of *charros* ('cowboys' or corrupt, unelected leaders) and argued that the PRI's televised propaganda conveyed a democratic image, but things were not really like that. He became increasingly aggressive, asking rhetorically whether they thought they had a good future ahead of them and maintaining that the PRI's sixty years in power had ruined the country. A young boy asked who Luis was for, and he repeated that Cuauhtémoc Cárdenas was the candidate of the poor. The boy continued, 'But sir, the PRI always wins; how is this possible?' Luis could only claim that the reason was massive fraud.

So as not to isolate himself from the group, Luis insisted on doing all the jobs, including tomato planting, which unfortunately he did not know how to do; so in a reversal of the teacher–student power relationship two of his students taught him how, but his pace was so slow that he fell behind from the beginning. When one of the students finished his furrow, he came back to help the teacher. Other workers were murmuring, and Luis overheard a girl say, 'Come on Lidia, help your teacher, it might earn you a 10 in the final exams for fifth grade.'

Luis received comments about the advantages of being a teacher rather than a farmworker, and he noticed that the workers were asking for fewer explanations and instead were now providing these themselves. Complaints arose about other teachers'

behaviour (an indirect criticism of him as a teacher) and the lack
of services in the town. Luis was getting frustrated by the workers'
apathy towards his political lectures. The last day of the week,
he was assigned a hard job without having to manoeuvre for it:
the foreman directly told him to spray pesticides with a hand
pump.

Luis liked the challenge, and it would allow him to work beside
a group of five young men between seventeen and nineteen years
old, one an ex-student, with whom he had had little contact. One
of them commented that he had not been able to finish secondary
school for lack of money. Luis considered that this a good
opportunity for another political lesson, and asked him how he
saw his future prospects. The boy appeared uninterested, and Luis
in his disappointment stopped working to observe the group. Their
movements appeared repetitive and uninteresting to him, until
suddenly he noticed that they were actually writing on the ground
with the pesticide: they would wave their spraying tubes to shoot
the liquid far past the plants themselves. It was a competition to
see what they could write. Luis strained to read what they were
writing: one was forming the letters of the name of a girl he liked;
another was drawing a heart with his girlfriend's initials. They
commented to each other about what they were writing, so Luis
decided to have a try himself. He wrote: 'Vota por Cárdenas'. They
read it slowly and started asking questions about who this man was.
Luis gave a short explanation, after which one of them said: 'What
a pity! If we had known this before, we would have taken the time
to get voters' registration cards, but since we didn't have them we
couldn't vote.' After some conversation, Luis mentioned that he
would not come back to work on Monday and one of the youngest
boys asked him mockingly, 'Don't screw it up, sir, you're not going
to back out now, are you?'

Vignette 2: Lola and the Janus Face of Solidarity

The following is a series of episodes structured as in a relay race
where the baton is passed from hand to hand: as researchers
exhausted their chance to go any further they could only pass on
the experience to a successor. Rogelio, whom we have already
introduced, pointed Lola out to me as 'one of the most skilled
women he had met in the tomato fields'. This alone would have
been enough to get me to meet her and interact with her group,

but Rogelio added that she was a very young unwed mother of two children. When I met her, I was even more curious, for I thought that behind this apparently undernourished woman whose gaze was lost on the horizon were many interwoven life-worlds.

I was only able to speak to her for twenty minutes during work, and she constantly cut herself off. I told her I was interested in writing a sociology book about farmworkers, and since she was a very capable worker I was interested in learning about her experience with the company. However, from the first moment I detected confusion as to my intentions in questioning her: she apparently could find no sense in it, and would give curt answers, obviously in order to get it over with. At that moment a male worker known to blackmail women workers sexually interrupted the conversation and insinuated to Lola: 'Hello, *camote* ['sweet potato', but figuratively 'lover'], you've got yourself one today!'

When he left, I kept trying to get her to talk, but she still seemed to be wondering if my interest in her life meant I was making a pass at her. She gave only direct, simple answers. Then, showing slight curiosity, she asked me what I was going to do with what I had written down in the field. I interpreted this as a way to end the conversation, since I had already explained.

Lola was sixteen years old, and had never lived outside the valley or worked anywhere but for tomato companies. Her only friends were people from work. A woman from the village where she lived had invited her to work for the company. Her family had never had land, and she had only studied until the fifth grade, explaining that she dropped out of school because her teacher was too grouchy. She declared that she saw no sense in marrying, and in any case it is no longer the custom to do so.

I was unable to talk with her again, but I overheard many comments about her. Some young men described her as a tough woman who made the bravest of them lose face when she asked them to make love in the cane fields. One day I saw her playing with a group of boys in a park beside the tomato farm during a break. Next to a swimming pool they had a big barrel, inside which one or two people could stand. The barrel could be turned by walking in it; but it could be turned much faster if pushed from the outside as well, which made it difficult to maintain one's balance inside. Most of the boys fell when the barrel was pushed hard, but Lola kept going. Then she demanded to go it alone and be pushed as hard as possible. She told them to go faster and faster, until the boys pushing cried out for help and three others took turns. A small crowd gathered to watch. I watched her for about five minutes, and all the time she kept her back straight and kept calling for the boys to push harder. I cannot forget her power to create space for herself in spite of the fact that others considered her to be of very low status. She died in the measles epidemic of 1990 for lack of medical attention.

Unfortunately, the gender boundary and my stiff style of carrying out field research prevented me from getting closer to Lola, so I had to pass the baton. At first I thought my wife might take over, since she was doing research in the village where Lola lived. However, her efforts ran into difficulties because she was working with a group of beekeepers, who were mostly wives and daughters of tomato producers who considered Lola to be poor and marginal. Also, Lola identified my wife with the beekeepers, so she was reluctant to open up to her. It was Hilda who took over.

Hilda is a medical doctor and close friend of mine, who had worked many years in Guadalajara working-class neighbourhoods and considered herself to be 'one of the people'. Recently she had been coordinating a health education project geared to housewives and peasant families near the project area. We shared a common concern for renewing the discourse of political activism. To illustrate her class identification and valorization of fieldwork: once we both attended a conference run by a social medicine graduate from the Universidad Metropolitana. The exposition on social epidemiology and the health/sickness process was sophisticated and well ordered. However, Hilda felt uneasy, and constantly made remarks like 'How is it possible for these upper-class ninnies to come and teach us what must be done with el pueblo ('the people') when they don't even know anything about it?' I answered that perhaps it was our own fault, and that people like her who had the knowledge and ability to present the situation in greater depth should take over the podium.

Hilda visited us often while we lived in the valley. She criticized us for having abandoned social practice and getting seduced by academia, but she was interested in the methodology we were trying out and eager to see for herself if it could help better understand the life-worlds of organized groups. She was curious to see what would come of it, and to her surprise interesting things did emerge. This is how she became involved in the project, even though she claimed she was not looking for anything specific to begin with.

Hilda was determined to win Lola's friendship to analyse the life histories of three families of rural workers. At first Hilda managed to establish trust by conversing in a relaxed way with Lola amid her everyday activities at home, playing with her children and helping out whenever she was allowed to.

I present some crucial moments of the relationship between Hilda and Lola (from Hilda's field notes), especially from the time they worked together planting tomatoes. Hilda was not only interested in an academic study, but wanted to feel what the workers like her friend Lola felt: so she decided to approach Lola as another worker. Hilda stressed that her main motive was solidarity. From previous conversations with Lola, Hilda had formulated a basic question: why was Lola's behaviour in the tomato fields so different from the marginality and anonymity of her village life?[14]

Hilda had to get up very early in the morning to meet the rest of the squad and wait for the truck that would take them to the fields. While she was waiting Lola poked her playfully from behind before jumping into the truck. 'You came', she said in a soft, slightly incredulous tone. Hilda was bewildered:

> I didn't know what to do lost in that world of people where all the women were dressed alike with their heads covered. I couldn't even recognize Lola and her friends. I had no idea where to go, but was shoved by the foreman into the truck. I had to obey for fear of losing the job, but I was sure it was a different vehicle from the one Lola had been assigned. Once on our way, I was overjoyed to find Lola in the front line of my truck. It was pure luck!

When they arrived they ate the breakfasts they had brought. Hilda remarked how ridiculous she felt eating quail's eggs and yoghurt while the rest ate tortillas and refried beans. She wanted to share her food, but the other women didn't like what she had. In the field she threw herself enthusiastically into her work job, but was soon far behind the rest. She was supposed to make a hole in the soil with her finger and set each plant carefully into it, but felt useless, tired and angry with her awkwardness. She looked for Lola and discovered she had already finished her row and was chatting with another worker. Hilda realized with desperation that she had only planted a third of the furrow. As she describes it, the day was a real drama:

> Sometimes there was no problem because the earth was soft, but it often happened that I thrust my finger into the soil like the tip of a spear, and found it painfully hitting against a damned stone. The mud had formed a glove over my hand that found its way under my fingernails, and in a short while it was pure Chinese torture. During those hard moments I turned around to look at those surrounding me, and much as I tried to copy their movements I just couldn't manage. I gave up and chose a posture that I felt suited me better: half kneeling, half sitting. That meant I would have to get up, walk and kneel again for each plant, which was a big waste of time.
>
> Each time a damn stone would touch the small bone, where my nerves lie almost at the surface of my skin, I felt a great pain, which cramped my body and made me want to cry. I was meditating on this when I looked up and could not find my measuring stick to measure the distance between plants. Surprised and furious, I asked my neighbour if she had seen it, and she told me a woman had taken it, pointing towards the end of the row. It was Lola. She had taken it and was now helping me plant. With her help I finished quickly and during the moments I rested beside her I felt superior to the rest who had not yet finished. I then realized we had not finished the furrow. There were about three metres to go, so I started working on them. But Lola stopped me, saying that if I finished they would make us help out the others. That meant doing the same for others as Lola had done for me, but I realized she had done it as a special favour. The foreman shouted at us and insisted we quit chatting and go and help the rest. I observed that there was a group of girls who enthusiastically applied themselves to the job as I had, but like me couldn't go faster. So it occurred to me to help one of them, and I did, realizing too late that I had betrayed an unwritten agreement with Lola. In the next furrow I paid dearly for this, since Lola didn't help me out at all.

Scrutinizing Political Agendas

Having related some of the critical circumstances in which encounters between researcher and researched took place, I will now trace some of the underlying political agendas that emerge from these texts. The fact that the students and neighbours of the teacher doing fieldwork were essentially unconvinced by his attempt to reject privileges, get involved in all types of tasks and understand them from the inside highlights his contradictory role in following what was in fact an ulterior agenda geared to helping an absent researcher. Also the teacher's aggressive political harangues revealed his personal political motives and image of the workers as dormant. The workers' explicit questions show that they sensed these contradictions.

Workers' agendas appear more confused. Do they fit the image of political backwardness and apathy? They may readily agree with Luis or me that electoral practices are corrupt and fraudulent, but they are pragmatic in meeting their everyday needs. They are used to talking with the winning politicians of the PRI, from whom they try to extract public services and other benefits in order to improve their living conditions. Thus they are not apathetic. Also they sought to advance their interests as students when they tried to win the teacher's favour. Likewise they got involved in the teachers' disputes over the quality of education and the use of resources in schools, all of which are political matters. Above all they express their disrespect for the bosses' misuse of pesticides by writing with the spraying tubes, as the first vignette shows, and, as the second vignette shows, for their preoccupation with output, by not helping their fellow workers finish their rows, thus ignoring the bosses' production targets.

The combination of secret and open agendas was more intricate in the second vignette. Changing perceptions of the researchers were influenced by both present and absent issues, motivations and strategies. The interaction between researchers and researched was circumscribed by physical, gender and class boundaries; indeed sometimes there was no interaction. Social constructs about Lola, one of those being researched, ranged from 'powerful woman worker' (on the part of the researchers) to 'powerless and invisible girl' (for other workers in her village).

As for the researchers, my plan to write a sociology book about farmworkers, presented as an open agenda, turned out to be largely meaningless in these encounters. Behind Hilda's engagement in the research project lay our initial construct of academia as a block to learning about the research process. Hilda's curiosity about the theoretical merits of an actor-oriented methodology fits with her notion that solidarity and sharing labour with workers were good tactics for understanding workers' life-worlds. However, the worker Lola rejected what the researcher Hilda considered to be solidarity (in the sense of doing what Lola defined as other workers' work) not because of 'false consciousness', but on the contrary because of her political awareness that it was detrimental to workers' interests. Luis' failed attempt to raise political consciousness also reflected differing worker and researcher agendas.

Emerging Political Discourse

The encounters depicted in this chapter highlight how social researchers followed different strategies and combined various forms of intervention (sociological experimentation, political indoctrination and worker solidarity). These differences emerged despite the fact that all the researchers worked within the framework of the same region, research project, topic, and type of labour unit, and occasionally even with the same workers. This shows the difficulty of applying homogeneous strategies, units of analysis and categories. In Autlán-El Grullo each researcher evolved his or her own relationship-building initiatives.[15] This runs counter to the picture of the sociologist who orchestrates social interaction to arrive at the order of things.

The vignettes show how identities, values and interests are changed by research practice. For example, the teacher almost lost the prestige he had formerly enjoyed because he participated in tomato work. The fieldwork interactions manifest different communicative codes, discourses, situational strategies, forms of personal testing, and both philosophical and technical explanations of work practices. Different communicative codes may employ polysemy in different ways: for example, 'hard' may only refer to a particular task for the naive researcher, but also to life as a whole for the worker. Linguistic variation expresses power imbalances and different sociological research tactics. This can be seen in the interaction between Rogelio and me or between the teacher and his pupils in the field.

Tensions frequently arose between researchers and workers when the former's good theoretical and political intentions led them to try altering taken-for-granted power differentials. Both the student workers' disregard of their teacher's political remarks and Rogelio's assertion that political issues were clear to workers and could be directly addressed can be viewed as misinterpretations or even a comedy of errors. There were also moments in which shared understandings emerged: the cooperation between Rogelio and some workers after his invitation to talk with the research team, Luis' final identification and rapport with the student workers, and the unwritten rules Hilda learned from the tomato workers.

Sometimes the dialogical element was externalized through a practical and material medium. As when, the pesticide spray-painting game, the key to communication lay in practical, non-discursive behaviour. Another example occurred when Hilda experienced worker solidarity. Only when Lola refused to give Hilda any further help did Hilda realize that she had broken unwritten rules of solidarity. More than any other event or conversation, this brought home to her an appreciation of work squads' work rhythms, discipline and social hierarchy.

Researchers' individual methodological paths bring out a basic point: the importance of spontaneous friendships as opposed to formal technical means like observation checklists or planned interviews for gaining access to crucial networks and events (although the latter means might still be indispensable at least as a way for researchers to identify themselves). In getting to know workers' everyday, critical social situations the researchers moved through from the camp to the fields to recreation sites. In the process, each came to appreciate workers' perspectives and to rely less on ideal–typical scenarios derived from sociological theory that divide up the workers' social world into formal activity fields such as 'the labour process', 'household reproduction' or 'the strike situation'.

Researchers' 'plunge into the garlic' of the people researched has a political dimension in so far as both parties communicate the complexities of power relationships. For example, they may become cognizant of the weaknesses of the powerful and the power of the weak, who are by consent or coercion part of the power relationship. Here my point of view differs from Schutz' distanced scientific neutrality (1962:54) or Garfinkel and Sacks' methodological indifference (1986:166). Abstaining from personal judgements or striving to be serious will not *per se* ensure acceptance or lead to deeper insights. On the contrary, researchers' claims of ascetic purity are claims of authority that overestimate their ability to empathize and analyse the social context.

There is, then, a new political discourse emerging from between the researcher and the people researched. Their dialectically negotiated agreements on the meanings of words and actions represent numerous politically significant accommodations in which discourse is a circumstantial social product of the particular people involved. As Foucault contends,

Dialogants can hardly agree to be deprived of that discourse in which they wish to be able to say immediately and directly what they think, believe or imagine. They prefer to deny that discourse is a complex differentiated practice, governed by analyzable rules and trans-formations rather than be deprived of that tender, consoling certainty of being able to change, if not the world, if not the life, at least their 'meaning' simply with a fresh word that can come only from themselves, and remain forever close to the source (1977:210).

The Sociological Relevance of Research Encounters

Several questions arise from these encounters. What allows us to characterize such seemingly trivial encounters as sociological? Is it the rough consent to interact that the researcher won from the researched? Is it the shared, overlapping interpretations of actions, interests or processes? Or is that in interactions distinctive socio-logical research concepts develop? Can we identify specific choices or procedures that constitute sociological analysis?

These are not intertwined, not isolated questions. If one accepts that the narratives of these encounters are not objective truth and that researchers can only partially record the people they interact with, then we have to ask more specifically about their significance: what do these encounters tell us about the heterogeneity of farmworkers and their conditions?

As the ethnographic vignettes illustrate, critical circumstances within dialogical encounters shape interactions and change the behaviours of both researcher and researched. This dynamic process generates new perspectives on both researchers' and tomato workers' life-worlds and the research process itself.

Sociological analysis emerges not in definitive answers to these methodological questions, but in the production of the analysis itself. The sociological text is an exercise in which the author recontextualizes the experiences and strategic performances of the research process. The notion of double hermeneutics need not imply a separation of the ethnographic moment from the analysis of findings. The vignettes emphasize that sociological research and analysis are part of the same process.

Analytical reconstruction and the reflexive relationships bet-ween researcher and researched are not cooked up *a posteriori*; they begin in field notes and end in drafts that appropriate words, acts and symbols from memories, recorded voices and filmed motion at desks with computers. Sociological analysis is complex and involves permanent reflection on crucial moments when interlocking theories developed in critical circumstances. Fieldwork also interweaves with other experiences and bodies of knowledge.

To conclude this chapter, I want to emphasize the need to abandon any single context for political discourse on tomato workers. Such discourse expresses heterogeneous ways in which workers organize their life-worlds. Moreover, this heterogeneity is the other side of the disappointment and realism expressed by the American researcher. But heterogeneity is not a magical explanatory word that can by itself substitute for the univocal categories of functionalism and fixed typologies. Heterogeneity should denote variations in strategies that develop in concrete situations. As I have shown in this chapter, such heterogeneity is also a property of the relationships that evolve between researchers and the people they research. This leads us to reassess the central analytical challenge of this book: tomato workers' heterogeneous combinations of resistance, avoidance behaviour and consent at work.

Notes

1. Here I consider De Vries' (1992a:78) suggestion that ethnography is not the isolated product of conversing subjects. Instead, all forms of dialogue involve power imbalances between the conversants, competing discourses and divergent interests.
2. This entails an interpretative interplay between social scientist and those whose activities constitute the subject-matter. Hence 'the theories and findings of social sciences cannot be kept wholly separated from the universe of meanings and action that they are about . . ... Lay actors are themselves social theorists, whose theories help to constitute the activities and institutions that are the object of study of specialized social observers' (Giddens 1984: xxxii–xxxiii; Giddens 1990:314).
3. The life-world has also been described as a fragmentary and momentary representation in social situations. Schutz and Luckmann (1973) write of 'the lived-in and taken-for-granted world' and Habermas (1987:119) of a 'horizon within which communicative actions

are always already moving'. Long revisits these concepts when he proposes conceiving of life-worlds as 'actor rather than observer defined' (Long 1989:247). Turner (1989) further clarifies the issue by defining the life-world as a habitat shared by both researcher and researched in social interaction. Stressing the concrete situation of 'feeling at home', he underlines people's ability to transform their contingent conditions into something liveable.

4. For Latour reflexivity can be achieved by making texts open to multiple interpretations. This contradicts naive beliefs in the authority of scientific texts. He emphasizes that readers and writers are political equals with respect to the explanandum: 'readers seem to be much more devious, much harder to take in, much cleverer in deconstruction . . . than is assumed by writers'. He concludes that 'we need to play down the exoticism of the other' (1988:168).

5. Researchers' authority is relative to particular audiences that can understand specific jargon. De Vries (1992a:80) points out that 'expert' researchers have the luxury of detaching themselves from experience, reflecting upon it and processing it conceptually. Through these authoritative scientific representations we shape bureaucratic policy and rural people's reality.

6. The researcher's authority arises from textual production, what Polier and Roseberry call a 'discourse on the discourse' (1989:252). This notion of authority refers to the distribution of knowledge that helps allocate and maintain credibility (Barnes 1986:185). Authority goes to those who can expect to be believed, at least by certain audiences.

7. De Vries (1992) questions how we can say anything about how others construct their worlds or represent them relative to our research practices. Ethnography should not be a devious method for reintroducing academic authority.

8. *Cacicazgo* refers to a set of relations with a dominant local leader, landowner or local politician (*cacique*). It implies economic and political power, influence and the capacity to manipulate other people's actions. *A la alta escuela* can be translated as 'in high style'.

9. Mely was the first worker with whom I made contact. Later I realized that she held a key job. As the first member of my happenstance research network, she suggested that I contact the workers she considered to be combative in terms of social class.

10. General Marcelino García Barragán had been Mexico's Defence Minister during the bloody repression of 1968. There are many stories about his influence in the region. Some accounts state that except for short periods when he left the political scene, for at least 40 years nobody in the main municipalities of the region became mayor without his approval.

11. Later I realized that when Rogelio said this, he referred to the unsuccessful regional agrarian struggle. His father had been one of the main instigators of the struggle in Autlán, and had always wanted to involve Rogelio and another son. Coincidentally, their land claim included 200 hectares currently being cultivated by the tomato company Rogelio worked for. In 1940 a group of peasants had invaded those lands and was expelled by the army. Several of those properties were in the hands of El General's relatives.

12. *Ejidatarios* are mostly small producers controlling less than 10 hectares of land allocated to them by the government as members of organized agrarian communities.

13. Horacia Fajardo and Miguel Delgado participated in these interactions with workers and offered me their field notes for constructing these accounts.

14. In addition to her low status as a worker, she lived in a small borrowed hut on the edge of the village. She kept very much to herself, and was looked down upon by everyone but tomato workers. The first time I looked for her in the village, people denied her existence. Thus she seemed marginal, invisible and anonymous.

15. De Vries (1992:55) conceives ethnography in terms of building a research network. The relationships that make up this network are multiplex, not single-stranded or univocal. As a result, researchers develop multiple dependencies.

CHAPTER THREE

Tomato Work

Introduction

In this chapter I construct micro-universes to interrelate the activities in different work spaces: fields, greenhouses, administrative offices and packing houses. A study of microlocalities has two ends: to identify how workers appropriate the workplace and to understand the flexibility with which those spaces are transformed on the job. However, the analysis is not limited to microlocalities; it makes connections with macrolocalities where businesses or financial institutions make decisions and where negotiations with regional, national and international institutions take place. The workplace is an important place to analyse the regional tomato industry's social and political organization.

This focus differs from others in which economic considerations are the basis for interpreting work processes as a by-product of the labour market. In fact workdays are not simple, even if they may seem repetitive at first glance. Daily routines can only be understood as part of a more complex network of activities. This entails that identifying factors that explain how conflicts were resolved at a specific time is not sufficient. Nor is it sufficient to find a homogeneous logic based on seriousness and efficiency, because jokes, evasions and disrupting established routine always occur and also require explanation.

My interpretation of tomato industry labour employs two key concepts: heterogeneity and diversity. Heterogeneity characterizes the workers and trusted personnel, who come from all over Mexico. Diversity characterizes the organizational styles of companies subject to daily problems and necessities. The experiences of industrial cultivation and local community socialization are not a homogenizing matrix. Heterogeneity includes differences in age, gender, ethnicity, skill levels, job type and permanence. It is crucial to understand how workers' multiple cultural repertoires shape task and role performance. Organizational schemes in space and time are shaped by worker initiatives, agendas and interpretations. Thus spaces where workers experience dramatic events, seek leisure or try to avoid difficulties have great significance.

This chapter is based on two main sources: workers' descriptions of themselves and their contexts; and my own observations of work situations. It is divided into four parts. The first offers a framework for understanding labour processes in the local/global nexus. The second illustrates different ways of representing work situations. The third explores the spectrum of worker heterogeneity and its relation to the labour market, and the fourth summarizes working conditions in the regional tomato industry.

The Globalization/Localization of Tomato Work

Tomato work is both an economic category and an epistemological/cultural construction. In line with Habermas' notion, labour is 'socially coordinated . . . rooted in culture and bound-up with forms of symbolic interaction' (Pusey 1987:28). Following van der Ploeg's (1990; 1992) approach, I view tomato work as a range of tasks that actors socially construct at work in Autlán-El Grullo valley tomato companies. Viewing tomato work as a social construction embraces productive, reproductive, political and economic relationships. It includes a panorama of practices, interconnected processes, power/knowledge techniques, norms, opinions, experiences, interests and forms of consensus and coordination. These allow for the collective completion of thousands of tasks at different levels and in different time-frames: daily, seasonally and annually. However, representing these facts means excluding others. Newby suggests that 'locating a study of farm workers is fraught with difficulties' (1977:123). Therefore, the goal is not to establish a typical empirical scenario, but to grasp a set of theoretical problems. As Jessop (1990) also stresses, my focus on workers' practices is a search for characteristics that are not determined at a more abstract level. As Marsden and Murdock comment, 'concrete situations have 'emergent properties' which extend beyond the immediate context giving structural regularities an indeterminate quality' (Marsden and Murdock 1990:31).[1]

Contemporary analyses of agricultural production focus on globalization and relocalization (cf. Marsden *et al.* 1992; van der Ploeg 1992). To show the relevance of current globalizing trends, van der Ploeg proposes that

> the actual (although far from complete) submission of agriculture to agribusiness, and to capital in a general sense, would be unthinkable if not accompanied or preceded by a contemporary (or prior) disconnection of farming activities from the local sets of social relations of production. These regulate the mobilisation, allocation and reproduction of land, labour, capital and required non-factor inputs (1992:23).

Thus from a global perspective driven by technological developments, the concrete local setting and entailed relations may disappear and be replaced by artificially created growth factors, general trends and standard procedures (van der Ploeg 1992). These overwhelming trends of technological progress conceal overlapping images of apparently archaic, ideologically condemned characteristics of agricultural labour processes. Despite agro-industry's diversity, innovativeness and flexibility in contracting, mobility of inputs and factors of production, as well as its novel, extended use of telecommunications and computers, everywhere there persists a mixture of advances and 'surviving' social practices with varied forms of exploitation and deprivation. Rural areas continue to be seen as labour reserves where low levels of unionization go hand-in-hand with sophisticated and costly outside expertise. This picture can be summarized as the persistent and increasing vulnerability of rural areas to rapid change (Marsden *et al.* 1992:3).

In the paradoxical process of relocalization, the locality disintegrates owing to alienation by new forms of technological development,[2] but human beings eventually come back to reassert the significance of locality within the discourse on global trends affecting the agricultural labour process. Such a view admits that workers' conditions of existence and reproduction are locally and regionally embedded. Moreover, they have an active role in the reorganization of national and international change, either because of or despite global interconnections. In van der Ploeg's terms relocalization means that the *art de la localité* can be constructed even where internationalization and homogenization dominate. Thus, the locality again becomes relevant, if not critical, for understanding agricultural labour processes. The issue to be examined is how working practices contribute to the emergence of local identities and to continuity or change. It is necessary to examine this theoretical axis of globalization/localization in the context of daily work practices and to see how transformations of working identities are reflected in those practices. This is the theme of the following sections.

The Complexities of Work

From my first day of accompanying workers in their everyday affairs, I got the impression that everything happened very fast. Everyone on the tomato farm seemed engaged in different routines, constantly talking to each other, interpreting orders and taking initiatives. I asked myself how I was going to follow simultaneously crucial issues and situations on five to ten different crews comprising up to 200 workers; remember thousands of words, opinions and characteristics to be recorded; make sense of new situations that constantly arose; and relate these to other events that I had already noted for analysis. Thus I wanted to follow a single methodology in a network including various crews of workers and other individuals. I was constantly losing control as I switched between groups of workers and subtasks.

Yet I cannot say that my notes from this sociological experience in the tomato fields are any less systematic because they analyse specific situations. Nor are they less enlightening because they interpret exploitative moments in the continual dialogue between me, workers and others in everyday contexts. This is not in principle a theoretical weakness. On the contrary, I would argue that concentrating on the concrete brought me to patterns of continuity in everyday labour practices. In this sense, chaos can be beneficial. Moreover, my aim in this section is to show that theorizing does not develop in a vacuum, but is continually constructed, which permits us to orient or simplify ethnographic narrative. The goal is not only to depict complexity or arrive at abstract categories, but to relate them to practice and their verbal representations.

A Visit to the Tomato Field on a Typical Friday

I first interacted with workers on the La Lima farm of the La Rosa Company one morning in November 1987, when most of them were cutting tomatoes. There was a group of workers between the rows of plants where I was walking with Rogelio the *cabo* (overseer) and Alejandro, who was in charge of irrigation. They were accompanying me, answering questions and interrogating me about my motives for visiting the company on orders from Chano, Alejandro's brother and the farm manager. Chano looked very happy that day, and repeatedly used his walkie-talkie – an authority symbol on the farm – to communicate with the owner and other departments of the company. He was hectically driving his pick-up from one end of the eighteen hectares of tomatoes to the other, stopping only to perform tasks or give instructions. At the same time, Rogelio and Alejandro were also keeping an eye on the workers, even though Rogelio explained that they already knew exactly what to do and he trusted them to do it efficiently. He said that the bosses gave absurd orders and 'the workers have a lot of initiative and think well', but feel constrained by the bosses' plans. Specifically, it was often those around the owner in the office doing the daily planning who restricted the workers' creativity and did not take their experience into account.[3]

One of the first questions I put to them concerned some teenage women workers' complaints of getting muddy from excessive water in the furrows. Rogelio said this was because of some absurd instructions from the bosses with which they had to comply. It had only been necessary to keep the soil moist, not swamp it, which hindered the work and made it uncomfortable. Alejandro told me about other absurd orders as Rogelio went to look after his workers. He monitored activities in several furrows, and twice stopped to show young workers how to select and cut ripe tomatoes. He explained that these workers were reluctant to obey his instructions, so he had been showing them how to distinguish the fading of the green at the top of the tomato as a sign of ripeness. When one of the young woman workers responded that the tomatoes were still not ripe, with a strong twist of his hands Rogelio tore a tomato in half. He showed her that the seeds were yellow and commented to me that that was the best moment to harvest a tomato.

The workers followed a clear plan – to cut row by row from the first furrow – and they deployed themselves according to how they completed the daily task block. The workers walked in the same direction coming or going on either side of the furrow, facing each other. An uncertain situation emerged when they tried to organize themselves to choose the furrows on which to start the second task block. At least two of the rows were more difficult to cut because they had numerous fallen plants and others were inundated, so nobody wanted to enter them. Normally, workers prefer to work on rows with fallen plants, because the *cabo* and the farm manager don't pressure them to cut all the ripe fruit, only the most visible ones, so that the workers can advance more quickly. But that day this was not allowed, because there was a good price on the market: so the workers used different tactics to avoid working in the difficult rows. Some slipped off to a nearby cane field, pretending that they had to go to the bathroom, while others tried to hide from the *cabo* and others openly ran and played without paying attention. The scarcity of drinking water was used as a pretext for spending more time waiting for the water carrier, who was usually late. Since no one seemed to want to begin, the *cabo* had to order his more loyal workers to start cutting.

Alejandro left because he had to irrigate the most distant section of the farm and went off with two helpers. The workers nearest to me with whom I was trying to converse now consisted of ten young women workers. They were joking, singing and sometimes playing among themselves. To some extent they were trying to attract the attention of the *cabo* and me. One of them pushed a companion to the ground; and so that everyone would notice she shouted, 'Look! Clara fell down!' Another wasn't doing anything, and complained about the puddles between the rows where she was working. One of the youngest hid herself amid the tallest plants so as to cover her body completely, and challenged Rogelio to figure out what she was doing. 'Maybe I've been playing cards here for ten minutes or more and you haven't noticed it. You're my accomplice; come and see what I'm doing.' Rogelio refused to get involved with her tricks, because other workers had already warned him what she was like.

After two hours, the farm manager approached me for the first time to ask how things were going. He explained that he was very busy at that moment and perhaps at lunch he could see me. He had come to offload plastic boxes at the end of the rows and to carry away full ones. This was an improvised task to replace one of the pick-up trucks that had just broken down. On another occasion he came to check on a group of workers and the voice of the boss's executive secretary could be heard over the walkie-talkie giving him specific instructions. Apparently the boss wanted to increase the quantity of tomatoes cut, and stressed that all saleable tomatoes, including those from fallen plants, had to be cut. She also asked for the approximate number of boxes likely to be filled that day. After the second task-block, a pick-up truck arrived with the woman timekeeper (*checadora de tiempo*) for all the farms. Some nearby workers immediately surrounded her truck and gave her the identification cards they had received at the beginning of the week (see Figure 2). She collected them in three different places. Her task is important for workers, who describe her as 'the one who gives us the day' (*la que nos pasa el día*). In principle nobody fails to present her their card, since not doing so means the company does not recognize their day's work. However, I later found out that her job is sometimes difficult and conflictual, especially in the case of workers who are sick or when she is expected to be an accomplice for workers privileged by the personnel manager, farm manager or *cabos*. Sometimes the company or its agents punish workers with a note on their card docking them the day or even taking away the weekly card. Usually the timekeeper confronts the workers and announces management decisions, so she is the first to receive protests or complaints from the punished workers. That day she confirmed to the farm manager that his estimate of eighty-four workers was correct.

To get a complete picture of a typical workday on a La Rosa Company farm, I needed additional information. I learned from the secretary who controls data on the workers that my visit was on the tenth day of the harvest, close to the peak of production. Three work crews were working. Two of them, with fifty-nine and thirty-five young women workers led by Rogelio and another local *cabo*, had the sole task of cutting tomatoes. The other crew, with eighteen men, mostly from outside the region and led by their own *cabo*, had tasks like lifting plants, arranging the strings for tying them up and applying fertilizer. Another six workers worked under the farm manager: a watchman, a water carrier, two irrigators and two helpers.

The Tomato Season

Considering the complexity and the number of surprises that arise in a workday, analysing an entire season turned out to be more

Figure 2.

difficult than anticipated, and the opportunity to get accurate information was limited. For researchers, access to and talks with good informants are crucial to solving such problems. Good informants are scarce and the researcher is lucky to find them. What characterizes a good informant? To express oneself clearly, concentrate on relevant information and have broad experience in pertinent activities are surely the marks of a good informant. The opportunity to interact with experienced, knowledgeable workers, administrators, and supervisors in principle should give the researcher reliable information.

Even though I collected many descriptions and definitions of the sequence of activities during the tomato season and listened to the main problems of experienced workers, I prefer to use a description by Polo, a young worker who had only been promoted to *cabo* the year before I began my fieldwork, supplemented by my own observations. At the beginning, this young man was afraid of my presence in the field, thinking that I had a hidden agenda for the company owner. After speaking with the foremen and farm manager, he became interested in talking to me.

He had been involved in tomato work for three years, and commented that he had obtained the position of *cabo* without having had particularly good relations with the company owner. This had surprised him. He explained in detail as we walked among the rows of tomatoes how things were organized in a tomato season. His narrative reveals his skills as a tomato worker, his acute understanding of tomato production and, more importantly, a discursive presentation of the practices passed on to him by co-workers, foremen and farm managers during the learning process that all workers ordinarily undergo. His narrative clearly depicts workers' common explanations. These illustrate how they carry out activities in what they consider the obvious or self-evident way.

I met Polo working in the field with his crew of twenty men, who come daily from his village, La Parota, which is one of the more distant in the region, about 100 km.[4] from Autlán. That day he was instructing his crew on how to tie tomato plants to sticks. He informed me the La Rosa Company season began in early summer and ranged from 120 to 150 days. The boss had explained to him that the season depended on the US market, the weather and plant diseases. He then quoted two La Rosa Company criteria for defining the season and its tasks:

All the tasks form a chain because they develop one after another very quickly. There is little time for each one. If you fail to do a task at the right moment, the next task will be affected.[5] Another important point is that the company's main form of organizing is the crew or collective team, ideally composed of up to thirty-five workers, which is considered the most one *cabo* can manage.

Preliminary Tasks

As we were engrossed in a long, structured conversation in the tomato furrows, I thought Polo might get into trouble for not supervising his workers. He replied, like Rogelio and Alejandro, that 'they know very well what to do and it's useless to pressure them'. He proceeded to describe the preliminary tasks, not all of which were performed on the farm, and many of which are consequently not his responsibility but rather that of the people in charge of the greenhouses, the machine shop and the soil laboratory. Polo explained that the greenhouse workers germinate the seeds and take care of the seedlings until they are ready to be planted. The greenhouses are isolated or in protected parts of the company farms. They have sophisticated equipment: sprinklers, fans, water tanks and warehouses (cf. Figure 3). Tomato plants are kept in the greenhouses for a maximum of twenty-five days before being transplanted to the fields. Meanwhile, in the fields a specialized crew of tractor drivers and three farmhands clean and plough the land, which takes one to three days, depending on the size of the farm.

Planting

According to Polo, the most demanding period of work is planting, which starts when the plants are taken from the styrofoam trays in the greenhouse. Planting normally takes ten days, depending on the weather, the size of the plot to be cultivated, the availability of workers and the wetness of the soil. It is crucial that the greenhouse plants be of good quality. The plants are placed in open boxes of solid plastic and are transported in various trucks, which go to the farms that have been prepped and watered. The tractor drivers design and furrow the rows.[6] Polo explained that planting depends very much on the quality of the preceding irrigation. If the land is too dry or wet, the tasks become harder and the risk of losing plants increases.

Planting is done so as to preserve sufficient wetness. Sometimes

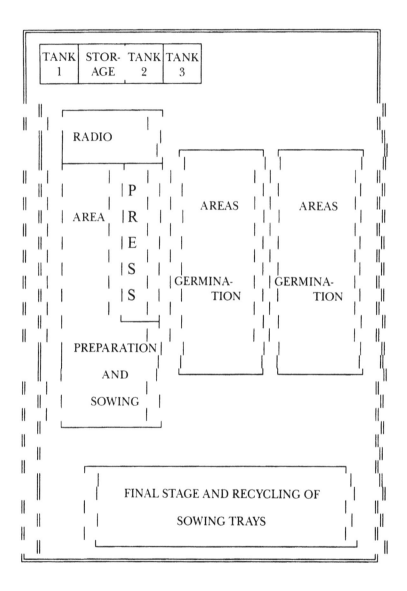

Figure 3. Working spaces within the greenhouse.

the sequence of planting changes because some areas dry out fast. The number and position of people planting depends on the length and evenness of the field. Planting requires precision and manual dexterity to make the 10–15 cm. holes for the plants. Women are deemed better at planting than men. The only tool used is a small stick to measure the distance between plants. Some workers also use the stick to make the hole, but this can slow one down; skilled workers only use their fingers. Normal positioning is as follows: eight women each take one row of a bed; four men each go between two rows to hand out plants to the women on either side. In this phase, the crews of workers are simply called planters (*sembradores*). They receive instructions from the foreman in charge of the crew or the farm manager. The priority is that the hole is large enough to hold all the plant's roots.

Cultivation
After planting come fumigation, hoeing, pruning and more irrigation. Fumigation is done by special crews of tractor drivers (see Figure 4), who work under the direction of an agronomist and the laboratory chiefs. Some *peones* (ordinary workers) report on pests and viruses, and sometimes collect sick plants for laboratory analysis. In stubborn cases fumigation is extended over up to five days. The *peones* spray with manual pumps throughout the cultivation period as necessary. When there are no complications, there are usually two fumigations, and the herbicide is chosen according to economic criteria, not environmental impact – a fact the company staff openly acknowledge. The first application is of *manzate or malathion*, and the next day the more powerful and expensive *methyl parathion* is used.

Cultivation practices changed drastically on farms that had recently installed drip irrigation systems; now some spraying and fertilizer applications came directly through those systems and were controlled by a crew of four workers and head laboratory personnel. Polo explained that, before pruning the plants, there are at least two hoeings, for which male workers are preferred. Hoeing is done in under ten days, after planting when the soil is neither dry nor wet; but it also depends on the amount of weed cover. Crews of twenty-five to thirty workers cover twenty hectares over six days. After hoeing, tractor drivers complete the cultivation by spreading more fertilizer and mounding the furrows.

The next task is pruning. For this, workers have to know the

Figure 4.

variety of tomato planted. For some varieties only the buds are pruned, for others, the foliage. Women workers are preferred for this task. The buds are cut to the level of the first flower. Pruning is combined with tying two plants to 1.2 m. bamboo stakes, which require holes about 50 cm. deep. The task of boring these holes is called the *poceada*. It is one of the heaviest jobs, and is done almost exclusively by male workers.

After pushing the sticks into the ground, the workers who string and tie the plants (*la hilada*) knot the stakes together (see Figure 5). According to Polo, female workers are preferred for this task. These workers are readily distinguished by the reels of string hanging from their waists. Some workers prefer to carry as many reels as they can, while others prefer to step outside the rows to get more reels. Every fifteen metres the *hilada* is interrupted, to avoid the possibility of large numbers of plants' being brought down together. Depending on plant size, up to ten strings can be tied together; but normally there are only six. This system is very delicate: a weak stake or a careless worker required that the plants be straightened and the string be retied. Another company was considering importing hard plastic stakes from the US or Japan, but had not yet done so because of the cost.

Sometimes plants do not grow straight, and develop other shoots. These are called *retoño mamón* (sucking buds) or *cogollo nacido* (sprouters). This entails further pruning, and can cause delay. Sometimes hoeing also needs to be done more than once or twice, although all cultivation tasks stop when most of the fruit reaches maturity.

The Harvest

The length of the harvest varies according to market conditions, the health of the plants and the availability of labour, which can be very unstable and sometimes becomes the crucial factor. The crews are simply called cutters (*cortadores*) (Figure 6). There is no declared preference for men or women.[7] Polo described different ways of organizing and controlling the crews. Some worked without pressure, following a normal pace for a particular shift length. Others did piecework (*trabajo por tarea*), with targets of 10, 20 or 30 kg. boxes per task block. The number of boxes per worker per day ranges from twenty to thirty-five (600 to 1050 kg.).

At the peak of production on the farm where Polo was working, 125 cutters worked on eighteen hectares, whereas at the beginning

Figure 5.

Figure 6.

and end of the harvest, only sixty-eight workers were involved (see Table 1).

The harvest stops when company owners consider that it is no longer profitable.[8] However, sometimes the harvest is extended for over a month. Polo explained that tomato cutters' main task is to look for tomatoes that have reached maturation point (*alcanzado el corte*). Bosses and farm managers repeatedly stress cutting tomatoes at the right time; they argue that tomatoes have to survive a lot of handling in under eight days before being sold. Especially when the possibilities of selling on the US market diminish, the company orders tomatoes to be cut for national consumption when they are turning red (*coloradeándose*).

Tomato Packing
The packing plant is organized like a factory. Workers are more confined to a single position and are frequently required to work overtime at least half the days during peak times. Their working conditions appear to be better than in the field: the packing plant is ventilated and covered by an enormous roof. They also receive from 5 to 10 per cent more pay than field *peones*.[9] Most of these workers belong to a trade union, but describe it as 'tame' and 'white' (false).[10] They regarded the unions as being directly supervised by the company owner, and therefore useless for defending their rights; they were only deemed to be good for taking their money (weekly dues were 2 per cent of gross salary) and for composing a list of workers. As long as one is on this list one can expect to work until the end of the season. The packing plant is only open for two months; workers do not pack all that time, and not all of them may participate during a season, depending on the size of the harvest.

Table 1. The Harvest on Polo's Farm, Boxes per Day

Day	Boxes	Day	Boxes	Day	Boxes
1	83	8	700	14	900
2	150	9	1245	15	780
3	233	10	1429	16	550
4	356	11	1495	17	325
5	328	12	1350	18	140
6	451	13	1220	19	7
7	600				

Most packing plant workers are skilled women from various regions of Mexico, although some of them have been living in Autlán for many years. Others are itinerant workers who follow the harvests north: from November to January they stay in Autlán; from January to May they go up to Sinaloa, Sonora and Baja California in the North-west; from September to November they go to Tamaulipas and San Luis Potosí in the North-east or Guanajuato, Morelos and Hidalgo in Central Mexico (see Map 2). Within the packing plant, workers are organized by circuits following the conveyor belts, on which tomatoes are classified by size, colour and condition. The best tomatoes are export quality; first and second class are for the national market; and third class is for regional consumption. But the criteria can vary (see Table 2). In the 1988 season, 235 workers worked in the packing plant in at least eight different job categories: general plant supervisor, his assistant (equivalent to a field *cabo*), carriers, boxmakers and assemblers (mainly men), selectors, classifiers and packers (mainly women).[11]

Company Institutional Styles and Worker Heterogeneity

Workday Priorities

This section and the following one interpret daily work interactions. Each activity reflects the great diversity of interests that converge at work, whether they be activities of workers in different departments or agents of different market levels or of commercial firms that deal with tomatoes and the inputs for producing them.

Table 2. Market Destination of Tomato Production (1985 Season, in Tons)

Quality	%	Local	Guadalajara	Mexico	Monterrey	USA
export	30.0					13,264
first	25.4			2,962	7,405	
second	23.4		2,962	7,405		
third	20.1	2,962				
unsold	3.1	1,150				

Source: SARH Report, March 1987 (approximate data).

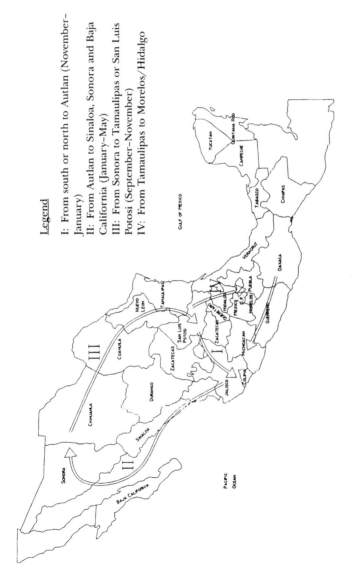

Legend

I: From south or north to Autlan (November–January)
II: From Autlan to Sinaloa, Sonora and Baja California (January–May)
III: From Sonora to Tamaulipas or San Luis Potosi (September–November)
IV: From Tamaulipas to Morelos/Hidalgo

Map 2. The cyclical migration of tomato packers.

Therefore even fragmentary everyday interactions include various offices, communities, camps, neighbourhoods, housing developments and schools.

All rural workers' lives – not just those of trusted employees or bosses – are complex, because in their interactions they share histories, values and cultural repertoires. There are diverse meanings behind explicit and implicit daily negotiations about sanitation problems, worker conflicts, reaffirming traditions, planning strategies, task implementation and space allocation. The work routine is never negotiated in a vacuum, and can be multiply motivated, but nothing about these daily interactions is trivial: they can be crucial for attaining tomato company goals and worker interests.

In the tomato fields, agendas and work plans are redesigned and negotiated every day, and before entering the fields workers must deal with household and community issues. Tomato workers start their workday between 4.30 and 5.30 a.m., depending on the location of their neighbourhoods and villages (see Figure 7 on the daily routine). The extent of involvement in other work depends on the distance and transportation quality between tomato farm and home community. These other tasks, like women workers' piecework sewing and embroidery or male workers' rural crafts, are carried out before, during and after work hours: thus a double or triple workday. Household activities, like food preparation, clothes-making, childcare, and marital and neighbourhood affairs, are the main concerns of female workers. It is not uncommon for male workers to begin very early in the morning and do a second job after work, such as trading, bricklaying, herding cattle, harvesting maize, helping butchers and transporting food and other goods.

Workers acknowledge the definition of workday priorities to be the prerogative of the company owners and managers.[12] These priorities include how to interpret when they have *alcanzado el corte*, which depends on individual and company factors but more importantly on US, national and local market conditions, weather, and regional technical, social and organizational conflicts – patterns of accommodation and pacing. Some workers described how workday priorities were discussed at the La Rosa Company following the rules set down by the former American owner twelve years earlier. There were short meetings every morning involving all the farm managers and foremen before they started work in

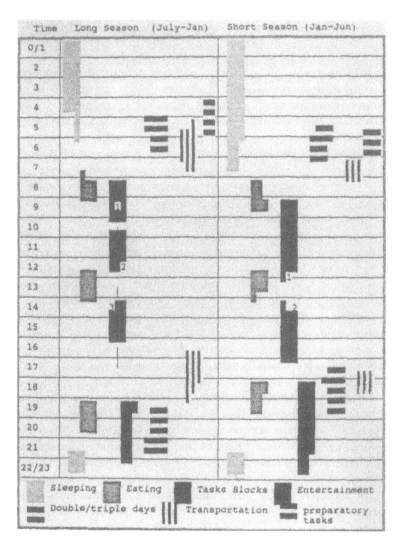

Figure 7. Daily rhythm and farming of tomato workers.

the field. Since then a more centralized procedure, involving only the new Mexican boss, two agronomists (the woman in charge of the laboratory and the man in charge of applying pesticides) and the man in charge of labour management (see Appendix 2 flow-chart), had taken the place of these. In contrast, in the Aréchiga Company the boss was both agronomist and timekeeper, and almost single-handedly decided on the daily schedule.

In both companies the pace of work depended on workers' responsiveness and initiative. Although the placement of workers in the workspace may formally comply with requirements, it does not always correspond to company planning: it is adjusted through explicit or implicit negotiation. Specialized workers may perform ordinary tasks and ordinary workers may do more skilled work. Sometimes workers or bosses introduce unexpected changes into the routine, as when a farm or packing plant is subdivided. For example, a section needing fumigation may be isolated from other sections; an area where rows of plants have fallen or been damaged may need most workers' attention for a whole day; part of the storage area may be converted to house skilled workers, to prepare extra inputs, or as a dance floor for a party; the machinery and tool area becomes a temporary storage area; the pump shed becomes a provisional packing plant; cultivated rows are used for leisure or for simultaneously completing three different tasks (culti-vation, tying up plants and harvesting); the eating area is moved according to the sun, the weather or fumigation; the owner's or farm manager's house is used for meetings or administration or as a guesthouse.

One incident clearly shows how the workers' spatial positioning contradicted the notion that the boss sets priorities, though their revision eventually served his interests. Ten minutes after the workday began at the Aréchiga Company, the workers were about to cut tomatoes as they had the day before. The boss came to tell the *cabo* who was acting farm manager that the workday plan had to be changed to take advantage of apparent stability in tomato prices on the US market. He ordered that workers be redistributed to tie up the thousands of fallen plants to avoid losing those tomatoes. Since these were the harvest's peak days, the *cabo* argued, 'More tomato will be lost if we stop cutting. We have to think about the whole farm and not just one area.' He gave him the concrete example of another occasion on which they put a group of workers to other tasks and the same boss had complained that more fruit was getting lost because it wasn't getting cut in time. The *cabo* added, 'You know because you as the authority have to make the decision.' The boss opted for supporting the *cabo*, and in that sense the workers' self-positioning prevailed.

Reassessing the Heterogeneity of Tomato Workers

We might suppose that workers' role in decision-making reflects heterogeneous behaviour embodied in life-worlds, cultural expressions, physical conditions, agendas and strategies. However, heterogeneity is not necessarily *a priori* for all workers, because we can only apprehend heterogeneity when it appears in face-to-face social interaction. It has to be seen as constant adaptation to circumstances, and it follows various paths. But circumstantiality is not the whole picture: people also act according to broader patterns. Thus more precise information on the workforce is required to understand the labour market or what others have called the fabric of *peones* (Astorga Lira 1985).

Counting Hands

Newby (1977) characterizes British farmworkers by the notion of social invisibility. This also aptly describes Mexican farmworkers in their circumstances. On the one hand, most of them are transported in trucks like cattle from their homes to the tomato fields, while key workers and company staff use vans and buses; on the other hand, they are socially invisible owing to their families' isolation. The places they inhabit have denigrating nicknames because of the poor housing in peripheral areas of town and the fact that their work achievements are not acknowledged like those of the owners (see Figure 8). Indeed, company management simply calls workers 'hands' (*manos*), as in English. But to count the thousands of hands at any point in the season is complicated. For this reason, the region's first tomato worker census is revealing.

Company personnel acknowledged that for many years nobody in the region had been able to count precisely the number of workers employed over the whole season or at different stages of production.[13] The first actual census of tomato workers in the region resulted from a joint effort by the Growers Association and the Mexican–Dutch research project. The researchers were always asking the companies for more precise data on the number and

Figure 8.

type of workers. For some owners this knowledge was a way of averting competition among companies searching for workers during critical shortages. The owners tried to turn the research team's constant requests for data to their advantage. After an agreement between one researcher and the Growers Association, a census was organized for the 1988 season and carried out over two days in November with company financial support.

The census indicates the number of tomato workers in the region; their gender, age, social status and job differences; how many are migrants; and their geographic origins. Counting the workers was surprisingly difficult, and required defining categories. For instance, it was hard to avoid double counting because of worker mobility: some were in two or more fields on the same day. To make the count more accurate, we made a direct count in the field and compared it to company data. On some farms the data were less reliable when the harvest was peaking, because the workers moved around constantly. Discrepancies between the census data and the payroll or other internal company information were incredibly numerous. I corroborated this with the La Rosa and Los Leones Companies. In the La Rosa Company, 767 more workers were registered for the whole season and than were counted by the census.[14] The Los Leones Company personnel manager commented that fluctuations had been enormous, and had hurt them at least five times that season. In a one-week period some 300 migrant workers from southern Mexico withdrew to attend traditional fiestas or had been hired by other companies offering higher wages. Thus, in the week when the census was carried out, they had 400 fewer workers.

The census reported that during two days of the 1988 harvest: (1) 4,735 tomato workers cultivated 1,367 hectares[15] for over twenty supervisors in the four main regional companies (La Rosa, Vergeles, Leones and Aréchiga); (2) 44.5 per cent (2,107) of these workers were women; (3) 86.0 per cent (4,105) of the workers were between eight and twenty-four years old, and 37.2 per cent (1,765) were under fifteen and therefore illegal; (4) 71.0 per cent (3,361) were temporary workers cutting tomatoes, whereas only 2.7 per cent (127) were skilled or administrative personnel like managers, accountants and supervisors, and of these a mere ten (7.9 per cent) were women; (5) of the 3,792 (80.1 per cent) working on the farms, only 231 (4.9 per cent of the total) were key workers like farm managers, foremen, and heads of irrigation and storage, whereas

942 worked in packing plants, departments and administrative offices, with jobs as secretaries, truck drivers, tractor drivers and specialized crews, etc.; and (6) 65.0 per cent (3,076) were from Jalisco and 35.5 per cent (1,659) from ten other states in Mexico.

For Grammont (1986) migrants are labourers who cannot return home at the weekend. This implies qualitative changes in working conditions, wages and cultural communication. On the other hand, local workers continue to have daily interaction with their homes and communities. Also there is an important difference between internal and external migration; this differentiates workers from other parts of Jalisco who can return home at the end of the workday from those who have to live in camps and temporary shelters.

Internal migrants come from diverse communities (see Map 3). In Autlán there are fewer workers from nearby villages and *ejidos* than from the principal towns of the region like El Grullo and Autlán.[16] There were 1,953 workers from these towns. Of all the tomato workers, 64 per cent (3,014) were Jalisco residents. Most skilled workers and staff as well as most of the illegal child and young student workers are in this group.[17] External migrants include workers from other states (see Map 4). Most of them (56.8 per cent) came from Aguascalientes and San Luis Potosí, whose rain-fed agriculture is similar to Autlán's. The Leones Company personnel manager stated that crews from San Luis Potosí and Aguascalientes are convenient because they are the most inclined to work and least likely to rebel. Indian workers from Guerrero and Oaxaca, who speak Native languages, were a second important group, but this manager described them as quarrelsome, quick to rebel or to go work for other companies, drug users and thieves. The 7 per cent from Sinaloa are among the skilled packers; these are itinerant workers who follow the harvest to different regions.

The census generalized tasks that in company registers are more clearly specified. It did not look at union membership, because of the unions' reputations. According to union data, in 1988 only 543 workers (11.5 per cent) were registered, and all of them worked in the La Rosa and Vergeles packing plants.

Labour Recruitment and the Labour Market

The literature on farmworkers generally describes the labour market as a quasi-mechanical system with unitary relationships

AYUTLA
3.0 %

UNION DE TULA
5.6 %

TONAYA
1.7 %

EL LIMON
2 %

EL GRULLO
11.2 %

CASIMIRO CASTILLO
6.3 %

TUXCACUESCO
2.2 %

CUAUTITLAN
5.2 %   AUTLAN
53.6 %   TOLIMAN
5.6 %

Source: Gonzalez, Humberto (1988). *Census of tomato workers.*

Map 3. Origin of the workers from Jalisco.

between buyers and sellers (cf. Marsden *et al.* 1992:11). Astorga
Lira (1985) looks upon the labour market as an exclusively
economic process in peripheral zones that produce *peones* for a
general labour market.[18] Brass (1990:52) shows how non-market
mechanisms like *enganche* bind peasants' labour power to particular
businesses. *Enganche* as practised in the Andes is a debt-bondage
system in which cash is advanced to peasants for emergencies like
funerals or religious *fiestas*. The borrower or a relative works the
debt off in mines or farms over a contractually stipulated period.
Sometimes the money is given to an intermediary with the job of
getting the peasant in debt and drawing up a contract. As Brass
comments, 'like slavery, this relationship entails the loss on the part
of a debtor and his family of the right to sell their labour-power at
prevailing free market rates during the period of bondage'. Fiona

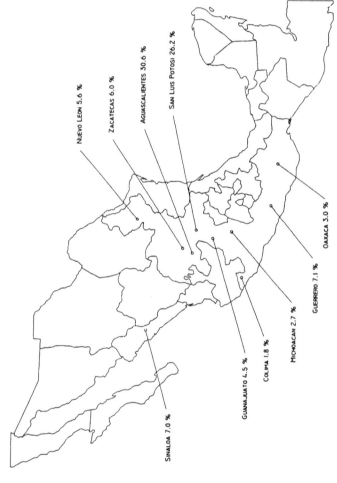

NUEVO LEON 5.6 %

ZACATECAS 6.0 %

AGUASCALIENTES 30.6 %

SAN LUIS POTOSI 26.2 %

SINALOA 7.0 %

GUANAJUATO 4.5 %

COLIMA 1.8 %

MICHOACAN 2.7 %

GUERRERO 7.1 %

OAXACA 3.0 %

Source: Gonzalez, Humberto (1988). *Census of tomato workers.*

Map 4. Origin of the (external migratory) workers.

Wilson (1986:3) documents a number of flexible means of operating the labour system with 'labour contractors, *enganchadores*,
paternalistic measures, wage increases, wage advances and in rare
cases debt bondage'.[19] For Mexico, Hirata describes a yearly
pattern of seasonal migration from poor peripheral mountain
regions to the prosperous valleys of Sinaloa:

> The period of time that highland inhabitants work their parcels is five
> to six months of the year. Most commonly, as soon as they harvest they
> have to look for work in other activities elsewhere in other regions.
> After maize or bean harvest they go down to the valleys to sign up for
> tomato planting. Labour recruiters, businesses and local authorities
> make extensive use of the media to ask thousands of people to come to
> work. When some problem (like the campaign against drug dealers)
> interrupts the migratory flow, as happened in 1983, workers become
> scarce, with the result that thousands of hectares are lost. People go
> back to the mountains when it is time to cultivate their own lands in
> February or March. This ritual is repeated every year; some groups leave
> and others stay. However, the more modern and affluent lifestyle in
> two or three valley urban centres remains very attractive (Hirata *et al.*
> 1986:105; author's translation).

Underlying such discussions of agricultural labour supply and
demand are images of rigid control exercised by employers over
worker recruitment and deployment. Hence the system is built on
the theoretical assumption that the prevailing centres of capitalist
production dominate the so-called peripheral economies. However, such a view is one-sided, because it emphasizes external
forces over workers' dynamic livelihood strategies. An alternative
interpretation would explore how planned efforts to hire workers
and workers' own self-employment practices are related. Workers
are not only cheap labour with little opportunity to negotiate their
wage, but capable and knowledgeable persons with particular skills
and commitments. They are also highly differentiated by gender,
class, ethnicity and economic status, as well as involved in various
power relationships. Low-status workers can be influential, so
one-way interpretations of the tomato industry labour market are
unsatisfactory. Workers and entrepreneurs agree that not enough
is done to ensure the recruitment of sufficient labour each year.
The labour market is more than a regional ghetto or closed system
of control; it is related to complex social, economic and political
processes (Summers, Horton and Gringeri 1990). As both workers

and company representatives say, the tomato labour market combines globalization and relocalization (cf. Marsden *et al.* 1990b and 1992; van der Ploeg 1992).

Hiring and Work

Crews of workers organize themselves in their home communities:

> Following their customs and proclivities, many workers approach the companies for work. They're motivated by the nearness of friends and relatives who help them in their effort to survive. If there are no major difficulties they can make up a group of more than two families. When the group sets up and stays together for a time, it can grow even more until it becomes a true crew which includes people from other localities.[20]

One Aréchiga Company *cabo* explained that ever since industrial horticulture came to the region, it has been thought that if a *cabo* did not know how to 'hook' (*enganchar*) or otherwise manage to interest a significant group of workers, he was considered practically useless. 'The selected *cabo*', he said 'has to try and contact as many workers as he can to justify his position. If he is capable of hiring a group as big as or bigger than the previous year he can continue to hold that position.' But these spontaneous organizational processes are not enough. One of the oldest workers explained that labour market fluctuations depend on variations in the area cultivated, which can exhaust locally available labour and give rise to planned recruitment. Workers seeking employment and companies seeking labour converge to extend labour recruitment beyond the region's traditional boundaries. Every year companies and workers make new contacts and set up networks in more distant regions of Mexico. Workers' descriptions of their search for work elucidate economic and social networks as well as the interaction between spontaneous and planned features. As a former timekeeper put it,

> Some people came to work accidentally. They heard information from the networks of tomato workers in other regions. These workers began with the idea of working for a short period without greater commitments. Other groups came to look for work when the sugarcane harvest ended in another region. Yet others come to Autlán after fulfilling their obligations as *ejidatarios*. These are the ones who sometimes stay on

for a whole season and manage to establish good relationships within the company. After working for one or two seasons they were asked to take responsibility for recruiting other workers. This way, several have become professional *enganchadores* who dedicate themselves to recruiting workers year after year.

This is not to assert that tomato companies lack established practices for dealing with uncertainties. They appoint special people to extend the search for workers to new regions. Nevertheless, the histories of those involved in searching for workers indicate that this recruiting practice[21] depends very much on specific circumstances that change every year. For instance, the La Rosa Company personnel manager travelled to different regions of Mexico in search of workers. He tried to contact the workers at their current workplaces, and discovered that they had already left for their home communities or had moved on to another labour centre. Knowing that people had few employment opportunities and poor land, he would invite people through the local media to come to work for the La Rosa Company, with mixed results. Some of those who eventually worked for the La Rosa company became very good recruiters in their regions of origin. Later his tactic was to target local *ejido* authorities and municipal representatives, who were very good at giving him tips about people looking for work. He preferred people organized in crews around well-known leaders, who were in most cases incorporated as foremen. He explained that the companies like to maintain relations with these distant workers and offer special prerequisites like extra salary, drinks and food for their families. However, this can have negative effects, because it can antagonize local workers.

Other recruiters described how companies established a system somewhat similar to but more flexible than Brass' *enganche* system: they lent money in advance to pay for transportation and food. The personnel manager or sometimes the boss himself would promise extra food allowances, shelter, parties, drinks, and payment for overtime or piecework. However, they asserted that such promises had the opposite effect when they were not kept. The promises unkept for many years in the region have to do with company housing, which in most cases is totally inadequate. Normally workers who come to work in Autlán cannot quit until they have paid back the money borrowed in advance. Workers describe this as very advantageous for the companies, but not definitively so, since they can change companies or simply go back to where they came from. Workers and entrepreneurs agree that companies are always under pressure to solve labour problems.[22] Entrepreneurs complain that worker shortages and mismanagement are why companies lose money, tomatoes and marketing opportunities. Another complaint of entrepreneurs is the labour piracy they suffer from other companies.

Hiring workers depends very much on the confidence between workers and company representatives. This became clear to me when I was talking with one of the most successful labour recruiters. That year, he had recruited 235 workers from San Luis Potosí, a day's bus-ride away. He had worked in Autlán for over five consecutive years. When asked about the procedure for recruiting workers, he found this question uninteresting and did not want to answer it, because he was angry about what he called the company's most recent 'robbery': not recognizing two days of overtime. He explained that this provoked a wildcat strike that lasted almost a whole day. At first, the workers blamed the time-keeper, but later concluded that the boss and the personnel manager were responsible. He complained that the company did not appreciate everything he did to look for workers, and that they caused him trouble because the most active strikers did not understand his accommodating attitude toward the company. He thought that the company was taking advantage because the tomato harvest was nearly finished. At that stage of the season, it was easier to risk losing fruit. After calming down, he explained to me that when the company needs workers, money is no object. They had phoned him many times to promise him extra benefits if he recruited more workers. He normally received the equivalent of $1,500 in advance to hire buses to transport people. This represented an enormous responsibility for him, and sometimes he could not sleep for fear of getting robbed and being unable to repay the money. Brokers like him are vulnerable to fluctuations in the labour market, to worker attitudes and to unforeseen losses.

The Complexities of Work Situations

In the foregoing overview of the workday, the tomato season, the setting of priorities and the labour market, I have examined from different angles the complexities of the labour process, in which changes in time and space interact with worker heterogeneity. The first part stressed the spontaneity of daily work. The second traced medium and long-term aspects of tomato work. The third focused on the mutual shaping of daily plans and improvisations in cultural discourse and socio-historical contexts. The fourth statistically analyses the labour force, and the fifth maps the mechanics of the labour market with worker and entrepreneur narratives.

I now interpret the dynamic character of the workplace. The position workers take up in the tomato rows, which corresponds with coordinated activities, appears as quite disorderly and serves many purposes. Hence, in order to unify daily work situations analytically and work out the rationales in the different placements of workers, I concentrate on the various ways they execute tasks, the gendered nature of tasks, the status and responsibility attached to them, and the relocalization of tomato work.

What Must Be Done in Tomato Work

There are as many definitions of the tomato work tasks done during a given day or season as there are workers. The best way to characterize this diversity is to identify the different ways of understanding tasks and working arrangements. I do this by examining three sets of notions that workers and staff use when dealing with production resources.

The first concerns the different means of apprehending the natural world: through plants, water, terrain, tools and above all tomatoes. Differences are expressed in terms of preference, essence and utility among other factors. Regardless of managers' different views, it is their business to see the natural world as manageable and profitable. Their concerns are related to productivity, scarcity, competence, losses and disease, which affect their earnings. Their notions of and relation to plants, tools and tomatoes are thus mediated by calculations of cost, time, and knowledge about final destinations and consumption.

Workers' concepts about the natural world vary greatly. In general, workers are more afraid than managers of pesticides' effects, not only as personal health risks and impediments to work, but because they believe their environment is deteriorating. Some are more concerned with making a living from tomatoes, and treat them as friends. Other groups more inclined to enjoying themselves and making their job as painless as possible have a more

utilitarian attitude toward the natural world. They like to appropriate rare tools as trophies and to use on other jobs. During
the harvest, tomato workers consume ripe tomatoes in their own
households or sell them locally. These are ordinary ways of
expropriating production – their way of rejecting the company's
planned final destination for the produce.

The second set of notions concerns the changing character
of tomato work and its negotiation, especially when technical
equipment is involved. For instance, when they collect sick plants
or do extra fumigations, department heads bring in workers from
other farms without consulting the *cabos*. Similarly managers and
cabos may appropriate central department resources like pick-up
trucks and tractors. This often entails altering the company´s daily
organizational chart. Whether seen from the perspective of the
central departments or of the specific farms, coordinating responsibility, roles and task sequencing cannot be rigid. Managing scarce
company resources, resolving organizational problems, controlling
plant health and mitigating climatic conditions cannot happen
without coordinated effort and willingness on the part of workers
and managers. It is easier to understand the motives informing
routine procedures by examining concrete tomato work situations
than by analysing central office plans. The biggest problem is not
the completeness of formal charts or work itineraries at the head
office, but what happens in on the ground on and between farms.
This applies especially to labour problems in terms of supply
and organization, and is mainly achieved through close contact:
(1) between *cabo* and networks of crew or *peones* or between
farm managers and department heads; and (2) by walkie-talkie and
management or migrant leader visits or less commonly by foremen
and workers doing specialized work. Through these networks of
concrete relations, problems are solved, communication is maintained between the central administration and the various levels
of the farm, and company plans are reformulated or ignored.

The extent and content of problem-solving depends on technical
problems in the situation and each company's priorities. The
Aréchiga Company, for example, is less rigid than most in its plans
regarding worker placement. But despite the differences at the
company level, on-the-ground problems get solved in a similar
pragmatic way. At the Aréchiga Company, workers resisted being
placed in some rows not because they were wet, but because of
prickly grass, which slows down the transport of tomato boxes and

makes it harder. However, the Aréchiga and La Rosa Company *cabos*' approaches were pragmatic; they rallied the best workers to support them in finishing the job, redrew the row plan and rotated the work – something quite beyond the planners' vision.

The third set of notions concerns workers' and the staff's use of power and knowledge. The definition and performance of tasks show how management decisions and positions affect the spatial array of workers. It is not enough to ask if workers are in their correct places and working efficiently. One must also look at how workers comply with company orders in terms of how they interpret affinity, strategy, commitment, marketing and organization. Sometimes workers withdraw from a situation or mock the *cabo*. Re-establishing order then depends more on kinship and other ties, like those to the *cabo* and management. Workers accommodate themselves to tasks and to migration through networks and knowledge. Instructions may be interpreted as hostile words from far away or as tantamount to talking with comrades in the rows. A relaxed environment may not reflect workers' planned strategy, but rather pragmatic outcomes like avoiding mud or seeking rows with fallen plants. Resistance can begin with one or two workers' simple refusal, yet eventually involve the whole farm. Knowledge of the market, working conditions, financial transactions and political relationships make bosses and managers provisionally more able to define tasks and priorities; but these are mediated by *cabos* who use personal relationships with workers to get unpopular tasks accepted, timekeepers who use the cards to sanction workers, unions managing lists of workers in the packing plant, and labour recruiters who know the details of labour availability. These mediation processes are critical to securing support and defusing conflict.

The Gendering of Tasks

Women make up almost half the tomato labour force, and, as we have seen, some tasks are gender-specific. Gender differences depend on specific task conditions and criteria, even though these are not blueprints. There is a shifting cultural construction of labour depending on circumstances. For example, both men and women hoe in different contexts. In Autlán hoeing concerns the changing character and contexts of tomato work and their negotiation, especially when technical equipment is involved. For instance, when they collect sick plants or do extra fumigations, department heads bring in workers from other farms without consulting the *cabos*. Similarly, managers and *cabos* may appropriate central department resources like pick-up trucks and tractors. This often entails altering the company's daily organizational chart. Whether seen from the perspective of the central departments or of the specific farms, coordinating responsibility, roles and task sequencing cannot be rigid.

Managing scarce company resources, resolving organizational problems, controlling plant health and mitigating climatic conditions cannot happen without coordinated effort and willingness on the part of workers and managers. It is easier to understand the motives confining routine procedures almost exclusively to male workers when they are seen to require more physical strength; but in Ixmiquilpan (Grammont 1986) both male and females do the hoeing, because women are paid less and easier to manage; efficiency is not given much importance. Bourdieu (1977) observes that hoeing for basic crop cultivation in Algeria is exclusively a woman's job. Martinez Alier (1971:87) notes that in Andalusia the definition of women's tasks varies according to economic, political and cultural criteria such as 'women are more docile than men', 'women are better at tasks which involve bending at the waist', 'women work more meticulously and are easier to supervise', or in general women are better suited to 'all tasks which require stooping or are light work'.

In Autlán, women are generally preferred for at least three tasks: planting, tying and pruning, on the basis of perceived differences in physical strength and skill. Planting requires accuracy and strong fingers to make holes that will cover each plant's roots. Pruning and tying plants calls for precision. A woman's light touch is valued for cutting young shoots and foliage and tying the right number of knots.

Making large holes for rods is seen as the heaviest task in tomato work, and requires another kind of strength; it is considered to be a more male task. For applying pesticides and driving tractors or trucks, the situation is more ambiguous, as experience, expertise and access to technological information are the valued traits. Women can drive tractors or trucks and deal with technical information just as they do when pruning, sowing and handling the plants in the greenhouses. Whether women are uninterested in maintaining trucks, pumps, engines and tools, or are more cautious about risky, unpleasant or unhealthy jobs like applying pesticides, or reject them for lack of previous experience is hard to know: but such jobs are out of reach for female workers. It seems to be taken for granted by everyone that such jobs are a male preserve, despite the fact women are acknowledged to be more responsible, orderly, and sober and lower-paid.

Only male workers are appointed to be farm managers; this may reveal male bias. The profile required for this job includes experience, expertise, access to information, initiative and the ability to exert authority. The manager must simultaneously deal with several tasks and crews of workers, intervene precisely and give strong instructions. Male executives consider that women are too gentle and fragile for this job. The bias towards men for such jobs is unjustified, and there are recent indications of change. Most positions of authority are still occupied by men, but now two women agronomists are department heads, and some key secretaries and administrative personnel are women. Nevertheless, women have the least eligible jobs in terms of pay and recognition. The preference for women in planting, selecting, classifying and packing reflects their dexterity and has led to some of the best women workers being promoted to *cabas*, but so far this has not given them access to other positions of authority. However, the key position of timekeeper requires different skills. At the La Rosa Company ethical assumptions underlie the notion that young educated women can perform this job better. A woman is thought more likely to be orderly and to have less propensity to accept bribes or accept corrupt practices. One area of responsibility to which women are promoted and for which they are given the corresponding wages is that of crew leader or *caba*. Like their male counterparts, these women may also be company labour recruiters who draw upon their networks.

Women workers often have to make lunch for their families before they dress and leave home for work. Such activities may seem simple, but are often complicated and time-consuming. Some women told me that they may spend almost an hour washing their clothes and dressing.

Variations in cultural expression between indigenous and non-indigenous migrant workers and between regional town and village workers are expressed in clothing style, such as the colour and brand of jeans. Despite the variations, *tomateras* have common ways of dressing (see Figure 9). This is not just a question of taste or

Figure 9.

economic constraint. It is also a question of protection against risks like skin exposure to pesticides. In this respect, women are more cautious than men. As one woman explained to me,

in cultivating tomatoes, the company frequently applies poisonous fumigants and insecticides. For that reason we have to protect ourselves. The plants constantly touch the workers' faces, and it is not uncommon for the poison to affect the skin, which can perhaps have bad consequences for our health. We use scarves to protect our faces. It is also common to wear at least two or three shirts to avoid direct exposure of the skin to the pesticides and diminish the effects of the sun, and to prevent the resin produced by the plants from sticking to our clothes.

Sometimes it is also a question of aesthetics. Women from San Luis Potosí are easily recognized by their use of several bandanas to protect the face instead of scarves. Normally women wear jeans and a skirt as well to avoid being scratched by the plants, and a skirt also comes in handy when you have to defecate in the cane fields. There is also imitation, competition and differentiation. They use accessories like cloth caps, miniskirts and jewellery to look more attractive.

Another important dimension of gender is the effect of household power relationships in the tomato fields and vice versa; as we saw in the discussion of priorities, home relationships are affected by work. Women in rural communities and urban neighbourhoods are often stereotyped as being confined to their households, obliged to help their husbands and look after their children (Cockcroft *et al.* 1982:48). These stereotypes are also applied to women working in the tomato industry, and may even apply to women migrant workers, who are still not free of household duties. This imposes a hectic schedule that drives them into isolation both on the farms and in the encampments where they live. Migrant women often carry their children on their backs or leave them under shade trees or improvised shelters where they work, making frequent visits to see to their needs (see Figure 10). Nevertheless, independent salaries for women and their older children and the opportunity to socialize with other workers, *cabos* and occasionally the bosses open up access to new resources, possible promotions and less isolated lives. This obviously modifies traditional images of subordinated women. Such images portray women as obeying or acquiescing to their husbands' and company representatives' orders. In some cases, the changing of roles has led to the

Figure 10.

breakdown of marriages; but in others, to the renegotiation of the marriage contract, which has ameliorated their situation.

Tasks and Relationships of Responsibility

I analyse the value assigned to specific tasks by looking at how responsibility or commitment is expressed and at the nature of the tasks themselves. *Peones* or crew members normally answer to the foremen and occasionally to farm managers or other company personnel. Migrant *peones* have the least responsibility of anyone on the farm; their points of linkage and mediation are their leaders. No more than ten of the twenty to thirty-five members of a crew are considered close to the *cabo* or farm manager, and these may be withdrawn to carry out special tasks and special activities. More responsibility is demanded of this minority than of the rest, who perform the same activity all day long. Another type of responsibility is demanded of department workers like the time-keeper, tractor and truck drivers, authorities and people with specific responsibility on the farm: *cabos* and managers. Irrigators, watchmen, storekeepers, water-carriers and helpers have yet another kind of responsibility, and carry out autonomous, specialized activities. Another point is that how tasks are perceived in terms of responsibility and commitment influences how the company organizes the hierarchy of tasks. This will obviously vary constantly in relation to specific factors like technology, availability of skills, and so on.

Unusual tasks that require only a short time to complete are usually accomplished by improvising and taking workers' suggestions. I observed two such tasks: helping the farm manager carry boxes of tomatoes after the pick-up truck broke down and helping the irrigator with an inundated plot. When there is special or unusual work like raising plants or hoeing over a prolonged period, one or all of a farm's crews may be dedicated to that activity. Such work usually stems from changes in priority or the need to do more demanding work that day.

Relocalizing Tomato Labour Processes

To make a final reflection on relocalization, van der Ploeg (1992:21) argues that 'the development of science-based technology materializes as the growing dislocation or independence of the different processes of production from those factors that initially composed its locality and diversity'. More specifically Goodman (1991:7) argues that 'since tomato production can be genetically engineered with relative ease it is used as a model system by leading agro-biotechnology companies . . . on the frontiers of agricultural innovation'. As we saw in descriptions of work, relocalization is an interactive process in which innovations and developments are not just formulae presented by commercial experts for tomato producers to achieve new market goals; instead, tomato workers and company staff also play a crucial role in achieving productive efficiency. Hence, local organizational forms are mixed with values and concepts internalized from transnational forms of organization, and sustainable yields result from the fusion of diverse potentialities adapted to local conditions. This presupposes a constant reproduction of the work process through the mutual influences of tradition and innovation.

As was seen in the case of the labour market, the interaction between self-recruitment and planned recruitment reflects multiple factors that cannot be reduced to a purely market framework. One has to conclude that in specific localities there is no modern operational scheme; there are hybrid social structures resulting from the conjuncture of different cultural features. In this sense locality constantly reflects changes in the identities of local actors. Many factors including the rate of technological change, availability of machinery, dominated/dominant cultural repertoires and knowledge/power techniques control such processes. Therefore, relocalization should not be interpreted as a transitional phase, after which one can expect a new model of development. Instead, it is a constantly changing, emergent pattern involving discontinuities with respect to earlier ordering schemes.

In fact, what happens in the fields and offices increasingly corresponds to the forms of dislocation, disconnection, disarticulation and fragmentation described by van der Ploeg. Performing blocks of tasks entails constantly negotiating the power/control system. In this process, both present and absent subjects intervene, whether foreign experts or workers of all levels. In the La Rosa Company, the most noticeable disconnection was between the less centralized operation of the farms and the more centralized operation of the departments. The managers and *cabos* are not directly responsible for specialized tasks, but they must understand and communicate the orders handed out for such tasks over the company radio system. Thus modern methods ironically both connect and disconnect new symbols of authority on the tomato farm. If in hacienda times the main overseer was identified by his beautiful horse and saddle, he is now identified by his walkie-talkie and pick-up truck. Just as in the past, this symbol reflects faster communication with the owner and the department heads, not a substantial change in the hierarchy or the autonomy with which workers carry out their tasks.

Other types of disconnection are what van der Ploeg calls the 'superfluity of the quality of the labour force'(1992:25). Within the region companies are still vulnerable to fluctuations in both the unskilled and skilled labour markets. There is also still a high valuation of the work of those involved in the different stages of tomato production, although the increased use of piecework to motivate workers to make extra efforts is sometimes detrimental to the quality of work performed, and shows the extent to which the company is subject to the requirements of the market. For example, how companies deal with the quality of rods for tying up plants is a weak point in the organization of tomato production. This reveals how companies still prefer to depend on cheap labour rather than expensive inputs. In other words, the balance cannot easily be standardized for all stages and tasks. This is true even when new technological developments could soon control the tomato ripening process (Goodman 1991). Such a development would surely change the criteria for *alcanzar el corte*, which rule the tomato season, but not universally nor at the same rate. Whatever the future holds, especially in Third World countries, worker initiatives and adaptations will again be a significant basis for negotiating more sustainable production. These could compete with the most sophisticated and expensive models of organization.

Conclusions

Whether Marxist, post-Marxist, functionalist or structuralist, much of the literature on the labour process and farmworkers implicitly or explicitly reproduces a dichotomous image of society based on the notion of development vs. underdevelopment. This leads to linking changes in working conditions to a conception of modernity and progress based on a rational or ideal model. Under such a model local circumstances, values and forms of organization are largely ignored. A commonly related weakness in this literature is that dynamic conditions and workers' heterogeneity are reduced to organizational variations on a general structure of production, and the workplace is synonymous with the shopfloor, supposedly subject to contractual limits and an overemphasis on control and surplus value extraction. Thus, the labour market, technology and standardization continue to be viewed as powerful external forces penetrating local processes, to which local producers are subject. These explanations do not take account of the fact that actors are not passive recipients of innovations, but agents capable of 'reinventing' the tomato work. As Hanna Arendt (1958) emphasized, creativity is always present in labour processes, but often left out of studies about them. In Chapters 5 and 6, I return to the question of creativity as I explore various forms of worker joking and avoidance behaviour.

In this chapter, I used scenarios including workday spontaneity, the stages of the season, farm hierarchy, worker heterogeneity and the labour market to develop a constructivist approach to everyday tomato work practices. I interpret tomato work as the effect of different cultural dimensions, thus abandoning the use of 'single signifier relations' (Calagione and Nugent 1992) to cover multiple realities. Analysing tasks and tomato workers' agendas, I observed how tomato work is gender-specific and embraces multiple ideological expressions. Power/knowledge techniques for implementing tomato work reflect different work contexts as well as migrant and local workers' changing trajectories. My examination of work priorities revealed that there are no scripts, but only shifting procedures at work in the hierarchies and job definitions, all subject to explicit or implicit forms of negotiation. How workers arranged themselves in the tomato rows did not comply with management's coordinated plans.

In the following chapters I deal with tensions in the apparently disordered labour process. These serve many purposes: if local tomato labour practices are discontinuous, how can we identify these discontinuities and relate verbal expressions to them? How can we reconcile routine, recurrent and concrete timing and spacing with the changing array of workers? If there is continual adjustment in tasks, self-recruitment in the market and a self-evident method for performing tasks, how do these mesh with everyday and long-term company planning? If companies develop tomato work in a deregulated, flexible contracting situation, how do they control it from a distance, and how are discipline and the coordination of tasks achieved?

Notes

1. In line with an anthropological tradition Long (1989:228-31) discusses the notion of emergent properties to understand small-scale interpersonal networks, institutional organizations of people and territory (e.g., state agencies). This focus on emergent properties allows Long and van der Ploeg (1992) to deconstruct deterministic notions and abandon structure as an explanatory factor. They call for more insight into the construction, reproduction and transformation of social relations, in which structure can be characterized as a fluid set of emergent properties.

2. At least six important forms of alienation occur in local agricultural production: (1) ecological; (2) the once integrated and autonomous structure of the labour process; (3) the quality of the labour force; (4) organization of time and space; (5) the linked evolution of specific qualities in specific end-products; and (6) the family as an organizing principle (van der Ploeg 1992:25).

3. See Appendix 2.

4. Some come from even further over the worst roads. It appears that the companies pay the teamsters' union to supply transportation.

5. Martínez-Alier (1971:68-9) stresses that in southern Spanish olive production, sequentiality is not absolutely rigid. Landowners have the notion that some tasks are essential while others are not. For instance, pruning, hoeing and mulching the trees can easily be skipped for a year, but weeding and harvesting irrigated crops are indispensable.

6. The landscape of tomato farms is symmetrical (Figure 11) and of standard design, as marked out by the tractors. They are internally divided by roads that allow trucks to bring in plants, fertilizers and other inputs and tractors to fumigate and cultivate. These roads separate the beds (sets of eight parallel rows where the tomatoes grow), within which there are narrow exits every seventy metres. At these exits the line of strings to fix the plants is interrupted to allow the workers access to the roads to pick up the plants and inputs. The plants are 40 cm. apart and two plants are attached to each rod.

7. Middleton (1988:34) analyses British harvests between 1690 and 1860 with an emphasis on the variable predominance of men or women.

Figure 11.

Shortages of male labour because of war or epidemics, the introduction of technological innovations like longer and heavier scythes
and other changes often produced a deskilling of men or women in
harvesting.

8. According to Chano, the farm manager, harvesting on a ranch like
   La Lima (with eighteen hectares) is commercially viable when 530
   boxes of tomatoes are cut per day. This means that only fifteen of
   the thirty harvest days were considered commercially viable that year,
   with the peak day yielding 1,495 boxes, but an average of 653 boxes
   per day over the 19 days listed in Table 1. Calculating the worker
   productivity ratio is based on *alcanzar el corte* (reaching the cutting
   point).

9. In the Mezquital Valley (the same area studied by Grammont), Luisa
   Paré (1980:130) found that packers could negotiate better conditions
   than *peones* owing to the prestige attached to this quality task, which
   only a few workers could perform.

10. This is a Mexican revolutionary term that refers to *hacendados'*
    attempt to keep government-expropriated hacienda land from falling
    into the hands of rebel *peones* by supporting their own *peones*.

11. Sinaloa has been the most important tomato-growing area of México
    since the 1960s. Martha Roldán (1980:41) describes the more com-
    plex organization of packing plants there. Tasks for women workers
    are divided into seven categories: packers, selectors, classifiers,
    reviewers, listers, boxtoppers and box sealers. Roldán identifies at
    least six other categories for men: freezer workers, wheelbarrow
    operators, container emptiers, labellers, stampers and stevedores.

12. Martinez-Alier (1971:40) describes how Andalusian owners, admin-
    istrators and large tenants make the decisions about the area
    and crop to be planted, machinery investments and maintenance,
    irrigation equipment and tools, and the definition of the tasks to be
    carried out. The main supervisor or farm manager does no manual
    work, but decides on the tasks everyone else carries out daily and
    has the power to recruit more workers. He also decides whether tasks
    are to be paid by the hour or as piecework. The owner may intervene
    in cases of conflict.

13. This was not for lack of data, since all the companies collected them,
    but because no sense could be made of them.

14. The census reported that the La Rosa Company had 800 workers on
    230 hectares, but there were 1,567 workers on the company roster.

15. The Autlán-El Grullo valley is small region compared to Sinaloa,
    Sonora, Baja California, Morelos, and Guanajuato, where in normal
    years over 100,000 hectares are cultivated. The 4,375 workers are a
    minuscule force compared to the more than one million mobilized
    every season in Sinaloa. Still, in 1987 Autlán's 15,847 tons of tomato

exports to the US represented 1.6 per cent of national production, making it the number five exporting region (González 1991:112). When the Autlán harvest goes to the US, it is the single largest source at the time.

16. This contradicts Astorga Lira's (1985) view of *peones* as linked to small-scale peasant economies.

17. The Mexican Constitution forbids employing children under fifteen years old. However, managers argue that they cannot stop hiring children because they provide essential income to their families, would themselves complain of enforcement, and receive the same salaries as adult workers. When companies have piecework, this is a disadvantage for children, who cannot work as fast as adults. Grammont (1986:91) reports that in Ixmiquilpan managers argue that children should receive lower wages because they are less skilled. Grammont also mentions that some bosses prefer to hire women and children because they are easier to control.

18. Astorga Lira (1985: 15) maps out supply and demand mechanisms for *peones* in the rural Mexican labour market. However, he fails to give a full account of the dynamic and heterogeneous production of *peones*. For him, *peones* are the majority of the economically active rural population. Despite describing types of *peones* ranging from permanent residents to temporary migrants, he stresses the lack of permanent employment and underplays the role of more established workers. He sees everyone who grows up in a peasant family and cannot afford land becoming a *peon* sooner or later.

19. For Brass (1990:52) the oral or written contract stipulates disadvantageous conditions for the worker such as low wages and hard work over a long period. As Paré (1980:130) indicates for the Mexican case, contracting is highly flexible and virtually deregulated. The contracts are ambiguous and verbal. Autlán is similar except for some key workers and union members.

20. Grammont (1986:55) states that in Ixmiquilpan, Hidalgo, migrant *peones* used to come as family or neighbourhood groups. First-time workers normally come through an established group; they rarely come alone. Graumans (1989:36) writes that in Tizapán, Jalisco, kinship is the most important factor in the composition of crews, and women do not normally mix with men. Crews had two types of workers: a fixed nucleus of permanent, generally young men or women and a changing nucleus of temporary workers. The latter included children, married women and old people.

21. Although some workers mentioned *enganche*, this practice is more flexible than the *enganche* system depicted by Brass. The bond is more fluid and the contracting more flexible. I therefore prefer to use the term 'recruiting practices'.

22. Paré (1980) and Grammont (1986) describe how *peones* are recruited at traffic lights, town markets or plazas in the main cities of the valley. Normally the supply of *peones* exceeds demand except at planting and harvesting.

CHAPTER FOUR

The Politics of Tomato Work:
Agribusiness in Autlán History

Introduction

This chapter explores how processes and events connect in a regional historical context. Case studies reveal typical images of a region as well as theoretical concepts that permit us to understand social power networks that reach far beyond the region. Even though Autlán is very different from Israel or California, it has social dynamics comparable with other localities. Therefore one must analyse the connections between the tomato fields, the marketing and financial spheres, and regional social institutions.

The goal is to distinguish the universal and that which originates in actors' everyday lives, by analysing power mechanisms and the relationships linking organizational schemes with other locations and times. Thus belonging to a local community means being simultaneously inside and outside, by exchanging a full range of influences. It also means attaching or detaching oneself to/from organized/spontaneous groups that may or may not be disposed to collaborate. The former possibility leads me to question social actors' universal heterogeneity. I view them as direct producers legitimizing the current social order.

In order to understand regional history, I concentrate on inherently dynamic conflicts and other political interactions. I position myself at intersections between life-worlds and social formation in order to reflect on overlapping styles of political culture and new forms of politics. I also explore the externalized and internalized influences used to construct regional identities. This will allow me to pinpoint what has characterized the Autlán Valley since the 1960s. It implies examining regional social development, agroindustrial and traditional work processes, and the mix of social organizational styles.

The chapter is divided into four sections. The first presents a framework for understanding political issues, practices and domains. The second takes a step back from historical processes to elaborate the cultural repertoires that characterize politics in the region. The third section emphasizes how a transnational company's externality nevertheless becomes internalized within local traditions of carrying out agricultural tasks and organizing rural life. It also throws light on how everyday work practices interweave companies' methods of local and long-distance control with workers' self-regulation. In the final remarks I offer a characterization of the region.

The Politics of Tomato Work

The politics of tomato work refers to power/knowledge relationships that emerge in tomato industry activities as workers, staff, politicians and others struggle and negotiate their interests and images. This differs from the concept of occupational community, an autonomous social and political field. It is important to work with the interweaving of public and private, individual and institutional, global and local, and the interlocking of politics in different domains where people attribute meaning to political actions. This is a manifold task: to acknowledge that politics is expressed through what people do, whether traditionally regarded as political behaviour or not, and to focus on the interconnections of political issues and everyday actions. It entails describing disputes over resources and strategies in different contexts and identifying the interrelations of the power/knowledge networks called into action.

The particular case I explore shows that in the Autlán valley some historical situations are seen as extraordinary: particular ways of renewing social contracts come to the fore and reshape the rules of the political game. The point is to understand what lies behind symbolic and effective authority, the rotation of persons in political positions, and policies and strategies developed by actors in different networks in ongoing institutional processes.[1] This implies that institutions are intrinsically neither essential nor totalities with global strategies for defining living conditions for their constituencies.[2] On the contrary, local institutions are dynamic processes embodying different actors' interconnected practices, strategies and tactics. These actors include political factions, social groups, peasants, landowners, merchants, farmworkers and company representatives.[3]

Thus, what is interesting to analyse in local politics are the regimes of practice. Foucault suggests that

> . . . the target of analysis is not 'institutions' 'theories' or 'ideology' but practices with the aim of grasping the conditions which make these acceptable at a given moment. Up to a point these practices possess their own specific regularities, logic, self-evidence, strategy and 'reason' and this is the question to analyze. In this sense, practices are understood as places where what is said and what is done, rules imposed and reasons given, the planned and the taken for granted meet and interconnect. To analyze 'regimes of practices' means to analyze programmes of conduct which have both prescriptive effects regarding what is to be done (effects of 'jurisdiction'), and codifying effects regarding what is to be known (effects of 'verediction') (1991:75).

Emergent Issues and Domains of the Politics of Tomato Work

Historians, politicians, entrepreneurs and ordinary people register the advent of the tomato companies as an important event in the region. This event was connected to local, national and transnational government and institutional practice, even though this fact does not register. When looking at company operations (Wickham 1983), one must bear in mind that they reflect government and institutional policies. Companies are attracted by government and other institutional initiatives like growers associations. These lead to standards of production quality and to meetings and rallies that affect workers' living conditions. Thus, how companies comply with bureaucratic procedures and regulations is part of a constant struggle for legitimacy in which the jobs created, wages paid, area cultivated, resources and inputs offered, and social security benefits made available are criteria considered when company finances come under review. When confronted by politicians and government agents, companies point to their contribution to 'the social peace and political stability of the region' even though wages, social security and indemnity payments scarcely reach the legal minimum.

Even though I give it particular emphasis in this chapter, the politics of tomato work cannot be reduced to government agents and companies. Behind the politics of tomato work, workers' initiatives play an important role. Thus, workers' working and living conditions are affected by economic circumstances, political negotiations between government agents and company owners, and negotiations between workers and company representatives. In any case, a dichotomy between internal and external government or between the politics of production and state politics must be avoided (Burawoy 1985).[4]

John Law (1986:234) identifies long-distance control as an effect of power reflected in networks of passive agents disciplined by and complying with powerful actors' or institutions' goals and projects. However, 'passive agents' is a problematic term, because passivity is relative. The interrelations between work situations presented in Chapter 3 demonstrate how following instructions is complexly merged with workers' multiple initiatives.

In tomato work long-distance control would describe the intersection of practices and coordination of tasks in order to *alcanzar el corte* and reach harvest targets. Establishing discipline complies less with general normative planning; instead disciplinary procedures intertwine complexly in tomato work. This implies that one cannot separate the standard calculations for production from tomato workers' living conditions and qualifications. Practical situations in which disciplinary procedures manifest themselves, albeit in a fragmentary or contradictory way, help map company management and reflect on the effects of jurisdiction. Companies do not need to negotiate every detail of daily life and work; they can follow established patterns.

The fact that productive tasks are largely coordinated without strong coercion sustains a more structural approach to work; but this still has difficulties. Burawoy (1985) refers to the factory regime as essential to his politics of production. This argument is unobjectionable in that 'an element of spontaneous consent combines with coercion to shape productive activities' (Burawoy 1979: xii). He locates the factory shopfloor as where management hegemony is born. However, he overextends the conclusion that hegemony means that workers participate in a consensus, that the practical implementation of company policy is coterminous with its normative framework.

The Birth of a *cacicazgo a la alta escuela*

This section deals with regional political culture and the tomato companies' historical background. I expand on Rogelio's image of the *cacicazgo* in Chapter 2. I take a *cacicazgo* to be the customary local model of power and authority. Rogelio explained how in order to guarantee access to land and political favours necessary for the stability of tomato production, the companies became part of the *cacique*'s networks. Rogelio also described how he had learned to look at municipal electoral politics with scepticism. I therefore began delving into the life of the *cacique* General García Barragán and his importance for the tomato industry through dialogues with Rogelio and other tomato workers, regional historians and intellectuals, *agraristas* and politicians, as well as data from local archives and newspapers. Talking with members of the General's clique, old peasants, ex-workers and other historical witnesses offered yet another perspective. The data presented in this section derive from this fieldwork material. Needless to say, this is not an exhaustive inquiry; it is only an attempt to understand political practice from different perspectives.

The General appeared able to unite political factions and promote the interests of many people in the region. Eventually, Autlán itself became his regional empire. In this way the persons, institutional forms and power contexts around this strongman's political and military career are important for understanding local politics. The General restructured political networks and established authority and discipline for over forty years, despite his interlocutors' varied regional cultural backgrounds. This necessitated coming to grips with the intricate organizing process of a political clique. His followers recreate the image of him as an influential political authority.

In the following sections I present historical and ethnographic data to show: (1) how a disciplined clique or network emerged under the General's command; (2) the role of discretion, persuasion, coercion and reciprocal favours; and (3) how the General's political defeat and ostracism and later the development of alternatives designed to support majority interests provide insights into how political strength can be forged into symbolic authority.

Overlapping Images of the Powerful

In the region stories abound about this strongman's advent. One of these stories, narrated by a local intellectual, tells of his father deserting him when he was very young. This forced his mother and brothers to migrate from their mountain village to Autlán, where she maintained them by washing clothes in the river. The General occasionally went back to those places to meditate (Fieldnotes, 24 January 1988). Because of his family's precarious position, as a teenager he joined in the 1910 revolution, and faced execution for supporting the Villistas, but managed to plead for mercy. Others spoke of how he advanced his career by currying favour with revolutionary groups and politicians. A local intellectual said, 'On the advice of the general who pardoned him, he learned to side with the winner and managed to stay in favour with those holding important positions in government, without losing face when he suffered defeats.' Thus, although his life history is mainly characterized by conflicts and intrigues, he cultivated the image of a military man loyal to Mexican institutions, despite various setbacks.[5]

In fact, for years the General was politically ostracized after being deposed as governor of Jalisco in 1947. In the 1950s there were rumours that he was preparing a military insurrection and demonstrations against the President and the PRI, but eventually he managed to regain the image of the loyal soldier. Under his command on 2 October 1968 hundreds of students were massacred when the Mexican Army broke up a massive protest in the Plaza de Las Tres Culturas in Tlatelolco in downtown Mexico City.[6] Roderic Camp (1992:28) quotes the General when he usurped the Mexican President's prerogative and made the crucial decision: '"OK, Mr. President, it is obvious something must be done. Unless you object, I am going to clear Tlaltelolco." Then General Barragán turned to his two aides and said, "I want the place cleared out." After it was over, he reported to the president, "Mr. President, the situation is clear."' Camp argues that the General's initiative under extreme political pressure overrode the President's discretion; many contemporary politicians interpreted it as a virtual *coup d'état*. Still, García Barragán managed to preserve his image as a soldier loyal to the nation and obedient to the civil powers.

How the General was Invoked as a Regional Authority

The General's first notable local political intervention was during the Cristero war of the late 1920s,[7] when the government decided to suppress all local uprisings. As head of the victorious federal army, the General influenced the selection of candidates for regional constituencies. His transformation from head of the army to general regional authority was facilitated by the fact that many land-hungry peasants and key leaders were impressed by his charisma and military bearing. According to one regional historian (Ernesto Medina Lima, interview, 11 March 1988), when the PRI took over most government positions, the General is noted in party archives as a distinguished member who had to be consulted when mayoral candidates were being selected. This destroyed 'the myth of the good times of democracy' cherished by the old people of the region, when candidates for the municipal administration from all competing parties were selected openly in public places through a traditional plebiscite. The PRI had briefly maintained the custom, but then suppressed it. Up to 1930, these plebiscites were dominated by Catholics, *agraristas* and liberals who did not agree with the ruling party or government.

The General was also called on to adjudicate serious conflicts within the ruling party or local councils. Citizens and PRIistas often had to wait for over a month for him to emit his decision from Mexico City or Guadalajara. In 1964, many people wanted to be mayor of Autlán, but were unable to get the PRI to agree on a candidate. To be nominated by the PRI was important, since PRI candidates usually won at least until 1988. When the General was Defence Minister he remained in touch with local events through close confidants who received the prospective candidates. Finally the General chose an unlikely candidate who was scarcely interested in the office. García informed the PRI leadership and the candidate only after the fact. Thus the General confirmed himself as an authority, 'obligatory passage point' (Callon 1986) and network director for those seeking solutions and benefits in critical political situations. He acted with discretion and surprise. The General gained the loyalty of the candidate, who could rely on his support and would govern in close contact with him. Such interventions show how the *cacique* becomes spokesman for both the ruling party and local citizens.

The General's Clique

According to the 1970 census, there were almost 100 professional politicians in the local bureaucratic institutions of Autlán (a town of some 40,000 inhabitants). For more than forty years rumours about the General's clique have persisted in these circles. Ernesto Medina Lima, a local historian, told me in an interview (11 March 1988) that the rumours depicted this clique as 'sons of the General', and that it emerged because the General was an introvert who liked to keep up with local events by talking with close friends; this clique was never acknowledged as a formal group and was allowed to recruit others as members of the political group according to the particular need of the time. Although the numbers and political affiliations of clique members varied, normally the group who shared information and plans with the General consisted of no more than fifteen people (of whom two were women). One or two of them were intellectuals, who did background reading for him and provided him with academic and media information.

The General visited Autlán at least once a month. Before the visit, close friends would spread the news that he would be there on a given day, sometimes adding information about the purpose of the visit, especially when important political moves were imminent. On the day of the visit groups of people (more men than women) waited outside his house to talk with him. During the visit the clique met regularly, sometimes inviting other politicians to negotiate or accept political positions. They organized social gatherings at the General's house, where they discussed local matters such as needed public services (roads, drinking water, etc.), how to get more land for small cultivators, improve housing and irrigation infrastructure, create agribusinesses, etc. Another *ejidatario* told how the General liked to reminisce about the Cristero war with his battlefield comrades, especially *agraristas* (Interview, Abel García Corona, Chacalito. Fieldnotes, 13 April 1988).

Establishing Discipline in the Clique

Discipline and discretion were developed differently in the General's clique than in Masonic or communist cells, which also existed in Autlán. The meaning of discipline varied according to circumstances, events, the character of the members and the style of the General. Contradictions emerged when serious political and

military matters mingled with trivial, domestic affairs. One clique
member recalled the disciplinary practice:

> As a military man, the General liked to emphasize macho characteristics
> and discipline (he never smoked or drank), but he was nevertheless
> fond of gossiping about friends and enemies. This could be difficult,
> since he was easily influenced by those wishing to have members
> excluded or gain political favour. This sometimes led to unjust actions.
> When indiscretion, a member's lack of discipline or inappropriate
> behaviour was in question, the accused was barred from the group until
> the issue was clarified. The outcome for the offender could be disgrace
> or regaining the General's trust. Discipline involved two crucial matters:
> the first concerned an accurate reading of the General's interests and
> completion of assignments; the second entailed sharing silence and
> acting with discretion in order to take advantage of the element of
> surprise. Rumours of extreme punishments were used as deterrents.
> In addition, an effective way to achieve discipline was to tell group
> members that they would be rewarded for their actions at the proper
> time.

Creating Social Control

The methods of promoting discipline and commitment went
beyond the clique. They attempted to gain broader influence in
the region, and as such were techniques for creating social control.
However, as mentioned, persuasion and coercion within the clique
were mainly tied to the General's personal style. For some, this
consisted mostly of unrefined behaviour such as coarse language.
These techniques created a network of sympathizers who, although
outside the clique and therefore not completely trusted, were at
the same time potential supporters who could be called upon for
political rallies and events. The motives of people seeking support
from the clique varied. Some were recommended by clique
members or by people connected with them. They came to seek
favours like the General's support in resolving problems, access to
important politicians, or work permits as migrant workers in the
United States. Hence, the clique used persuasive methods, such as
providing opportunities, solving problems and granting favours,
to broaden the group of sympathizers and to promote particular
projects and candidates for political office. These processes were
developed over a long period of time.

There were situations, judged as politically sensitive, in which
persuasion or coercion were more intricately interwoven. These

included complaints against priests involved in politics,[8] skirmishes between corrupt politicians, and accusations against liberals, communists and other caciques. The General sought to be directly involved on these occasions. More problematic situations, like murder fugitives, were considered to be situations that only the General could sort out (another point in the 'geography of obligatory points of passage'). In some situations, the wife, mother or sister of the accused pleaded for protection from the General. These cases were treated with more care, and the General offered his personal intervention to individuals he thought might eventually be trusted to carry out delicate jobs for the army. Some of these people became his personal bodyguards.

The fear of coercion was evidenced on two occasions: once when the clique was dominant in the late 1930s and 1940s, and again in the 1960s when it was in decline. In the early 1940s, one member of the clique was killed in a personal quarrel by a member of a rich family also involved in local politics. The murderer got away, but some months later he and some close relatives were ambushed by strangers who were never caught. It was rumoured that this revenge was from the General's 'invisible hand'. This swift justice reinforced group commitment and broadcast a message to their enemies: it was hard to escape, and retaliation could be extreme. But coercion also frightened and alienated large sectors of the public.

The other case occurred during the Cuban revolution in the early 1960s, and coincided with counter-propaganda to prevent Mexico from going communist. A priest who headed a movement with the slogan 'Catholicism Yes! Communism No!' accused the principal of a recently created high school in Autlán who was also one of the best doctors in town of being a communist. A student committee in close contact with the priest and members of the school board organized a strike and demanded that the principal be fired for being authoritarian, communist and homosexual. Actually, the principal had made himself *persona non grata* among political groups of various persuasions. These included the General's clique, rich merchants and Catholics; but the doctor was widely respected in a region where doctors were scarce. Indeed, some of his most faithful patients were members of the clique, and the General himself had consulted him.

The stated issue was how he managed the school, but the real issue was that he was judged to be politically dangerous because of his growing influence over students. He was becoming too influential in the region because of articles critical of local politicians that he had written in a local newspaper. In the face of this conflict, the General's clique made an unexpected alliance with the priests and merchants who were his traditional enemies. The General personally called in the principal and told him that he would not be responsible for his safety unless he left the area immediately: so he left, and the school was closed for over a year. This may have created some confusion in the group because of changing political alliances; but it reinforced the clique's acceptance among a large sector of the population.

The Effects of Defeat

A methodological observation: these historical events are largely informant interpretations. Many of them came from landless tomato workers who recreated the past in the light of their life experiences and current circumstances in particular. There were big gaps in their narratives, with adverse events like the General's political ostracism and final defeat between 1947 and 1961 poorly defined. Perhaps the fact that the General died at peace with the world on 3 September 1979, again at the top, influenced this.[9] The fact that members of the clique and their descendants still occupy important political positions may also have influenced the interpretations. At the time of my fieldwork, at least two of the General's closest relatives became important national and regional-level politicians: one son was national president of the PRI and later a cabinet minister, and a nephew became the region's congressional deputy. This is yet another reason why members of the clique would not talk about past hard times. I had to question them more precisely to obtain a fuller picture. In contrast, some workers and radical *agraristas* who were also former clique members recounted the era of political defeat in detail at times. They were then confronting the PRI in the 1988 electoral campaign and felt betrayed by agrarian policies that in their radical perspective did not address their problems.

How Agraristas Reinvented the General's Authority

The General's authority was socially constructed and forged by both his followers and his enemies. Ex-*agraristas* in the Cristero war associated the General and his clique with their defiance of the *hacendados*. Since the late 1930s, radical *agraristas* transformed political values, interests and the course of events in local political domains and within the clique. These radical *agraristas* pushed general demands like expropriating and redistributing big properties, using government resources and organization to create *ejidos*. Other specific demands included increasing access to credit, agricultural inputs and machinery for small-scale peasant producers and *ejidos*. In fact, the General, as some of these radicals described him, was indifferent to the *agrarista* cause. He and his clique had nothing to do with initiating the *agrarista* movement in the region, although they eventually benefited from it in many ways.

The man who had promoted the *agrarista* movement in the 1930s was a retired soldier, Jesús Ochoa Ruíz, who had come from Michoacán to work in Autlán as head of the Agrarian Reform Department. He was involved in land struggles and had witnessed the agrarian policy developed by President Cárdenas in Michoacán. The *agrarista* cause could count on a core group of 35 leaders and more than 70 *ejidos* throughout the coastal area. In fact, during his period the main land distribution and creation of *ejidos* took place in the region.

Struggling for at least three years, organizing the *ejidos* to get credit from the government bank and supporting groups of land claimants, Ruíz was able to coordinate massive demonstrations of considerable political strength. One of these took place when he was running as a PRIista in the Autlán municipal elections against the General's brother, another PRIista supported by local landowners and merchants and previously selected by the General. With the support of the *agraristas* and *ejidatarios*, Ruíz won by a large majority in what was to be the last plebiscite organized by the ruling party, and he became municipal president. Afterwards, he approached the General and his clique. He and the General had met in the army, but had not become friends. He clearly stated (Interview, 17 March 1988) that at that time the General did not identify with the *agraristas*. Although he was respected by them, they considered him distant, for he preferred interacting with small groups of community leaders rather than large groups of peasants. The General's image changed for the *ejidatarios* and he identified more with their interests when Ruíz promoted him politically in the late 1930s.

This move turned out to be advantageous for both sides. A few days earlier Ruíz had lost his job in the Department of Agrarian Reform because of political pressure from wealthy landowners and politicians who had the support of the Governor. They also tried to get him to leave the region; but since he had a close relationship with the General (then head of Mexico's military college) and his clique, he managed to stay and fulfil his promises to the *agraristas*. One such promise was to return arms to the *ejidos* and their leaders. He was also able to re-establish contact with politicians and agrarian reform functionaries to settle unsolved land claims.

With the creation of armed groups to defend *ejidos* some *agraristas* and land-seekers became bolder. This coincided with closer relationships between the General and *agrarista* leaders who had joined the clique after Ruíz did. In this new era of friendship, the General asked to use some communal plots to feed army horses, and soldiers taking care of the horses interacted with *ejidatarios*. The *ejidatarios* interpreted this as an alliance with the government, and this gave them the courage to invade plots disputed with neighbouring landowners. There are indications that *ejidatarios* extended their fences to cultivate such areas or cut wood from them (Interview, Miguel Nieves, head of Las Paredes *ejido*, 2 April 1988).

Despite all this, the General himself continued to be uninterested in the *agrarista* cause. Ruíz recognized that the General was in favour of some landowners in the clique. It was not easy for *agraristas* in the clique to be heard or to contact politicians and functionaries. They wasted time lobbying, and complained that the General was more willing to support them personally than to comply with the collective demands of their agrarian communities. For example, when someone approached him with an *ejido* problem, he would inquire instead about their personal needs.

The *agraristas* also had to deal with problems with the General, as when he asked for *ejido* labour to cultivate his farms. It is rumoured that the General acquired these farms when he was Governor of Jalisco by appropriating private landholdings legally disputed by *ejidos*.[10] Meanwhile agrarian leaders managed to convince *ejido* members that if they supported the General with unpaid labour, he would reciprocate by helping to resolve land disputes or to expand their *ejidos*. They were also aware that by allowing him to pasture army horses on communal land, they were allowing the General to pocket the army budget for animal feed.

The most critical of my informants claimed that the General had enriched himself and his family at the expense of the agrarian community, manipulated agrarian unrest, and infiltrated his supporters into *agrarista* circles in order to control the 35 radical leaders (Interview, Manuel Núñez, president of the Comité de Vigilancia of the Autlán *ejido*, 16 January 1988).

The General's association with the *agraristas* took place under Lázaro Cárdenas. Cárdenas favoured the *agrarista* movement, which in any case was winning the battle at that point: so the General had to identify himself as being in its favour. It is difficult to establish how many interventions were made on behalf of the *ejidos* through the General. There was some land distribution and credit for cultivation inputs to *ejidos* while the General was governor. Without such benefits it is unlikely that people would have supported him, hoped for his favour, or created the image of him as a pro-*agrarista* leader. However, the General was skilled at exploiting ties with landlords and rich merchants as well as peasant groups.

The Agraristas against the President

As portrayed in Muriá's *Historia de Jalisco* (1982:606), the most humiliating moment in the General's career was when he was deposed as Governor of Jalisco in 1947 by the Chamber of Deputies. This body was dominated by Jesús González Gallo, the man who succeeded him. González Gallo had the support of President Miguel Alemán, with whom the General was not even on speaking terms. The reason for his dismissal was his refusal to publish an official decree extending the tenure of the office from four to six years, which would have favoured his successor. In fact, the General was involved in a very complicated political struggle.

The General used his close communication with *agrarista* leaders to organize voters against the PRI in the 1952 elections. At the time the PRI was headed by his two worst enemies, Governor González Gallo and President Alemán. Under the umbrella of the *agrarista* movement the so-called Henriquista Party (after General Henríquez Guzmán) was formed to deepen opposition to the national and regional governments. Castañeda Jiménez (1987) refers to the persistent rumours that President Alemán was seeking re-election (something prohibited by the Constitution): this unified politicians, activists and above all soldiers of various political persuasions in opposition. They formed a Confederation of People's Parties (Confederación de Partidos Populares). The Confederation's candidate for the presidency was General García Barragán's good friend, General Henríquez Guzmán. The opposition party's immediate aim was to avoid Alemán's re-election; but they lost the contest against a new candidate promoted by President Alemán himself.

Given that the Confederation was organized in haste, it conducted a very successful campaign and put the PRI under considerable pressure at the national level. Within the region the Confederation won by a large majority in the elections. It was acknowledged that the strength of the Henriquistas stemmed from strong support by *ejidatarios*, land-seekers and farmworkers. However, none of the victorious mayors and deputies were recognized by the incoming government of the region, who installed only PRIistas.

The municipalities of the Jalisco coast, the General's centre of operations, were ungovernable for the PRI appointees. The new Governor tried to create his own network of Gallistas to control the Henriquistas. The Gallistas unsuccessfully tried to corrupt *agrarista* leaders and divide Henriquistas. They in turn retaliated by invading lands and obstructing local authorities. Later, there was a rumour that General García Barragán was organizing an armed revolt with *ejidatarios* from the coast. The General was dismissed, and he retired to Guadalajara. When the rumour of the insurrection emerged, the General came under surveillance by soldiers loyal to the President, and was virtually banished from the coastal region, including Autlán, for many years. The rumour of armed revolt was also a pretext for prosecuting leaders who caused unrest in the region. Ruíz was again chosen as a special target for attack: he was accused of murder, eventually had to abandon the region, and became a federal customs officer. However, despite such measures, the Gallistas never totally dismantled the Henriquistas.

The local intellectual Gregorio Rivera (Interview, 24 January 1988) interpreted this at least ten-year period as a power vacuum, because, after their unacknowledged electoral victory, the Henriquistas could not remain mobilized, and survived only in a defensive posture. Some *agraristas* opted to negotiate with the Gallistas to participate again in local politics. Others became more desperate. They went to the General's house and called him and Henríquez Guzmán cowards. One of the most radical Henriquistas lost all his savings and livestock. There was a rumour that the Government had bribed Henríquez with several million pesos (then hundreds of thousands of dollars), a factory and special concessions from the army. In view of the débâcle, García Barragán recommended returning to the PRI. The Gallistas regained the confidence of the region and collaborated with hostile Henriquistas by offering inputs, credit, the means to cultivate and more jobs. They discussed alternative ways of developing the regional economy after irrigation infrastructure was completed in the early 1960s; but land reform was not part of this scenario. Governor Gallo and his successors[11] appeared ready to deliver fertilizers, ploughs, cattle and machinery to improve *ejido* production, but were unable to establish direct contact with *ejidatarios* and communities; instead, they were forced to use a member of the General's clique to provide services and benefits to the *ejidos*.

Thus, the power vacuum was a period of power struggles and negotiations. While the Henriquistas maintained a degree of legitimacy and authority among *ejido* leaders, the PRI stayed in office and had administrative roles. However, the General's reappearance on the political scene in 1964 as Defence Minister brought new changes. Although he never regained the governorship for his followers, he reshaped networks and promoted his followers to important national and Jalisco municipal posts, above all in the coastal region. However, after Henriquismo the political spectrum changed, and the local groups including *agraristas*, merchants and Catholics become more linked. This had another effect: expectations in Autlán rose in hopes that the General's power would revitalize the regional economy. A sugar mill became the centre of attention for most people in the region.

The Empowerment of Sugar Producers

The idea of establishing a sugar mill in the region had been suggested as early as 1950 by a radical *agrarista* clique member. As Defence Minister, the General promoted the project despite state government apathy, and the governor was forced to go along. This project allowed *agraristas* to recover their political influence in the region. In 1965, a recession and unemployment hit the region after

Autlán's mining company closed down and a five-year canteloupe boom ended, so there was broad support for building a sugar mill; a pro-mill committee was set up.[12] This committee represented a new alliance among local political interests, including the Chamber of Commerce, municipal government and *ejidos*; domesticated *agraristas* now worked closely with rich merchants and large landowners. In fact, the landowner who became secretary of the committee was a pardoned *Cristero*. However, the committee's president was Espinosa the Ugly, a radical *agrarista* who had suggested installing a mill over ten years earlier. There are indications that this committee acted in close collaboration with the General.

The committee functioned for over two years, and helped persuade *ejidatarios* and Autlán residents to sign petitions to the President and national institution responsible for sugar mills. When the government set up a commission of experts to find the best place in the region for a mill, the committee offered to survey the land and showed functionaries around the region. According to one of these functionaries, the committee won over the experts, who reported favourably on installing the sugar mill in Autlán. General García Barragán's presence at the final discussions among sugar mill experts, the President and the Minister was instrumental in getting a machinery package that had just arrived from France and had been destined for another region of Mexico allocated to Autlán. More visible and effective for convincing people in Autlán of his support was his personal donation of the land on which the mill was to be built. However, this land had been sought by land claimants for many years (cf. Van der Zaag 1992:44).

The sugar mill reactivated the regional economy by gradually bringing almost 6,000 hectares of irrigated land into sugarcane production, which directly benefited over 1,000 families of *ejidatarios* and 200 landowners from Autlán and El Grullo. This meant access to credit, technical assistance, agricultural inputs and machinery, as well as 250 mill jobs and over 4,000 jobs for cane-cutters. Most of these benefits went to ex-Henriquista *ejidatarios* who were unconditionally loyal to the PRI (van der Zaag 1992:44; Guzmán Flores 1995). Most informants agree that the sugar mill culminated García Barragán's dream of developing 'his region'. After his death in 1979, a monument to the General bearing the legend 'To a soldier loyal to the nation' was erected in Autlán; this affirms his image as benefactor of the region.

Autlán and the Politics of Tomato Production

I now explore how regional tomato companies fit into the above-described local politics in terms of political competition between the tomato growers' and sugarcane producers' associations. I also look at crucial junctures when the clique and General García Barragán himself guaranteed the continuity of tomato production. Finally, I examine tomato workers' self-discipline and how they create social life.

From 1969 until the time of my fieldwork (1987–8), the five main tomato companies in the region had increased the area they cultivated to 1,365 hectares, including 300 of El Operado irrigation scheme's 9,000 hectares. However, company managers described their operations as 'enterprises on wheels' to highlight their fragility and uncertain future. Poor harvests had forced at least two companies to close during those eighteen years, and more have folded since then. The region's tomato industry had always been enmeshed in political conflict, and the need to gain legitimacy socially (as a source of employment), economically (in terms of profits and technological advances), politically (in terms of relationships with politicians and other influential groups) and vis-à-vis sugarcane producers, other farmers, companies, workers and government agents.

Although these conflicts did not manifest themselves stridently, they revealed 'the maintenance of the origins of the local society in the present' (Latour 1986). Tomato industry-related issues such as pollution, lowering of the water table, financial solvency, and compliance with labour and tax regulations (like paying the minimum wage) are best understood in relation to political constraints and competition for space, resources and labour.

Relocalization

The origins of horticultural production in the region can be traced back to the 1950s (cf. Arce 1990), although people have long known how to practise irrigation and take advantage of the area's hot climate. In 1962, the neighbouring areas of El Limón and El Grullo began a five-year cycle of canteloupe production that brought foreign companies into contact with local producers and exhausted the fertility of the soil (Arce 1990:2). The tomato boom started in late 1968, when the US company Griffin & Brand rented

38 hectares of land from an Autlán private farmer. This initiated a new trend in regional agriculture. In addition to renting land, the Griffin & Brand contract had two very attractive clauses for local producers: the installation of infrastructure construction and new equipment, both of which would be left in place after the contract expired. The contract also increased employment and technologically transformed agricultural tasks.

Companies came to the region with labour organizational plans from Cuba, Venezuela, the US and other parts of Mexico. Workers and administrative personnel were brought in from the US and elsewhere in Mexico as production designers and instructors in new cultivation methods. Company representatives deemed them useful for adapting the area's microclimate to the transnational tomato industry. The imported production model was based on efficiency and maintained a politically neutral image; the companies appeared uninterested in developing political ties, and focused on technology, marketing and international contacts.

Some workers claimed that tomato cultivation was not unknown in the region. The novelty was technical innovation, which favoured mass production and organization in compliance with market quality standards. Workers maintained that the Americans' concern was to introduce a new way of producing tomatoes, a new standard of living and an entrepreneurial lifestyle. This seduced some local landowners, who were willing to copy the method and dedicate more land to the activity.

One might have expected transnational companies to take over the best irrigated land from the recently inaugurated federal government infrastructure; but in fact they failed to enlist many *ejidatarios* and owners. Instead, the companies faced hostility from sugarcane cultivators, whose leaders identified the companies with new landowners who threatened the canegrowers' own recent regional dominance (since the 1968 installation of the sugar mill). Hence 'the incoming agro-export companies were forced to organize their ventures on non-irrigated land' (Arce 1990:5).[13] The company tactic of renting neighbouring plots over consecutive years to obtain quick profits from tomato production was partially successful. Companies were continuously searching for new lands, and wanted to pay as little as possible for them, an attitude characterized as a 'mining mentality' (van der Zaag 1992:39). Often, after three consecutive years of production on the same plot, viruses and nematodes increased and yields fell. At the end of the contract, these plots were often depleted and unsuitable for tomato production. Elimination of the pests is difficult, and made the low rents unprofitable.

Despite this, the companies' introduction of new economic practices initially raised expectations. Rental income, high wages and investment meant more cash for agricultural production, changed thousands of regional families' daily routines and ways of performing agricultural tasks, and entailed changes in power relations. Even though it is more heterogeneous, tomato production brings to mind Burawoy's concept of the factory regime. The difficulty with Burawoy's concept is that it suggests a coherently reproduced, institutionalized pattern. To understand the changing forms and intersecting practices of tomato work one must examine issues that emerge in concrete domains, the global/local nexus (Robertson 1990), and the effects of jurisdiction and verediction (in Foucault's terms) in tomato work practices.

There is also the problem of historical explanation and locating the intersection between customary forms and innovation. For example, resorting to political networks to maintain control and working in crews are customary cultural forms; current operations are reshaped by workers' and landowners' accumulated experiences. For example, the eight-hour workday with a one-hour lunchbreak was a novelty at first; it was difficult to persuade local workers accustomed to working until sundown not to work overtime. Also, companies were initially willing to pay comparatively high wages, equivalent to those in the US. But one local landowner who rented out land was afraid this would lead to a general regional wage increase, with which other farmers and small landowners would be unable to compete. So only smaller increases were allowed, in order to preserve the local bourgeoisie.

Companies' Search for Legitimacy

The changes introduced by the tomato companies were numerous and noticeable. New disciplinary schemes involved multiple cultural expressions, including worker self-discipline. Two concrete situations show how companies established control and preserved a stable, legitimate political environment in which to exercise authority. The first occurred on a La Rosa Company farm when eighty workers spontaneously put pressure on the company by capturing a foreman it had brought in from another region. The workers had complained of low wages and bad treatment from this foreman. The foreman threatened to use the gun that he carried with him, while the workers had knives and machetes. The American owner and company manager was quickly informed and intervened to avoid people getting killed. For the workers there were two immediate, positive results: the foreman was disarmed and fired, and they received the extra wages they were asking for. But, being recorded in company files for future use, the workers who received the higher wages were blacklisted and later fired one by one.

The companies accumulated experience on how to cope with internal conflicts in the labour camps. Solutions were sometimes achieved through key workers, without police support. At other times, the companies bribed the local police to intervene in some farms and camps. During the tomato industry's brief history in the region (1969–92), the companies asked twice for direct, external government intervention to settle strikes. Both times this involved both legal and illegal mediation by Defence Minister García Barragán, a key federal, regional and local government contact when companies and workers could not reach agreement. Once, when a strike continued for over two days and threatened to get out of hand, it was violently repressed by the army and police; the leaders were later simply reported as 'missing'. In another case, the local branch of a national union was disciplined when a top union official negotiated too unfavourable a contract. In both cases, there were unofficial talks between the companies and members of the General's clique to ensure quick action.

Government violence or manipulation in labour conflicts was hidden behind company legitimacy constructed with various rhetorics and expressed in political rallies, parties and propaganda with slogans like 'This company produces high-quality tomatoes, creates thousands of jobs and benefits the nation.' (This is ironic since the owners are foreigners.) Company legitimacy is complex, and embedded in the struggle for regional political stability. This struggle pits the need to ameliorate poor living conditions against the need for profits, and management's status and power against that of farmers and workers.

Negotiating Living Conditions with the Tomato Growers' Union

Repression and manipulation played important roles in resolving conflicts, but were only used in exceptional circumstances. To guarantee everyday discipline, other measures were more effective and politically less costly. These included lobbying and bribing government officials. Workers saw repression as a significant obstacle to organizing a union. They acknowledge that their failure to form an effective union resulted more from company surveillance than worker hesitance. But despite being effective, this surveillance is not unproblematic. Surveillance, increasing competition for resources and leadership among companies, sugar producers, the General's clique, other politicians and tomato workers are all part of the conflicts continually negotiated in the disciplinary framework.

González (1991) mentions the Mexican government's 1975 initiative to strengthen the unionization of producers. In principle this was part of an agricultural modernizing program to allow more autonomy and improve companies' capacity to compete for international markets (cf. Van der Zaag 1992:36). However, the unionization of rural producers and farmers disturbed General García Barragán, who felt his empire invaded by socialist initiatives from President Echeverría and his relatives, from whom he had distanced himself after 1968.[14] Although he continued to support the sugar producers' union, the General did not support the federal initiative and unsuccessfully tried to curb such unions, in which some members of his own clique were involved. He was opposed because the new *Asociación Local de Productores de Tomate*, which included the five main companies, old hacienda owners and landowners, could make quick profits and become politically independent. The General saw the unions as part of Echeverría's political networks, which did not fall under the PRI's traditional local organizing scheme and/or his clique's control. This stand was so extreme that García's own nephew disobeyed him and supported the new associations' search for more resources and government support (González 1994).

In theory, a tomato growers' association would have led to better inter-company communication on technological problems, scarce resources and labour problems (in particular how to apply progressive Mexican labour laws). Entrepreneurs involved in local politics would regard the laws as ideologically unobjectionable advances of the Mexican revolution. However, to compete, companies interpreted the legislation for their own political advantage and conceded only minimal social security benefits, pensions, indemnity payments and wage increases. The law is more often used tactically to attract workers from other companies. But there are common points of interest, and so competing companies share information on how to dodge the strict application of the law, which they consider economically unsustainable. They have a policy of dividing and dismissing subversive workers, and depoliticization and avoiding negotiation. Companies describe 'acting with discretion', which means restricting economic concessions, as managers' greatest skill. This skill is intuitive and subject to pragmatic considerations rather than guided by a rigid framework; companies often try to improve the pensions, social security and living conditions of their most skilled workers. Thus, legal definitions are constrained by historical situations, including the workers' claims.

However, the analysis of how workplace discipline is established would not be complete if other related contexts were omitted. In reality, company strength is relative, especially in economic terms, owing to the risks of agricultural production: one company owner compared it to a crapshoot. They must continually weigh external and internal constraints and opportunities, and recruit people into their networks to prevent problems and search for new solutions. Their vigilance may be explained by the political threat of spontaneous or organized workers' movements, which happens from time to time. Such practical manoeuvres are an opportunity to understand political stability, how the rules for negotiating wages and working conditions are established, and how companies concede the minimum, but are obliged to reckon with workers' previous gains.

Such gains are neither substantial nor definitive, since they are often specific to particular situations, like the dismissal of the foreman or a temporary wage increase. Nevertheless, the memory of organized strikes or defiance has more effect than an imaginary threat. Bosses realize that mass actions are unpredictable and can never be underestimated. If poor work discipline coincides with a bad season, the company could be in a precarious position. Thus, economic calculations are less important in determining concessions than political calculations that identify the timing and spacing of the minimum practical symbolic concession. Dissipating collective demands and avoiding mass worker mobilizations can hang on such calculations.

It is therefore no accident that managers and owners frequently assume a dual position in relation to workers. In order to avoid granting wage demands and prerequisites, they argue that they will be bankrupt or in the red at the end of the season. They may also complain about workers' lack of commitment to the company and poor work. According to another company owner, local workers 'have bad habits due to the fact that they can easily find another job in the area without committing themselves to a permanent obligation'. Companies acknowledge that they cannot completely control workers. Their approach to discipline is to get some advantage from and counter the bad effects of labour desertion. Thus the picture is not one-sided; workers themselves are part of the equation.

How Workers Recreate the Social Life of the Tomato Companies

As Chapter 3 showed, the job opportunities created by the companies amount to four workers for each new hectare cultivated. In 1988, this meant almost 5,000 jobs. This is the companies' strongest argument for legitimacy, used in negotiating with the government for taxes, credit and concessions. But one might also argue that legitimacy comes from workers who become self-disciplined and skilled in their work. This argument will be discussed here, as it pertains to other parts of the analysis.

For many years, working for the companies has been a common activity for large sectors of local communities, especially young people. Some, native to the valley, consider that these jobs mostly favour poor families, particularly women, young people and children, who have not previously done farm work. This is because tomato work is considered easy, less responsible and suitable for people unable to compete for better jobs. Some permanent workers are disenchanted because wages are falling. Only for children and women whose husbands cannot maintain them is tomato work still a good option.

For youngsters, tomato work is also fun. For women it means breaking out of the domestic mould (Verhulst 1988:67). More radical women workers believe that tomato work has changed regional cultural patterns, because as hundreds of women went into tomato work it became accepted that they work outside the home; but for others, working women are promiscuous. Tomato work involves people in a socialization process that changes the routine of living on isolated farms or in boring neighbourhoods. For landless people it means opening up other possibilities for survival. Most workers claim to have found new networks and lifestyles. They say that, despite the low wages, the work is interesting. Some go on to permanent work in the industry, others connect with other activities and regions; but for the majority it is only a transitory survival activity.

Looking back at workers like Rogelio, Alejandro and Polo in Chapter 3, one might think that the following statement by Bourdieu (1977:18) is somewhat extraterrestrial: 'if agents are possessed by their habitus[15] more than they possess it, this is because it acts within them as the organizing principle of their actions, and because this modus operandi informing all thought and action (including thought of action) reveals itself in the opus operatum'.

If one takes Bourdieu's dictum seriously it means believing that native experiences of the social world can never grasp the system of objective relations governing it. Hence workers' accounts and the researcher's second-hand accounts grounded in workers' accounts are objectively insufficient for explaining the meaningful world of tomato work. Bourdieu's privileging of data like statistics, prices and curves to characterize living conditions and working routines under institutional and hierarchical control is consistent with this. One implication is that workers are unable to create and maintain self-discipline; they have to follow the instructions of company planners. If the habitus is taken as a material basis or advanced strategy for control this means that workers cannot discipline by themselves. This notion of habitus is worthless for dealing with workers' taken-for-granted, emergent ways of doing work (regulated improvisation in Bourdieu's terms) as depicted in Chapter 3.

Taken-for-granted ways of working and worker self-discipline refers to workers' assumption that the tomato business is known and describable in terms of workplaces, changes in routine, common movements, familiar words, tacit actions, silences and common sense. However, these expressions of the self-evident are not shared by all tomato workers. The ethnographic material in this book suggests that we can distinguish five ways of under-standing how workers apply self-discipline in tomato work.

First, they know what they are doing, when they are performing well and how deliberately to do things carelessly. Second, they know some management instructions are absurd, and how to behave to respond to them. Third, workers discern the opportune moments for taking the initiative and doing more than they are asked or paid for, knowing that this benefits the foreman, the manager or the owner more than themselves, and that it does not guarantee better wages or treatment. Fourth, workers may prefer to accommodate themselves to tasks rather than be coerced, as this gives them more room to manoeuvre. Fifth, workers like to choose the constraints and opportunities for change and to avoid suicidal moves. Hence they acknowledge and comply variably with their exploitation and subordination.

Conclusion: Multiple Histories, One Region?

To conclude this chapter, I reflect on how this experimental sociological exercise differs from traditional studies on regional *cacicazgos* and transnational enclaves as commonly used (and abused) in the Latin American sociological and political economic literature of the 1960s and 1970s. I also spell out some implications of the interwoven historical processes narrated above. Autlán does not have one history but several. Regional *cacicazgos* and agro-export enclaves are socially constructed in multifarious ways by many actors, including local intellectuals and historians, members of political cliques, *agraristas*, merchants, Catholics, and workers, not just *caciques*, transnational owners or major politicians.

My inquiry into the regional origins of tomato production and its politics reveals complexly interrelated networks. Rotations in command and changes in networks reflect expected and unexpected actions in institutional domains, including the Autlán municipal government, the Agrarian Reform office, church, high school, *ejidos*, tomato companies and sugar mill, as well as national and regional contexts like the Presidency, ministries and state government. Arenas like the General's house, company planning departments, the Producers' Association, the spontaneous workers' union, wage and benefits negotiations, and daily conflicts became reference points for emergent issues like the image of authority and its uses, company legitimacy in the region, disciplinary modalities, social control and contingent institutional norms. These defined local politics.

The outcome is twofold. First, the customary local *cacicazgo* ceased to be the stable province of the powerful and entered a conflictive, unpredictable cycle of victory and defeat. Second, the apolitical modelling of transnational operations in terms of efficiency, technology and marketing became hybrid: the political mechanisms of customary forms, alliances, friendship ties and loyalty became the effective means of guaranteeing productive continuity. A social order with ongoing routines and patterns emerged as a product of negotiated political stability. This order gave precedents for agreements and innovations without having to negotiate everything afresh. Such a social order does not comply precisely with the letter of the law or planners' instructions.

New ways of selecting candidates for municipal elections, solving problems outside the legal framework (for example, pardoning murderers, vendettas, lynchings), distribution of resources, and above all changes in the command of interconnected networks shape the modalities of power within the *cacicazgo*. The clique and other groups employ techniques and tactics like closed meetings, information flows, political favours, ideological alignments, submission, discretion, surprise, radicalism, confrontation and withdrawal. Both modalities and techniques of power shed light on regional social patterns as the sum of social demands on authority to sort out problems and decide on behalf of the federal government to their advantage.

In company history, early entrepreneurs' 'mining mentality' is part of the constantly shifting positions amid labour conflict, interest group competition, bankruptcy, land, water and labour scarcity, pests, and environmental degradation. This shift in the modalities of power allowed for power-sharing with farmers who rented out land to them, government agents, the *cacique* and politicians (who were important mediators and did surveillance for the companies), and with workers (who displayed initiative, self-discipline and organization). Techniques for sharing legal knowledge to deal with labour matters, coordinating the Producers' Association to cope with financial and technical constraints, operated in tandem with minimum concessions, covert coercion, blatant repression, and constant, defensive vigilance. These modalities of power show how women, children and landless people find alternative forms of survival without developing permanent commitments to tomato companies, which in turn characterize themselves as constantly on the move.

This account shows how changing images and deployments of authority are the key to understanding local political matters. These images reveal the dynamic interconnections within diverse domains (Willener 1975). For instance, the General's often contradictory image as a military man and political figure was forged by followers, occasional allies and enemies under different circumstances, and expressed changing meanings outside the official political calendar. Among the list of qualities attributed to the General's authority were 'decides in the final instance, overriding the prerogative of the President', 'intervenes in situations beyond the law', and 'acts with an invisible hand', to more specific qualities such as 'chooses mayors in the region', 'represents the interests of the citizens and ruling party alike', and 'can reunite political factions'. This exercise of authority entailed mutual participation, as was clear with the empowerment of *agraristas*. The General had to defend their interests as his own, and *agraristas* considered him their benefactor despite the fact that radical leaders viewed him as apathetic to the *agrarista* cause. Still, they used the General's charisma to defy landowners and influence local elections.

In the companies under critical circumstances a flexible image of corporate authority could override the rigid organizational chart; but their political game was never totally under their own control. They had to enlist other forces from within and beyond the region, like government representatives, to manage labour problems, scarce resources and land invasions. Therefore some of the pioneering US owners referred to the twenty-year tomato boom as a 'miracle', in the face of bankruptcies, pests and personnel changes. Because there was no secure future for the regional tomato industry, company flexibility and survival were linked to winning legitimacy, a contested issue subject to continuous negotiation. Companies were legitimated and made politically viable by economics and technology, but also by politically astute labour management and alliances with other forces. This required contributing to local political stability by keeping their promises to produce a certain quantity and quality of tomato, generate jobs, boost the regional economy and bring services and social security to the population.

Discipline and social control also reveal the interconnections between social domains. Discipline tells us about the composition of linked forces and operating strategies (Foucault 1977:162). As we saw in Chapter 3 and the last section, discipline means negotiating values, task definitions and procedures. It is difficult to disentangle external models from customary forms of tomato work, and transformations constantly occur. For example, scheduling changes affect social routines in the local communities. It is often difficult to link features with corresponding forms, since socialization patterns overlap in time and place.

In concrete processes, such as changing disciplinary practices in the clique, the shift in membership indicates the targeted and targeting forces as trustworthy, discreet, capable, and as linked to *agraristas*, landowners, merchants, Catholics and liberals. However, discipline includes self-discipline, and this is only possible through effective recruitment and shared interests. Workers have little commitment to the job, and take it easy when they can. Companies profit from low wages and benefits. In the clique members imposed self-discipline to retain the General's trust.

The historical process frequently raised the issue of short- and long-distance normative and institutional control. The political rhetoric at different moments and in different domains was a pragmatic way of defining legality in elections, management and labour relations; the law is selective. Thus known written codes are not the definitive rules of the political game. Informal political negotiations are often more effective. However, such negotiations are grounded in political calculations. The researcher can only partially see their connections to past processes and their future implications.

As the third section showed, despite the companies' fragmentary and changeable agreements and norms, negotiating living standards lets them manage labour conflicts, such as the tendency to leave for other jobs. Although these agreements may not be formal contracts and procedures, they are practical examples. Thus they are precedents with prescriptive effects and rhetorical force for future situations.

A final reflection on the region is pertinent here. It is problematic clearly and securely to bound a region legally, geographically and historically, because it is difficult to characterize the changing symbolic and physical boundaries of unfolding social networks. However, despite the persistence of multiple locales in the Autlán valley, the region nevertheless has kept its own distinctiveness. It is the product of collective and individual actors' constant efforts to reinvent the region through dreams, self-organization and recruitment by others, promoting specific projects like the irrigation system, the sugar mill, and the tomato industry. These aim to have widespread regional effects that cannot be ignored. They influence political stability and the potential development of various activities by linking people's everyday lives with job opportunities; but the people of the Autlán valley transform the meanings of these projects.

Notes

1. Callon (1986a,b) conceives of actor networks as flexible structures mobilized in complex, intertwined power relationships. This is different from the usual sense of social network, which entails interrelated actor-units that, in Carlos and Anderson's (1981) terms are hierarchical and systemic. Callon and Latour call their approach to studying power relationships the 'sociology of translation', which aims to identify the methods by which an actor recruits others. These methods involve: (1) the definition of roles and placement of actors in scenarios; (2) the strategies by which actors render their worlds indispensable to others by creating a geography with obligatory points of passage; and (3) the displacement imposed upon others as they are forced to follow this itinerary. This geography of obligatory points of passage helps understand how actors' projects, initiatives and resources become so involved with others that they cannot act otherwise. It does not imply that they pursue a determined scheme or strategy.

2. I follow Elias' concept of institutions as 'consisting of nothing but the actions of people . . . which were neither intended or planned by any single individual in the form they actually take' (1978:xvi). Elias also considers institutions to be parts of a global civilization that is a product of the 'many single plans and actions of men that give rise to changes and patterns that no individual person has planned or created' (1982:230).

3. Carlos and Anderson (1981) show the importance of networks in Mexican political activity. They argue that networks cut across formal political institutions and often act quite independently of them. However, these authors view these networks' dynamics as quasi-mechanical, overemphasize their coerciveness and start describing from the top down (cf. Cornelius and Craig 1988). Lacking is an account of how networks' legitimacy is built up, varied, interrupted and interconnected, or how people from the middle or bottom are

recruited. The description of network maintenance and creation says little about conflict in resource distribution and power struggles. For an exhaustive analysis of power networks in Mexican politics, see De la Peña (1986).

4. Burawoy (1985:11) distinguishes between the politics of production and state politics, with the latter being the politics of politics. This leads to viewing the productive process misleadingly as semi-autonomous, and attributing superiority to state politics or meta-politics. This perspective is consistent with Burawoy's earlier work (1979:xii), which he defined as an 'attempt to understand how consent is produced at the point of production independent of schooling, family life, mass media, the state and so forth'. Rather than identifying domains as autonomous, I reflect on the politics of tomato work in terms of emerging issues and interconnected domains. This means exploring how schooling, family life, mass media and state policies are manifested in production and become interrelated through actors' emerging political discourses.

5. I look at images here in the sense suggested by Willener (1975), i.e. as conveying not only individual features but representing images of society. Willener offers this argument to understand the conceptions that workers have of society. He reminds us that actors are not only the products of a situation, but that they contribute to producing that situation. He emphasizes the potential of images for revealing social processes by pointing to the interrelation of the actions as image-producing situations and the images as actions producing (or continuing) situations.

6. Student protests had lasted over two months. At the time Mexico was preparing to host the Olympic Games. International media coverage of the event put more pressure on the government. The political climate deteriorated rapidly as the starting date for the Olympics approached and negotiations between student leaders and politicians failed to end the conflict.

7. The war took place in four western states, including Jalisco, between 1926 and 1930. Many priests and some bishops collaborated with the *hacendados*, military deserters and peasants to defend their religious beliefs, and organized an armed rebellion against the government. The result of this conflict was an overextended conflict between the Church and the Mexican State. The General was the head of the federal army and a volunteer rural militia mostly composed of landless people and *ejidatarios* who had taken over land expropriated from the *haciendas*.

8. Liberals and some members of the army had radical interpretations of the Mexican Constitution, especially in relation to Church involvement in political affairs. Article 130 established the separation of Church and State and forbade priests to participate in

politics. This was especially controversial in a former war area like Jalisco.

9. In an short biography Castañeda Jiménez (1987:54) explains that 'peaceful' meant that the General was interested in the needs of Autlán, in contact with his clique and good friends until the last, and trying to eliminate any idea of a *cacicazgo* from the minds of his followers and sympathizers.

10. Van der Zaag (1992:27) states 'that under suspicious circumstances the General acquired (shortly after becoming Governor) 40 hectares of land which officially belonged to the *ejido* of Ayuquila. General García Barragán bought a *trapiche* [a disused, ox-driven sugar mill] and let some of his soldiers and peasants work the land and cultivate sugar cane.'

11. Muriá (1982) shows that Governor Gallo's influence, agrarian policy and governing style reached into the next two governments (1948–66).

12. This committee was initiated in response to a request by the national leader of the caneworkers, a Jaliscan who wanted a group from Autlán to lobby the Cabinet for a mill. This leader acted in close coordination with the General and the Ministers of Education and Agriculture, who were also from Jalisco. This committee bombarded the President and other Ministers with telegrams asking for the mill (Guzmán Flores 1995). They argued that Autlán desperately needed a new source of jobs, and got a group of volunteer farmers to start producing in the valley.

13. The tomato companies' rental of lands from small producers and *ejidatarios* outside the irrigation network was disadvantageous (Arce 1990). The *ejidatarios* were unable to obtain credit, technology and other inputs to develop even basic grains, let alone tomatoes or sugarcane, so they stopped producing. They opted instead to migrate or to cultivate less fertile land in the valley without the above benefits, or rented out their more fertile land. Land rental does not reduce to simple economic or political factors. The agrarian legal framework, although slightly modified in 1918, 1934 and 1976, still prohibited renting out *ejidos*, but did not prevent it in practice. The *salinista* reform (1991) allowed the selling and renting of land from *ejidos*. It also aims to put an end to land distribution. This fact had a major impact in Chiapas, and is invoked as one of the important factors in the Indians' uprising (Harvey 1994).

14. Camp (1992:28) describes this mutual distancing between two politicians who played important roles in the repression of 1968. Before the Tlatelolco massacre, Echeverría was Interior Minister and sought a negotiated solution. When he become President he openly, if discreetly, criticized the massacre, and indirectly blamed García Barragán.

15. Bourdieu (1977) offers various different definitions of the habitus. Perhaps the clearest is the 'embodiment of subjective and objective history' but some are contradictory: 'Habitus is the result of an organizing action with a meaning close to that word such as structure', 'a way of being', 'a habitual state (especially of the body and group)', 'a predisposition, tendency, propensity or inclination'. The problem is the unresolved tension between the 'generative principle of regulated improvisations or the necessary improvisation of everyday strategies' (ibid.:78,179), and a 'system of dispositions or the mechanical assembly or preformed programme' (ibid.: 214,218).

CHAPTER FIVE

On Workers' Power and Skills

Introduction

Powerless, poor, unfree, oppressed, socially isolated, deferential, disorganized and subordinated are some of the terms that the extensive, pessimistic social science literature uses to characterize the asymmetry of farmworkers' power/knowledge relations. Even if academically flawless and supported by ideological and methodological 'isms', the analytic corollaries of such notions are uninteresting and frustrating. If one does not describe subordinated people's hard lives and maintain the omnipresence of a power/knowledge differential between farmworkers and bosses, managers, and politicians one gets accused of not being objective. Yet such analyses suggest that workers cannot win important power struggles or company promotions. Instead, as I argue in Chapter 1, by presenting such differentials as ironic conditions, we avoid interpreting them as being definitive. This also points to a difficult analytic issue. It may be easy to see when an individual or group within a power structure lacks power or abandons it. However, when power seems to manifest the collective will of many individuals and groups under a leader, *cacique*, politician or capitalist, it is not so easy to see where that power resides or originated (cf. Villarreal 1994:18).[1] Nor is it easy to see how the disadvantaged have power or how the powerful may be vulnerable.

If I cannot objectively place tomato workers in rigidly asymmetrical power networks and demonstrate their disadvantaged living conditions, in this chapter I can offer a second look at what workers do in their everyday lives and what this means politically. My aim is to destabilize the tendency to take domination as a given, and instead to analyse interactions that reveal the

complex, contradictory and provisional nature of human interaction.

Academic texts and especially everyday reflection see the
achievement of power/knowledge positions as mysterious. These
positions are presented as pre-arranged moves, secrets, privilege
obtained through strategies. However, such privileges, secrets and
moves are always embodied in negotiations that are part of the
risks and the routines of everyday life. Thus, the mystery is not in
the existence of secrets, but in how these overlap with other
expressions of everyday affairs. Hence an analysis of power
mechanisms and positions that seeks a stable model for explaining
or reproducing the logic of social relationships is not useful. Power
neither explains nor establishes the order of things. To analyse
power relationships it is necessary to risk instability and maintain
a degree of ironic relativism in order to dismantle fixed notions of
domination. As Latour has argued, 'when actors and points of view
are aligned, then we enter a stable definition of society that looks
like domination. When actors are unstable and the observers'
points of view shift endlessly we are entering a highly unstable and
negotiated situation in which domination is not completely exerted'
(1991:129). Thus one can see more clearly that power must be
explained through action (Latour 1986:265); this implies that
power is a set of constantly shifting combinations.[2]

In this chapter, I construct contexts for a dynamic analysis of
power/knowledge relations in various interactions (cf. Long
1992:27). That is, I understand power/knowledge relations
through their effects. Although I consider power to be something
that happens,[3] 'it can only be seen through its practice, by focusing
on the ways in which techniques are deployed and on the
construction of social forces (fluid networks) that give it existence'
(cf. Villarreal 1994). However, in analysing power as constructed
by the will of others the analysis is always fragmentary and
incomplete. This is because power practices are the illusion of
people who think that they are obeyed or believe that it is possible
to identify fleeting instances of collective will in which it is not
clear who obeys whom or under what circumstances.

I discuss the problematic nature of power/knowledge relations
based on the analysis of two situations of the type Long (1986;
1988; 1989) calls 'social interfaces'.[4] The first is a forgotten story
which certain workers occasionally recall among friends. It is about
a worker who replaced an engineer as head of the greenhouses,

reversing the new management's tendency to substitute professionals for manual workers. It describes how the worker won
his battle with the boss at the Rosa Company after a change of
ownership had modified organizational patterns. The reper-
cussions of this change forced the company again to rearrange the
whole organizational scheme, including firing the man viewed in
Autlán as the boss.

The second situation emerged during my fieldwork and caught
my attention because it called for a deeper review of technological
change's local effects. A middle-level skilled worker ridiculed an
international drip irrigation expert precisely when he was
instructing the bosses and professionals about the advantages of
cutting-edge technology and how to operate the new equipment.
This was recounted to me by workers and technicians on the
course, which had been organized by the Unión Nacional de
Productores de Hortalizas (National Horticultural Producers
Union, UNPH).

The Ethnographic Construction of Worker Power

Through these ethnographic accounts, I examine how workers
struggle for power and are recognized as capable at work in
greenhouses and irrigation systems. There are two reasons for this
recognition: (1) their skill at directing production, because they
give appropriate orders; and (2) their knowledge of the workplace.
Implicit in the former is a political argument that questions two
assumptions: (1) the ideal of substituting agronomists or engineers
for workers in positions of technical and organizational responsibility; and (2) the belief that trained experts have more knowledge
than manual workers.

According to company hierarchies, the workers involved in these
events were not in the most important departments for decision-
making on the organization of tomato work, and they were neither
the best paid nor the best qualified in terms of formal training:
they possessed no certificates or diplomas. I will now explain
ethnographically how some company workers and managers
invoked worker power. This results from my research, and is based
on interaction with two social networks. In those networks, the
positions taken by one group of workers acquired important
meaning in so far as they were recognized at times as the general

sense of all the workers. This happened despite the fact that, for most of these workers, the events about which these positions were expressed were not well known. We are dealing with a specific discursive formation that could only be perceived under special conditions. It is interesting to determine how these workers were transformed into symbolic authorities not only in the eyes of other workers, who saw them as the most capable among them, but also in the eyes of bosses and managers.

As in Chapter 2, this again brings me to the question of how the political character of ethnographic analysis is reformulated in the dialogue between the researcher and the people researched. Workers impose their political views and emphasize what is most important to them. Their point of view is a kind of sabotage that forces the interpretation in a different direction. Once this focus is adopted, new challenges can be posed. This entailed that I could find different ways to reconstruct the event; this is exactly what happened when I tried to investigate in detail the 'forgotten story' of the reinstated worker.

Everyday Political Struggles in Tomato Work

An Unexpected Conflict: The Worker who Replaced the Agronomist

On 8 November 1987, a typical day two months after starting my fieldwork, apparently nothing unusual was happening. As a way of breaking the routine of waiting for the next orders from the boss, two workers with whom I had become friends poured out their accumulated resentment. They told me the story of a worker who knew and could do more than the head of the company. 'Don't you agree,' one of them asked rhetorically, 'that workers are justified in ignoring senseless orders?' This question prompted me to investigate the social networks of the workers in the story. I became excited about chatting with combative workers with interesting stories. I understood that the question was not at all innocent, and that it was another attempt to draw out my political sympathies.

Rogelio, the man who had posed the question, continued without waiting for my reply: 'It's just that the office plans don't work . . . they have to be made in the field. How different things will be the day that students learn through practice and not purely from a distance like they're accustomed to do.' Alejandro, the other worker, added 'It's like what happened three years ago in the greenhouse. Because of ill will they dismissed Ricardo [the department head] and replaced him with a woman agronomist but when she didn't work out they had to bring Ricardo back in order to get the work done, because only a worker knows what's best in practice.'

The Fulfilment of the Worker's Prophecy

The new company had had three consecutive catastrophic seasons, which obliged them to change bosses. The chief financial officer of the company came from Guadalajara to introduce the new manager to the workers and the rest of the personnel. This man immediately called for Ricardo, the ex-head of the greenhouse, and asked him to return to his post. When the new manager spoke to the worker, he explained that he had consulted various people and they had all recommended that for 'the progress of the company' he should return to his position in the greenhouse. Ricardo recalled how the context made for a calm negotiation:

> I told him that I would accept as long as we could agree on my salary and so I asked for the same salary as the agronomist. He accepted my argument with few objections. My reasoning was that if her work cost a lot but wasn't worth anything, why was mine, which was proven for eleven years, not going to be valued, and it worked.

The Political Nature of the Confrontation

More to the point, it should be noted that 'it was about a political problem'. This is how the reinstated worker himself openly and decisively summarized what happened:

> When the old gringo owner sold the company to his Mexican partners, they put a relative who was an engineer in charge of the company, but who was very conceited and wanted to impose things that were unacceptable to the workers, who knew more than he did. This created a hostile climate, which the manager interpreted as undermining his authority in the field. He reacted violently and irrationally, arguing that it was a matter of opposition to change. Well, I certainly am older than he is and have greater seniority in managing the greenhouses. Because of this he accused me of being corrupt and not wanting to change. His solutions were quite arbitrary. He switched me to another department

without much explanation. He humiliated me and reduced my wages . . . Faced with these facts, out of dignity or stupidity I took a position of silent resistance; I avoided openly confronting him and devoted myself to prophesying to my friends about the fiasco of these little Made in Mexico engineers. What made it worth continuing to work in the company was that the owner, who knew the rumours about me, didn't dare scold me.

The Agronomist's Version: 'The Problem Arose Because I was a Woman.'

Jeanette, who had graduated from the university five years earlier, did not like recalling those difficult times. She has assimilated them as details caused by her being a pioneering woman, since she had had the fortune to be one of the first female graduates of the agronomy department of the local university. She nonetheless agreed with Ricardo that the conflict was political, though their notions of the political differed.

> It's that people aren't used to seeing a woman engineer. So many of the workers were always complaining that things went better when the other worker was in charge of the greenhouse, and they frankly admitted that it was because they couldn't stand having a woman tell them what they had to do, especially in the field. They envied me because they said I worked less and earned more. That's why there was a problem and I had to leave the greenhouse. It wasn't a technical disaster but rather bad years, because the other companies didn't manage to produce much either owing to the virus that plagued the region.

Jeanette recognized that when she was put in charge she did not know much, but the boss had insisted that he would support her while she was learning the job. She said she did everything the boss ordered her to and demanded that the workers comply with those instructions.

Constructing the Context, Part I: How the American Entrepreneur Developed a Successful Company

To a degree one could infer that the two main protagonists' versions of the conflict clearly express their differences of class and gender. They are self-explanatory and perhaps influenced by different ideological biases, but neither provides a complete picture of the conflict; for that it was necessary to broaden the context. To that end, I provide two kinds of ethnographic accounts, one concerning the origins of the company, the other about the two workers' life histories and careers. In so doing, I am not attempting to give an objective account but to clarify the actors' life-worlds from an actor-oriented analytical perspective. The purpose is offer greater understanding of what generated the conflict.

My methodological procedures agree with Latour's suggestion (1986) of going back in time to rebuild the social origins of power networks that still underlie interactions. This provides reference points from which it is possible to reconstruct the development of the power network (ibid.:270). However, in the case of the origins of the company, this was not immediately possible, since the retired American entrepreneur, a key figure who could help me through the impasse of the two versions, was missing. The 'gringo', as he was called, became for me the 'great absentee', who had long since retired and was now selling property and living in a tourist paradise far from the region. I sought him out twice, but it was not easy to motivate this old entrepreneur to retell his story. The first time he was quite resistant, saying 'Well, it's that I don't want to get into problems; as a foreigner one can't talk about the government and how things are in a country. It exposes one a lot.' But on the second try the mention of friends with whom he sympathized made him more trusting, and he told me of experiences from three periods in his life: when he was a pilot in the US Air Force during the Second World War; an ex-tomato entrepreneur expelled from Cuba by Fidel Castro; and a pioneer of tomato production in the Autlán valley.

The entrepreneur, whom I call Jeff, boasted that despite the risks he was economically successful when he retired. However, he emphasized that, in the field, production is a very inexact science, and what gives results one day is no good the next. Moreover, with tomatoes what matter is practice, not theory; if all the available technology was ideally applied, it would fail through being uneconomical. Jeff recognized that several workers contributed to his success, because, despite earning little, they knew how to think on the job. Their practical experience enabled them to think through what was needed in tomato work. But the reason the tomato industry had been such a good business for him was because of the ideal climate and the large number of tomatoes sold on the Mexican domestic market: 'With the Mexicans' *salsa* culture, something happens here that happens in no other country: the percentage of the product that gets marketed is very high.'

The Innovation of the Greenhouse   The greenhouse epitomized Jeff's contention that the ideal deployment of technology is not always profitable. He decided to introduce greenhouses because too many tender young plants were damaged outdoors and their replacement was too costly. A partner who was a US banker took on the job of setting up visits to other greenhouses and helped find technicians to install them in México, but Jeff was very frustrated with these technicians' work: 'They were very inflexible and wanted to do everything like in Florida.' The solution he arrived at was to combine some of the things done in the US with what local workers could do in practice: 'In México they have neither money nor sufficient resources to set up sophisticated electronic equipment, and we had to keep making changes as we went along because it was very expensive to bring everything from the United States.'

The Company Work System   Jeff explained that many of the military concepts that he learned in the Air Force were useful to him in organizing his company. One of them was knowing how to select the right people for the job in question:

> It's that you don't need to have experienced, highly paid people for everything. What you need is to train new people who have no established work habits but know how to work. Sometimes it's bothersome to work with experienced pilots because it's difficult to get rid of their bad habits and they don't adapt to handling new planes.

Another concept was to hold work planning meetings:

> It's that every day you're playing with capital and with the livelihoods of a lot of people who think differently. In the air squadron, you had to find constant forms of communication with the colonel to plan and specify situations on the different battle fronts. In the company, we adopted a system of holding meetings with the ten farm managers [trusted workers] each day before beginning work. They had the right to protest and even upbraid me, but once it was agreed what was going to be done, everybody disciplined themselves.

Constructing the Context, Part II: The Two Careers

Ricardo: The Local Teacher   Ricardo is important because although he has never set foot in a university, he is known by the workers as 'the Prof' and 'Doc' for knowing a lot of things. Despite his poverty, which was highlighted by the fact there were seventeen people in his family, he finished his education. Lacking economic resources, Ricardo could scarcely imagine getting past sixth grade; but thanks to one of his teachers, who considered him very capable, when he finished sixth grade, he was invited by her to give classes to the pupils who were behind in their studies. Ricardo says of those years, 'I didn't make much back then, but it was good for the experience and I kept learning. But that only lasted for five years, and I had to break it off because I got seriously ill.'

The Natural Healer   At twenty-two, Ricardo was on the brink of death. Not even the so-called medical specialists could diagnose his complaints; official medicine had simply declared him beyond help. His parents gave what little they had at their disposal and tried every kind of therapy: *curanderos*, cleansings, herbalists and famous doctors, but everything seemed in vain. Ricardo emphasized, 'all hope had been lost and those docs were such bastards that they dared to prophesy that I only had three days left to live'. Without giving up, they turned at last to Don Daniel, a natural healer from El Grullo.[5] After diagnosing him through his iris, Don Daniel assured Ricardo that despite his weakness, his body was not so contaminated. Don Daniel said he had faith that Ricardo would respond to treatment. For three months Ricardo followed a disciplined programme of hydrotherapy, infusions, drinks and a strict diet, and he returned to normal.

Don Daniel noticed that Ricardo was interested in natural medicine, and invited him to study and train with him to be a natural medicine instructor. He worked for Don Daniel for four years.

> I liked the idea that medicine was there to serve, and should not be used to make a business out of health. He personally enjoyed giving me classes, suggested readings and sent me off to research natural reactions and treatments in different regions such as the sierra and coast. Don Daniel also wanted me to collect plants and tea recipes and other therapeutic treatments that were practised locally. Through daily contact with Don Daniel I acquired the habit of taking notes on every case to monitor patients' evolving reactions. Ironically, when Don Daniel died some of his disciples who were businessmen took over the centre and turned it into a business. I felt displaced and decided to leave.

The Experienced Worker   Ricardo began his work for the tomato company as a *peon*. Over time, because of his ability, he was made the foreman of a group of workers. From there he was promoted to the greenhouse, where he learned a great deal from German instructors the company had brought in from the United States to train fifteen workers selected by the company. He followed them closely over the short two-month period of the course, and he hounded them with relentless questions. Ricardo was the only one of the fifteen to complete the course, and proudly states that he still has the notebook with the instructors' comments. Ricardo still makes a habit of taking daily notes about what happens in the greenhouse and what the plants need, just as natural healers are accustomed to doing. He considers that the autonomy he enjoys in his department was won during the time of the gringo and after overcoming various conflicts. Ricardo gave an example:

> . . . it was about applying a fungicide, and Jeff sent me without giving clear instructions or informing me of the contents, so I decided not to apply it. The gringo got really mad because I didn't apply it. When I saw him angry, I retorted that he should take the trouble to explain the fungicide's purpose, since I wasn't going to risk my job by making a mistake. Now even angrier, Jeff answered that if he sent me to do it, it was because he would assume responsibility. I insisted more strongly, 'You as the boss would put the blame on me if the application of the fungicide was mistaken.' This just enraged him further to the point that he reminded me that he was the one who signed my check. I was also fed up, and told him that he hadn't bought me, and that whenever he wanted, the job was free. In the end the gringo ended up apologizing, because, as *patrón*, he acknowledged that they make him a lot of money and he respects them for that.

Ricardo had good *rapport* with the new boss who reinstated him, especially because the boss let Ricardo do things in his own way. This included his father's custom of sowing on days when the moon was full and his preference for the natural treatment of plants, thus avoiding the excessive use of herbicides and fungicides. He liked to spread rumours about their polluting effects and unnecessary use.

The Trusted Secretary: Jeannette's Career   Jeff, who lived across the street from Jeannette, asked her to work for him after she finished high school. He asked her because he knew she spoke English.

Jeannette's mother negotiated with Jeff that Jeannette's acceptance of employment be conditioned on his support for her completing her professional studies. Jeannette began working in the office, and was put in charge of the English reports sent each month to the other American partners. She also handled the payroll, balanced the bank accounts, and did the correspondence and all the company paperwork. It was a job that cost her a lot, especially when she had to spend more time on her university coursework.

The Engineer   After getting her agronomy degree, Jeannette kept working for the company and its new owners. She enjoyed it when they gave her more responsibility, such as being in charge of fertilizing, tracking down viruses and, what she considered most important, preventing financial losses due to people who did not work hard. She also liked to consult with the boss frequently and oversee all the responsibilities for work in the field. She admitted that the boss treated her as a confidante and told her all his problems. She preferred that the boss comment on or read for her all the advertising pamphlets on pesticides and technology, because she didn't like big books. She put the disaster in the greenhouse behind her and felt that she came out ahead, since the professional experience she was acquiring allowed her to surpass those who wanted to sink her. She pointed out 'in salary and know-how I'm leaving them behind and I already beat them, because now I'm better off, I keep making progress and I've earned the trust of the boss, who is my confidant'.

However, Jeannette admitted that she had also learned much from those subordinates who wished to improve themselves. According to her these were a minority, since most of them waited to be given orders: 'Do it this way and that's it, because they don't like to get ahead and they're not interested in understanding the details of the technological change taking place.' In her opinion, what some workers rejected most were the instructions for applying chemicals, which is also a feature that had changed since when the gringo was the owner. Perhaps this was due to the fact that the land did not need so many chemicals back then.

For Jeannette, the workers' reluctance to follow instructions on applying chemicals would be resolved by the new, foolproof drip irrigation system. The proper dosage of the chemical to be applied would simply be put into the pumping equipment. Although there is still a lot that is not known about pesticides' so-called side-effects and very little has been done in the region for effective biological pest control, Jeannette considered the existing pest and weed control system advanced and safe. The company's procedure for applying pesticides began when the plant disease was diagnosed. Economic considerations were the first priority: what was in the warehouse was used first, starting with the cheapest and going to the most expensive. When the pest could not be controlled, they sought help from the outside, ordinarily requesting consultations from the people in charge of commercial houses. She considered this to be a beneficial relationship for the company, since in that way the company obtained much up-to-date information about technical advances and their applications, even though she knew beforehand that these houses' main objective was to sell. Her executive approach to her work entailed a loss of anonymity, which pains her. Men know her as 'the engineer'. But she is very proud of her new, powerful pick-up truck, to which she has added a feminine touch with special carpets and by keeping it clean and sweet-smelling.

The Company's Changing Context and Worker Power

I now reflect on the political transformations that occurred. I first examine the usefulness of the ethnographic narrative and of the concept of social interface (Long 1989). Once the researcher manages to penetrate the local social networks, s/he can understand and even identify with some of the interests of the actors whom s/he engages in dialogue. The interaction allows one to understand the actors' arguments – no matter how fragmentary or outdated they may be, which then become meaningful and allow one to connect the events. It allows one to group participants and reveal alliances and established associations among people of different networks, and apparently incompatible life-worlds, like the gringo.

The nature of the conflict between the two employees and the manager was readily acknowledged by all three as political, but was generally perceived as a dispute over power and authority in the heart of the company. In contrast, the workers formulated it as a specific problem about decision-making in the greenhouses. However, there are three different interpretations of the conflict's origin. It is intriguing to explain how and why different ideological representations supporting divergent interests develop in similar contexts on the basis of the same information. The analytical challenge is twofold. On the one hand, we need to understand how contrasting interests form part of historically connected power practices. On the other, once the mutual links are established, one must ask about the coherence between the rhetoric and practice of actors who appear less transparent because they express themselves in terms of sex or class. The point is that if company hegemony is considered stable and only momentarily interrupted, this keeps us from seeing the importance of the political effects of changing the greenhouse director. The reduction of the conflict to a momentary obstacle only serves to reinforce the prevailing logic of domination. The ethnographic narratives reflect the complexity of the conflict and in fact undermine hegemonic company relations in reconstructed imagination.

I will now break down the actors' interests and attitudes to better understand the power interests that operate in the social networks mobilized in the conflict. The dismissed agronomist interpreted the conflict from a gender perspective. Her argument was not an abstract discussion about women's rights, but a pragmatic one, which assumed that women face difficulties when they want to pursue their interests professionally. Jeannette used several techniques to achieve her goals. One of these was to work closely with the boss and win his trust. Another was to support the policy of technological change and the company's commercial interests. An especially beneficial strategy was to collaborate with the company in controlling the workers by eradicating their reluctance towards technological change.

As a result of her collaboration with the boss, she felt entitled to confront workers who in her opinion did not like receiving orders from a woman. For her, the three catastrophic seasons did not represent a political defeat. At most they were upsetting events that could be explained as the result of a technical failure (the spread of a virus) that also affected other tomato producers in the region.

The reinstated worker and his fellow workers interpreted the conflict as an issue of class. For Ricardo, it stemmed from a disagreement with an arbitrary *patrón* who humiliated him and cut his salary. His tactic was to avoid direct confrontation and to engage in silent, subversive resistance. He also spread rumours and gossiped to close friends. Gradually, he built an oppositional network among the greenhouse workers, who were later able to express their criticism more openly as the harvest kept failing.

After negotiating better working conditions he established some autonomy in the greenhouse, even though this distanced him from the small group of company decision-makers of which Jeannette was a member. Hence, although his reinstatement acknowledged the workers' ability and contributions, it also created resentment in the boss, who was reluctant to include difficult or rebellious workers like Ricardo in everyday discussions and planning. This in itself was a company strategy to prevent him from rising any higher or obtaining privileges.

The boss's interpretation of the conflict reflects his need to re-establish company discipline after technological solutions failed. Although he tried to disqualify those who confronted him as corrupt and opposed to change, this was not enough to keep workers from disobeying his instructions in the greenhouse and undermining his authority in the company. Facing the failures and consequent political risks, his successor abandoned disciplinary measures against the worker but also encouraged the small group of decision-makers, the use of technical language, the appointment of professionals and their training. He promoted the idea that the conflict was due to a virus, a technical problem common to the region. In this way, the virus was a fortuitous pretext, a natural disaster and an external cause that could easily explain away mismanagement mistakes. After three years, most local and migrant workers had no idea about the conflict, but the select group concerned with daily planning was completely aware of it. For them it was something in the past, which concerned only the greenhouse.

The accounts of the conflict are useful because they highlight how some workers become powerful, if only for fleeting moments, and because they shed light on how the management of power networks passes into different hands. Political concerns about power issues are continually expressed and open to multiple interpretations. Although momentarily contested, the historical tendency to replace workers with agronomists or engineers did not stop, but became a more subtle form of creating power differentials. The issue became more complicated and resulted in more than simply creating positions for professionals or removing others for manual workers. Although the conflict created discontinuities in work organization, it did not lead to fundamental change. The destabilization of work routines was actually useful, because it reflected the interlocking points of contact[6] among social networks that create continuity in daily life. Identifying these interlocking points of contact clarifies Law's phrase, 'to understand what it is that stabilises social relations is to generate power effects' (1991:66).

Underlying the conflict was a shift in management style due to a change in ownership. These workers regarded the shift as a drastic break because at least ten workers who had actively participated in the company's daily planning and decision-making suddenly stopped doing so. What they had seen as a democratic style suddenly disappeared. Although some workers like Rogelio criticized this style as a scheme for getting the workers' best ideas for free, it increased motivation and gave workers more control. In any case, the workers noticed the difference immediately and interpreted it as a more centralized and authoritarian management style. The atmosphere of openness in which farm and department heads talked with the boss was now replaced by a gang of four, which included the dismissed agronomist, the head of personnel (another experienced worker), the accountant and the local manager. Workers now had to take daily work orders from this group.

Worker Power

For one group of workers, reinstating Ricardo led to the emergence of a symbolic image in which 'the powerful one was the worker who knew more than the boss and had managed to destroy his authority as company chief'. In fact, this sensibility typifies workers, who like to assert and maintain their autonomy within the workplace, where they do actually exercise authority. This is expressed as 'Only the worker knows what is best in practice.' However, this did not represent a major change, as would be the case of worker self-management or in a bottom-up decision-making model. From the point of view of company managers like Jeannette and the new local boss, the image of worker power evaporated quickly once Ricardo was reinstated. In the end, owner control was less endangered when the conflict and rebellion diminished, and they even thought that they had gained more legitimacy.

The reinstated worker continued to enjoy greater autonomy in managing the greenhouse, although he later recognized that this resulted in his feeling more isolated. This enjoyment of greater autonomy is what Gorz (1980) refers to as 'uncaptured effort that all human work comprises and which is defended by the worker as a sovereign praxis'. In this case, the power exercised by workers implied at least two of the types of power Law describes: the 'power to' negotiate his salary and manage the greenhouse in his own way and the 'power over' – to influence, enrol and control workers in disobedience and rumours. One could even say that, if only for fleeting moments, there were discretionary power and power effects when Ricardo received unanimous support on being reinstated in the greenhouses for the good of the company.

Although worker power is a social practice, it can only be located in concrete social networks, work situations and spaces. It eventually spilled over and influenced the company's whole work process. In this regard it matters less that this can be judged as beneficial for company interests, which will always capitalize on or control their workers' efforts. The American founder expressed this well when he recognized that 'workers play a very important role in the success of the company in that they earn so little but are very capable when it comes to understanding how to do tomato work'.

The image of worker power embodied in those champions who have more authority and wisdom than the boss imagines a type of ironic vengeance. This contradicts the perception of workers as submissive and obliged to obey the instructions of a boss who in turn bases his authority on prerogative and not on the viability and coherence of his orders. The image of workers' power also extends to an ideological argument for defending the school of life in which the workers nursed their knowledge against the stereotyped procedures of expert, academic knowledge. In any case, workers frequently express their awareness of managers' and technicians' planning mistakes from a critical angle that asserts that it is simply impossible to control everything from the office.

Worker Skills and the Local Effects of Technological Transfers

The second ethnographic narrative explores other power/knowledge effects under circumstances connected in many ways to the previous case. Some of the participants were the same, although the context and script were different. This account stresses how transferring technology sets off multiple local effects which deepen differences in power/knowledge and make them more subtle. The situation concretely demonstrates the tomato companies' emphasis on doing a more efficient job by adapting technological packages and reinforcing the technical training of their professional staffs.

Chimino's Prank on the Israeli Expert

Thursday, 7 October 1988 was a great day for the Asociación de Productores Agrícolas de Autlán (Autlán Agricultural Producers Association).[7] That day a course on drip irrigation, given by a team of Israeli experts and headed by the Director of Experimental Plant Genetics of the Neissman Institute, ended.[8] The professor had demonstrated that the drip irrigation equipment of the region was not operating at full potential, and claimed that this was because it was badly designed or poorly operated by the technician or workers in charge (cf. Annex 3, Regional Information Newspaper #481, October 1988:7).

Of course, the newspaper account made no mention of the fact that Chimino, a worker responsible for operating some of this 'inefficient' irrigation equipment, had given Professor Abi a hard time and mocked his attempt to corroborate his claim with a field test. Two days later I heard several versions of this event from course participants and one of the other researchers who was present. This prompted me to contact Chimino himself. During pauses in his maintenance work on the irrigation equipment, he related,

There were many weird things that day. A lot of people arrived very early to the airport ranch, including the boss and my superior, *Ingeniera* Jeanette, who was also taking the course. I noticed that they came prepared: they brought cameras, calculators and even land maps. I didn't count them all, but there were like twenty-five and they were taking notes and all. It was said that there were some extensionists from Baja California working for Banrural and a tall, thin gringo they called Pieter. The Israeli professor approached me and said: 'Look, get the equipment working.' Then he started with his babbling and he tried to direct the students yelling, 'Let's proceed...'. Here he paused and asked me in a low voice, 'What are you going to do? What are you going to do?'. I told him, 'Well, I'm going to start draining and clean the well.' The professor started yelling again so the students could hear him, 'First we are draining the water from the well . . .'. 'Yeah, yeah,' I interrupted, 'here I come with the water', and warned him that I was only going to put in 600 gallons, since that was the usual amount here because there were only seven valves to distribute the water through the equipment. The professor kept watching the pressure gauge. When he saw that the pressure level was not what he expected, he began to shout louder and gesticulate for more pressure. I contradicted him, 'It's just that I have only seven valves. Where do you think I'm going to put so much water?' But he didn't appear to hear what I was telling him, and kept yelling at me, 'You give it more pressure. Don't you see that here on this gauge there should be more pressure?' For a few moments I gave it more pressure, but only so that he could see that the equipment did have the capacity. Then I stopped, because if I had continued I was going to damage the most distant sections, where for sure hoses and sprinkler heads would burst from the excess pressure.

When the professor again noticed that I had lowered the pressure, he got mad and started to shout louder. And it was then when we started getting more stubborn. He told the students, 'Look! Look!' and he pointed to one of the pressure gauges, which was oscillating quickly and didn't function well, and that was why the equipment wasn't delivering the correct pressure. I again contradicted him, 'No way, it's giving me the pressure that I want.' He got even madder and told me, 'Let's see the pressure on the other gauge', which according to him proved his point of view. He called the students again, 'Look closely. This gauge has low exit pressure.' I again contradicted him, 'That's what I want, that the stream stay small so it falls at the base of the plants.' But he kept insisting that he needed more pressure, and I kept contradicting him, 'That's it for me, because I'm sure neither you nor the rest are going to fix the broken hoses and blown sprinklers in the far sections.' Since he couldn't convince me or shut me up, he seemed to leave me alone. He took out his calculator and went with the group of students to straighten out his calculations. Finally he repeated his conclusion, 'This equipment is badly designed and operated.'

Chimino interpreted this as a personal insult, and reacted angrily when he heard the professor say to the students 'It's just that they need to clean the tanks every five minutes.'[9] On hearing this, Chimino contradicted him, and pointed out that because of the condition of the wells it was only necessary to clean them twice a day. Chimino could not understand how they were going to irrigate if they were cleaning every couple of minutes. Since the professor kept insisting on giving it more pressure, it occurred to Chimino to have a bet with him to go out and see what happened at the far ends of the equipment to determine who was right. Chimino explained,

I had to again specify the terms of the bet and what each of us maintained. 'You say that with the pressure I'm giving the equipment we have a medium stream leaving the equipment but a little, inadequate stream getting to the plants. But I say you're wrong. I'm using a smaller stream of water than you want, but I assure you that it's big enough to reach the plants because you haven't taken into account that the terrain has a slope at both ends.' I invited him to join me and verify who was right. We went to see and when he got there he was surprised and didn't say a word.

Back at the pumphouse, the professor again insisted that the equipment was badly designed and didn't work. On the other hand, the equipment that he showed the course participants and that they were offering for sale to the companies had no problems. He tried to challenge Chimino by asking how much the equipment had cost. Chimino turned to his boss and told him, "'They're talking to you here, you have to answer this." The boss stated that it cost US $1,200 per hectare. The professor immediately counterattacked, "Now you see, so much money down the drain because the equipment doesn't work and this kid who doesn't know how to irrigate.'"

Feeling more insulted, Chimino again interrupted and shouted louder than before, 'I showed you that I do know how to irrigate and that the equipment doesn't break on me but if what you want to do is sell machinery, start off saying clearly that that's why you came. That's another matter. That way you could have avoided having to insult a person.' Chimino then asked the professor, 'How about if I hit you in the head with a bottle?' Again angry, the professor answered, 'Look, even though I'm old, I can still defend myself.' Chimino laughed,

> You see, it's the same thing. You also react like anyone else. I didn't want to offend you, but that's what happened. You arrive here wanting to sell people fancy shoes when you see they're wearing torn sneakers. So that things are clear, if what you want is to sell, then offer your product and don't say ours doesn't work and that we don't know how to irrigate.

Constructing the Context, Part III
Before discussing this altercation, I will first present a summary of Chimino's life history and part of the speech by the president of the UNPH at the closing ceremony of the drip irrigation course. These provide a useful elements for understanding the case. I also

add interpretations from other participants whom I asked about the circumstances in which the encounter had developed and what it meant for the tomato companies.

Chimino's Background   He is one of the more unusual members of the company and is easily recognizable. He was described to me as 'crazy, smiles and talks a lot, and is responsible for the irrigation equipment'. At the same time he was 'the fearless worker, intelligent and resourceful'. Chimino was the oldest of thirteen children and had just turned thirty. He had to break off his studies early and go to work in order to help his mother maintain the family after his father abandoned them. Maybe that is why he likes to say that with effort he can just about sign his name, but can't write at all, although recently, under pressure from the company, he has begun to do so, and even uses a calculator to get the correct mixture of fertilizer and pesticides that they dilute in the irrigation pumps. This is why he is trying to go to night school for adults, so he can get 'a job that's better than dog's work'.

His appearance is completely informal. Short in stature, he dresses strangely for where he lives, because he keeps wearing the same clothes he bought when he lived in a black neighbourhood in the US. He also likes to show off the tattoos he had painted on both arms there to help identify him with the *cholos* (gang members) of the Mexican *barrio*. However, Chimino is also an experienced and responsible worker who has managed to rise through several positions in the company, which has helped him to save a little money. He is proud to own his own house. His boss respects his adaptability and readiness to learn new things. For instance, while still only an inexperienced boy, he began driving tractors, and above all dared to install the irrigation equipment using only the provisional plans provided by the American salesman; overwhelmed by the enormous demand for irrigation equipment in the region, the salesman had left others to install it. This made Chimino an important worker for the company. He knows how to use the majestic language of 'Let's do it' or 'Let's plant.' He defends the company's work, adapting and innovating to maintain the equipment at lower cost. Despite his seeming talkativeness, he is very sure of himself, will not be put down by anyone, and knows the appropriate moment to ask for a rise, because he does not like conflict. On the other hand, he glories in driving the company's most dilapidated vehicle, because he is 'not interested in a new one instead of a better salary'.

The Closing Ceremony   Jeannette looked very elegant but nervous for her presentation at the end of the course. She was part of the group the Israelis designated as more advanced; they were to present a design of the ideal equipment, based on measurements of the terrain and available equipment. The instructors introduced the presenters, requested that they use the technical terms learned in the course, and helped them to clarify confusing points. Jeannette was to discuss the cost of equipment. She concluded that it cost $2,890 per hectare, which seemed too high for two owners who had asked about financing and repayment terms. The Israeli professor intervened and said that costs would decline in the medium term, because the equipment lasts a long time. In five years they would scarcely need to do more than replace hose. The rest would remain intact.

The crowning moment of the course, only the second of its kind held in Mexico, was the final address by the general director of the UNPH, the course's sponsor. For him, the purpose was to give the members current technical knowledge. He began by emphasizing the UNPH's efforts at finding the best technology in the world: from the US, Japan, Holland, Spain and Israel. For him, the Israelis were in the vanguard in many areas of agricultural production and technological knowledge.

After congratulating the local association for endeavouring to organize a course that demonstrated their desire for progress, he prophesied that in the near future they would eliminate the unimaginable irrationality of inefficiently managed investments in costly irrigation equipment. He considered that with such courses, the UNPH was getting up to speed and responding to the challenges of modernization and competition, since only in that way is it possible to overcome the irrationality of the fact that countries as distant as Chile, Holland and Israel are beating Mexico in the US market.

He concluded that the key to explaining this inefficiency was that the tomato companies' planning continues to be based on fundamental weaknesses: the economic advantages of cheap labour and the low value of the Mexican peso. In the future cheap labour and a devalued peso would be insufficient, because it is necessary to master new technology and face the challenges of modernization to be more productive. 'I am convinced that the step taken tonight can guarantee better technical management, which will achieve greater efficiency in vegetable production', he said.

Analysis

The Construction and Effects of 'Official' Truth   The language used
on the course and especially in the closing ceremony conveyed the
idea that tomato companies and entrepreneurs not only represented the interests of the region but to some extent heralded a
strategy to recover a cutting-edge position in the Mexican market
and compete with US, Chilean, Dutch and Israeli producers. The
tomato companies continually used this argument in their struggle
for legitimacy in the face of political attacks. The course itself tried
to demonstrate that the region was progressing and reaching its
goals of increasing production. The transfer of modern technology
was viewed as a guarantee of success, since new equipment was
more capable of controlling plant pests and diseases with better-
regulated application of pesticides and fertilizers. As a corollary,
such measures would help recover better market position.

   This discursive formation was very much in tune with the festive
atmosphere of the closing ceremony. Consequently, arguments like
those of the Israeli professor concerning poorly designed and
incompetently operated irrigation equipment as well as the
UNPH's national representative's denunciation of irrationality
became dogmas used to explain past and present results and
predictions of a better future for the regional tomato industry. This
was the UNPH representative's main argument for getting ready
to compete and attain better market position. This also entailed
that companies had to master new imported technologies and
abandon the intrinsic weaknesses of cheap labour and the financial
fictions based on the constant devaluation of the peso. The
accusation against unscrupulous equipment designers that they put
such equipment in the hands of workers uninformed about
technological advances was seen as a thing of the past, like putting
sophisticated and costly aeroplanes in the hands of inexperienced
pilots. (Note that this point was totally opposed to the thinking of
the American, who considered expert pilots to be less open to new
ideas.) At the same time, the successful areas were precisely those
most criticized by the UNPH representative.

   Workers like Chimino do not have a voice, and are even
considered less rational in the logic of official truth. Therefore it
is not surprising that the verbal confrontation between Chimino
and the expert had been ignored or seen as irrelevant: this is a
visible effect of power/knowledge differences within specific

networks. To counteract that effect, I was curious to find out the course participants' reactions to this confrontation. I talked informally with twelve of them, but only two of them had noticed the depth of the conflict. The rest had only thought, 'What a stubborn worker!'

One of the participants was a chemist. In the course he had given a session on soil analysis. For him the course represented an objective step forward for the region, and he could not disagree with the official version, even though he was not very optimistic about any immediate benefits. From his point of view, the course was another step in the socialization of knowledge. He believed that in the present context of change, the companies showed the way to gain access to international experts. In the past, foreign influence was almost totalitarian. They left no room for local initiatives in their courses, to the point of dictating where one should place one's feet in the greenhouse; and the bosses themselves did not know the content of those courses.

The chemist also recognized that recent visits by Autlán companies' technical personnel to tomato farms in the US, Spain, Holland and Israel were fruitful for organizing tomato production more efficiently. He interpreted the altercation between Chimino and the Israeli as a struggle between expert and practical know-ledge, and an example of the different ways of diagnosing and evaluating technical production problems. For him, scientists and technicians are more insecure in their knowledge than ordinary people and peasants, because their practice proceeds according to a theoretical position derived from some notion of scientific knowledge. They are accustomed to checking everything with exact mathematical procedures. Peasants and lay people, on the contrary, address problems with a surer, more pragmatic vision, because for them the issue is to make their everyday situation more liveable.

The other participant who expressed his awareness of the alter-cation was an agronomist working for a government institution, who had been one of the most brilliant students on the course. He considered that Chimino had really called into question the expert's teachings. Although he thought that Chimino was right in so far as he demonstrated his knowledge of the field, he questioned whether Chimino could give a technical explanation of that knowledge.

Defining Worker Skills   To understand how the image of a skilful worker is created and maintained, it is necessary to look beyond their individual achievements. If we were only dealing with individual ability, we could look at their life histories. However, it is more important to examine how this image is connected to specific social processes. This means asking how images of skill and ability are constructed in different situations and are seen as important; or, in short, how the most capable tomato workers are valorized.

For some workers who identified with a collective management that promoted the company's progressive interests, the era of the 'democratic dream' under the American owner fostered images of skilful workers in a competitive environment of incentives. However, this was not a monolithic interpretation, because others saw it as a time when workers who made the company product cheaper were identified as capable. In both perspectives, the key to being considered skilful was that there was no favouritism or imposition by the owner to valorize the workers, but valorization depended, for example, on the ready acceptance in particular departments of the company of the most qualified workers. With the more centralizing style and other changes introduced by the new owners, the profile of able workers changed. The favouritism of the boss and his trusted group of decision-makers appeared more important. They chose the most loyal workers, whom they liked and who shared their interests in undertaking certain tasks and functions. However, the criterion still exists that some workers deserve general recognition, and they remain on an imaginary list of the most skilled, whether in the bosses' or workers' heads. Chimino seemed to be one of these.

In any case, the meaning underlying the idea of a skilled worker is a matter of interpretation. In Chimino's case, the boss appreciated his adaptability and readiness to learn new things, which coincided with Chimino's own view that being more capable and skilful was a question of attitude and being open to opportunities. Being a skilled worker therefore means being good at negotiating a better salary and working conditions that avoid 'working like a dog'. Some among his colleagues identify his skill as part of his bold adventurousness to take on any job. In practise, being a qualified worker means being able to solve problems, manage scarce resources, test things out, invent and adapt. This also means being more productive for the company without expecting great rewards.

Of course, Chimino's personal circumstances and the environment in which he grew up are part of what socialized him to develop his abilities. Forced as a teenager to face the rigours of life because father abandoned the family, he became engaged in a career or lifestyle full of challenges and adventures. His various experiences predisposed him to face challenges and learn from them. Therefore it is not hard to understand why Chimino has a critical and subversive attitude toward experts. In the altercation he was very confident of his practical ability and knowledge. He felt that the irrigation equipment was his, since for him it represented one of the most noticeable achievements in his career. Having precise knowledge of local conditions was another advantage for Chimino, which enabled him to adapt to any equipment the company bought, whether from an American or an Israeli. This gave him the security of knowing he was more capable than the ordinary worker, and put him in a position from which to combat the international expert's arrogance.

But although being a skilled worker is a distinction and should imply privileges and better positions within the company, the ethnographic account shows that it does not automatically carry with it immediate rewards. For instance, despite his greater skill, Chimino never replaced his superior, Jeanette. Winning the bet with the expert meant no immediate profit, like winning a contract for installing new irrigation equipment.

The Criticism from Below: Technology is a Commercial Procedure and the Course is Brainwashing to Increase Privileges   A 'second-rate' worker winning a bet with a prestigious international expert is ironic and has critical epistemological and political implications. Perhaps Chimino cannot use technical language, but the majority of the course participants' ignorance of the altercation disqualifies his practical knowledge. At stake is how scientific value is attributed to things and actions, as well as how this influences power/ knowledge networks. Because scientific value is overvalued, workers' practical knowledge and skills are undervalued. However, the confrontation in the field relativized both kinds of knowledge, and showed how such knowledges are circumscribed by their respective analytical arenas and audiences. The expert's routine and recommendations were inappropriate for local conditions, but nevertheless became the official truth, and the worker's knowledge and practice were ignored or trivialized for not being scientific and mathematical. Even in the local newspaper only the official truth was recognized. Yet one cannot hide the political effects of this worker's prank: it showed the importance of workers' skills for transferring technologies, and thus demystified the most sophisticated means of implementing that transfer.

This point leads us to reflect on the epistemological and political implications. It is practically impossible to formulate a criterion free of all ideological bias or to conceal the political–economic interests of prevailing official, institutional truth. Thus a research perspective centred on the social actor and the concept of interface shows its analytic strength. That is, by following actors and their actions, researchers can bring to the analysis an understanding of social processes that are often diluted in fleeting moments of everyday interaction. Frequently critical dimensions are associated with absent or less visible actors. Therefore they present themselves as illogical or easily dismissed, localized resistance. If researchers can bring this absent character to their analysis, we can better comprehend the meaning of changes, however small they may be, which are hidden in everyday life.

Chimino's criticisms were direct and radical. He characterized the course as generally unsatisfactory, expensive and useless because from his point of view it did not take account of the needs and conditions of the terrain, and immediately noticed some of the bosses' hesitancy about the high cost of new equipment. At the same time, he questioned the ability and motives of the people who took the course when he said that his superior, Jeannette, was never going to handle this equipment directly. He saw the course as a brainwashing to reinforce the privileged. He was convinced that Jeannette had nothing new to teach him about the current equipment. Nevertheless, Chimino's resistance moulds his superior's style of intervention and the forms of controlling irrigation. As a result of the course, Chimino predicted more work, especially in terms of water recycling and tank cleaning, without greater irrigation efficiency. For Chimino a corollary of the course was that technological transfers are paired with an underlying commercial strategy. On this last point, Chimino's language about a bottle to the expert's head unmasked the hidden agenda and tactics of selling new equipment. Indeed, the commercial interests revealed themselves more explicitly in the students' presentations at the closing ceremony.

Chimino's suspicion of hidden motives behind the technological management and transfer training agrees with Long and Villarreal (1993), who established that knowledge processes are dynamic and problematic because they entail transformations of meanings; they are not just transfers of ideas or technology from one individual or social unit to another. Moreover, knowledge and technology are informed by ideological biases in struggles and negotiations to advance business, political and personal interests. Finally, as the American entrepreneur emphasized, there is not just one external scientific or technological model to apply, but thousands of adaptations and contributions by the participants in the productive process. In these contributions and adaptations, the workers' skills can mean bigger profits in tomato production. Thus, there is no pure science and technology, but only artefacts in the hands of actors struggling to advance their interests through the enrolment of clients, pupils and allies.

Chimino's perspective on the course as a way of advancing technicians' careers shows how new forms of information control are articulated through technical language and calculation procedures. Chimino also thought that the course put information into Jeannette's hands that would enable her to control him and through her calculations exert more pressure for applying pesticides, which means immediately reinforcing the hierarchy. This leads to a final reflection on the role of calculation, mathematics and the image of teamwork in defining the scientist and technician. There is an overload of ideological expressions and discourses that emphasize the need to modernize and automate production. These are not neutral, since they portray entre-preneurs and managers as promoters, great friends and masters of science and technology. In accord with that logic, sophisticated language, credentials and titles become the prerequisites for climb-ing the company hierarchy, and widen the gap between workers and managers. Gorz (1980a,b:172) argues that the calculation, information and language used to highlight superiority and difference in salaries and prerogatives are of little or no practical use in the workplace.[10] As for the teamwork perspective, which has been presented as distinctive of managers, it can also be seen among experienced workers, who exercise it in practice without the need to attend special courses.

Conclusions

This chapter has shown that an analysis of social situations focused on the effects of power/knowledge is useful for understanding the complex and frequently contradictory human relations involved in tomato work politics. I also showed how the changing face of power, even though it is only perceived momentarily, can be analysed without the need to start from a fixed scheme of domination, and without having to wait for a complete transformation of the political system.

In terms of changes in the Rosa Company's hegemonic hierarchy, understanding discontinuities as part of one single process of continuous domination gives good results. These discontinuities included ownership and middle- to upper-level management changes, authority conflict, production failures and organizational style. These visible spatio-temporal discontinuities put us in touch with various interconnected social forms to which they are not reducible. This brings up the importance of developing a theoretical strategy that allows us to build what I called in Chapter 1 a local theory based on interlocking interactions and events. This means that events like the training course, artefacts like technology, the know-how to implement it and, above all, the intervening actors' power and skills are interlocking points that allow us to understand apparently incompatible but interrelated life-worlds and what destabilizes social networks and power relationships. Looking at interlocking points or what Long and van der Ploeg (1992) call interlocking projects is the interweaving of action and context, and is also the reflection of states of mind entertained and forms of speech used in the networks by people in everyday situations.

Interacting people fuse and share knowledge, transform meaning (Long and Villarreal 1993) and maintain or mobilize networks. Although this sometimes becomes highly conflictive and visible, it is difficult to grasp in its routine operation. The interlocking points are blurred in everyday affairs, and this is what frequently makes understanding people's alliances and associations problematic. In the conflict between Ricardo and Jeannette, her explanation was revealed as a puzzling ideological discourse. It was an orthodox feminist discourse: a subordinated woman diagnosing victimization by macho workers. However, this discourse was also a subtle, pragmatic political manoeuvre by an unforgiving woman who wanted to advance her career structure in the company.

As far as the class position of the worker was concerned, the transformation of meaning was tied to his search for autonomy. The dismantling of his oppositional attitude came after he was conceded a semi-autonomous albeit isolated *modus vivendi* as greenhouse manager. Other interesting transformations came after abandoning the authoritarian pretensions of the deposed boss. To re-establish control over the power network and confront possible resistance, the new boss made concessions to some but not all the actors involved in the everyday planning of work.

Following workers through a series of interactions exposes the fragility of the status quo, the inconsistencies of the official truth, the provisionality of company hierarchies, and the rupture of ideological and historical trends despite their continued prevalence. The logic in which these are grounded does not correspond to objective values and truths, but to situationally contextualized political negotiations, resources management and commercial operations.

The worker power which sometimes emerged in abrupt, collective interruptions of the productive process was most often exerted as a diffuse collection of initiatives, a provisional set of coalitions, and a mixture of strategies. Following the specifics of ongoing current struggles for power/knowledge allowed me to conceive of a technology of power used by workers who have distinctive techniques and characteristic individual and group rather than mass interests. Hence, the amalgam of images that workers projected consisted not only of those of weak, submissive and apathetic workers worried only for their survival, but also of those of tactical collaborators making situational alliances with the boss and managers. Above all were the images of self-reliance and subversion, calculating opportunism, semi-autonomy, the propagation of rumours against the use of pesticides or management mistakes, and defiance of authority by encouraging others to use their political networks.

The dominant ideological tendency to substitute technical professionals for manual workers on the grounds of complex productive problems cannot ignore workers' important contributions. Skilled workers make a difference in terms of making investments more profitable and reformulating local conditions of production, including making sophisticated technology ecologically more viable. This leads me to look more critically at propaganda, and to make a final comment on the connections between the local and the global. The picture presented by the American entrepreneur and the opinions of the workers illustrate how localities are imbued with knowledge and technical procedures that take account of workers' and managers' needs and capabilities. This perspective can be more fruitful than rigidly following models imported from Florida or Israel. It is no surprise that attention to cultural tastes and expressions like Mexicans' penchant for *salsa* is a more successful organizational strategy for the tomato industry than idealized automated technology transfers.

Notes

1. Villarreal suggests that power negotiations should be not depicted as big issues or discussions about legal frameworks, but as practical moves about specific norms, ideas, values, interests and feelings in circumstantial 'points of consensus'. She also maintains that by agreeing with or dissenting from these points of consensus, people can connect or fragment social networks and change political loyalties. Maintaining power networks is less a question of building institutions and structural hierarchies than of offering initiatives and enrolling people in projects to create manoeuvring room (cf. Long 1984).
2. Latour insists that this methodological emphasis could make a radical difference in the analysis. He suggests that 'we do not have to start from stable actors, from stable statements, from stable repertoires of beliefs and interests, nor even from stable observers. And still, we regain the durability of social assemblage' (1991:129).
3. Law (1991:165) distinguishes four conceptions of power that are already developed in the sociological discussion: 'power to', 'power over', 'power/storage' and 'power discretion'. He asserts that these should be linked to a fifth notion of power/effects, which stresses ongoing social relations. He argues that 'power to' and 'power over' may sometimes be stored and used in a discretionary and calculating manner. But he warns that these forms have to be treated as relational products: to store power or have discretion over its development is to experience the effects of a network of relations.
4. Long defines social interfaces as 'the critical points of intersection or confrontation between groups or social units representing

different interests, resources and levels of power. Analyzing interface situations aims to bring out the dynamic character of the interactions that take place and show how the goals, perceptions, interests, and relationships of the various actors are reshaped as a result of the interactions, leading to a "new" interface encounter the next time round' (1989:254).

5. Don Daniel was a follower of the well known Chilean natural healer, Manuel Lezaeta. Don Daniel, also the son of a poor farmworker, developed his career under circumstances like Ricardo's, curing himself after being discarded by the medical profession for being beyond help. He set up a natural healing centre in the region and continued his homoeopathic and natural medicine studies. He was prosecuted by Mexican health authorities for practising medicine without formal credentials. Don Daniel's centre now has an international reputation (and high fees) and is visited by people from all over the world.

6. Long and van der Ploeg (1992:23) argue that series of specific inter-locking actor projects create, reproduce and transform structures.

7. Chapter 4 gives an account of the origins of this association, to which tomato producers and company owners are affiliated.

8. Twenty people took time off to attend the month-long course, among them technicians and engineers working for companies and government institutions. Some students and company bosses also participated. The companies paid US $1,000 for each participant to attend. Jeannette was one of the two women agronomists to receive the training, which consisted of three lectures a day on drip irrigation systems, with practical field demonstrations in the last week. The confrontation between Chimino and the course director took place during the first of these demonstrations.

9. This was a recommendation to improve the efficiency of the equip-ment, something he had continually repeated throughout the course.

10. Gorz interviewed French workers and confirmed that what exists is a kind of cultural symbolism that has to do more with social conventions than with solving practical production problems.

CHAPTER SIX

The Force of Irony and the Irony of Power

This chapter addresses how subordinated people accumulate, exercise and concede power. As Chapter 5 showed, worker power happens from time to time, but not everyone notices it, and it entails inverted meanings. In this chapter I analyse expressions of political power shrouded in group anonymity. We are dealing with contradictory appearances, since there is never total subordination. All the flows or trajectories that constitute the collective profile of power cannot be specified because they are concealed under various appearances of (in)subordination. However, one can reconstruct how mass power operates in everyday life. Ultimately, the power of the (in)subordinate is as complicated as any other type of power. Its conceptualization requires a complex exposition.

Three ethnographic interactions will serve to analyse the power of the subordinated in diverse work and domestic situations. To interpret the meanings in these interactions I employ the notions of ironic practices and contingent utopias. Irony helps workers to recover their dignity against the stereotypes and prejudices of company personnel, other workers and the researcher. With the notion of contingent utopia I want to refute the idea that because they are subjected to alienating living conditions, workers cannot think or systematically articulate their power strategies.

The chapter is divided in four sections. The first presents the ethnographic narratives and shows how context and workers' social action are interwoven. The second interprets these interactions and looks deeper into the theoretical and methodological implications of ironic practices. The third introduces the notion of contingent utopia to explain how farmworkers' life-worlds can change. The last section synthesizes the styles of power of the subordinated.

The Social Constitution of Irony

This section offers ethnographic material on collective behaviour in the workplace. These behavioural patterns are reshaped by new kinds of action. Hence, ironic conditions in workplace situations are not structural constraints; they are contexts prompted by workers' boldness. As I look at workers' ironic practices I pay attention to their states of mind and figures of speech. This entails understanding practical logics as modes of self-sufficiency, even though they may appear to employ negative methods, like promoting apathy and denigrating the established order.

From Isolated to Collective Games

In my fieldwork I did not seek to record every interruption of the work rhythm that might have implied non-compliance with company norms. It would probably have been impossible or very contrived in any case. However, my field notes record responses to company instructions ranging from irresponsibility to diligence. The accompanying attitudes ranged from seriousness to happiness and exasperating triviality to subtle *double entendres*. Amid this diversity I noted a marked preference for jokes, mockery, ridicule and games.

For the moment, I will not go into detail about issues like class consciousness and collective action (which would entail a different analysis), but about the strategies workers most often resorted to: mockery of authority, themselves and their conditions. Games[1] include both present and absent persons, and they end as fast as they begin; but the nearest in proximity are the most frequent objects of play. For example, some of the most common games are competitions to see who can throw a tomato the furthest, tomato fights in which the fruits fly from row to row, and hiding tools, clothes, lunchbags or other property.

Three months after starting fieldwork I decided to focus on games, and began to record some recurrent activities, such as how tomato cutters took advantage of the physical position they had to maintain. They worked on the same plants from adjacent rows, which gave them the opportunity to touch or hold hands. This could be affectionate or mocking, especially when women worked with men. The woman might say, 'I'm stealing you!' at the same time as she scratched the man's hand with a thorn.[2] Some pranks targeted unpopular people: the pranksters put obstacles in the row to delay their victims and provoke a management scolding, or hid their lunchbags to make them return late to work. Some pranks went so far as to hamper all the work on a farm or sector of the company, as when the pranksters deflated a company truck or tractor tyre. Theft of tomatoes, tools or other agricultural products like fertilizers and pesticides are taken as pranks. The most celebrated achievements are the sexual challenges and games that people claim have taken place in the canefields. Such behaviours allowed me to decipher meanings, but were mostly isolated and vanished as soon as they began. When the games lasted longer, involved a whole group or mixed with other actions, I understood larger contexts. I present three of these situations in more detail.

External Intervention: The Sociologist and the Snake

The Context
The first situation took place on two of the last days of the harvest, when the atmosphere seemed more relaxed. The *cuadrilla* (crew) had forty-five people, mostly young and female and all from two neighbouring villages. The twenty hectares of tomatoes belonged to a small entrepreneur, a nephew of General García Barragán, but the land was rented from an *ejido*. This was the only land the *tomatero* had planted that season, and it was the last of the five years that his company would cultivate it before returning it along with a well he had drilled and some other infrastructure to the *ejidatarios*. This last fact drew the attention of the research team, and we planned to study the imminent change from three angles: the behaviour of the entrepreneur, the *ejidatarios* and the workers. This was the purpose of my relationship to this crew.

I started by conducting interviews with them according to the research team's guidelines. We wanted to discover their views on the history of the crop, the organization of the work process and the consequences that the change would have for them and their families. Since I had never met any of them before, I also had to collect basic information. The crew leader and *tomatero*'s son provided some general information, and after interviewing two workers I felt I had a more comprehensive view of the situation. Still, I was dissatisfied with the results, and felt that to keep on interviewing would be to go around in circles. I did not know how

to continue, so I started an informal conversation with some of
the crew members.

The Interaction

I was standing between the furrows where five cutters were
working, and one of them was telling one riddle after another. He
tried several on me, scrutinizing my capacity to catch his double
meanings: '*Tú me pegas, yo me enojo, tú me juegas el manojo, ¿qué es?*'
('You hit me. I get angry. You play with my thing. What is it?').
When I didn't answer, he laughed and said it was a bell. I felt
disconcerted and defensively took out my notebook and started
writing it all down. That emphasized my externality to the group,
so the game of jokes and notes began.

The storyteller pressured me to show what I was writing. I
explained that I was recording his jokes and riddles and generally
how they liked to pass the time. This relaxed the five cutters, who
continued to test me with their jokes and biting riddles.[3] For a while
they kept asking if I knew their jokes, but only requested that I
write them down. The laughter from our small group caught the
attention of the rest of the crew, especially some of the young
women, who approached to see what was going on. The first
storyteller noticed this, and as an effect of the *modus vivendi*
(Goffman 1959:21) he lowered his voice, asked me to come closer
and said it embarrassed him to let the girls listen. At the same time,
suggestions as to what jokes the group should tell me started
coming from other workers in more distant furrows, who passed
the word along. They mentioned the one about the siren and
others about a donkey and the ocean, nuns, a parrot and a
disfigured man.

The women's curiosity was growing, and when they reached the
end of their furrow they moved to a closer row. Others who had
just been listening also approached and started telling jokes they
knew. However, an old man smelling of alcohol murmured, 'I don't
take the bait; who knows what things this guy's jotting down for
the boss?' While they were telling me jokes, I overheard the women
telling jokes among themselves. They were urging Chayo, apparently the boldest of the group, to come up to me and tell them.
She finally mustered the courage,[4] approached me from behind
and said, 'If you want to hear some good ones, come back with us
and we'll tell them to you.' I entered their circle as Chayo shyly
laughed and the others urged her to start. She asked me, 'Let's

see, tell me, in what way are a woman and a tomato alike?' I couldn't answer so she told me, '*Que los dos le quitan lo bravo al chile.*' (It's that they both take the hotness out of the chili pepper.) She was using the common *double entendre* of *bravo* to mean sexually hot and *chile* to represent the penis. I was feeling really uncomfortable, and must have shown it, because they started acting a bit more sympathetic, but still asked mockingly if I was bashful and if I was married. They had to be patient while I finished writing down one joke before they could tell another. I was relieved when a man called me from another furrow to tell me some jokes that he said I really had to write down. This request was followed by several others from different parts of the field. Obviously word had got around, and I went from one end of the farm to the other.

Although that Friday's work was almost done, the game seemed to have no end. The *jefe* (foreman and shift supervisor) called everyone to gather around him so that he could communicate the boss's message that since the price of tomatoes had risen and the fruit was still in good condition, it would be necessary to organize an extra work group for the coming Sunday.[5] Almost no one paid any attention, and after the interruption they returned to the joke-telling game with more enthusiasm. They even called the *jefe* and asked him to tell some jokes, which he did. Before leaving, they invited me to return the next day and to bring a tape recorder so that I would not get tired from so much writing.

The next day I returned with the tape recorder, since I felt authorized by them to use it. However, the atmosphere had changed: they seemed to recoil from the apparatus as if unknown ears would be listening. The old man seemed to have convinced the others, and he repeated his suspicions about my motives for asking questions: 'See, I told you this guy was *rayando* (getting paid) at our expense, and maybe he'll even sell a book of our jokes!' The situation was uncertain for me. When I tried to start a dialogue with other workers, I felt that the conversation was strained.

Suddenly, some loud shrieks were heard: 'Catch it! Trap it! Don't let it go!' Two workers were darting between furrows to catch some animal. They called on others for help, several men took control of the situation, and they circled a large *chirrionera* snake, so called because it lashes its tail and can strike hard. Several men were holding it, until the one who had been telling most of the jokes began to toss the reptile around. He started with the women, and it became a collective game of double meanings: *se te mete la viborita* ('the little snake is getting inside you'), *que te pica* ('it's biting you'). After incorporating me into these games, they asked me to record them and they listened to the tapes in a circle around me. The snake aroused new jokes and riddles. The day passed quickly amid the joke-telling, and at quitting time the *jefe* repeated his request for an extra group to work on Sunday. However, people did not seem to hear him. That Sunday the *jefe* and the boss's son were obliged to visit the workers house by house, and even so only managed to get half the group to work the extra shift, despite the promise of soft drinks and double pay.

The Nail-cutting and the Birthday Party

The Context
This situation includes two contrasting episodes in the same greenhouse of a tomato company I call Leones: the nail-cutting occurred one day at the peak of planting activity,[6] and the party in honour of Alfonso, the greenhouse boss, was held when work was very slow. Leones had prepared 200 hectares for planting, the largest single area of land under tomato cultivation in the region. At one point there were fifteen workers, but when the work was pressing there were as many as ninety-five. On the day of the nail-cutting about forty-five women and thirty-five men were at work in the greenhouse. Most came from different *barrios* (neighbourhoods) of Autlán, the most important town in the region. Many were students taking advantage of their vacations to work. Five of them were particularly conspicuous because they were agronomy students at the state university in the region. They were addressed respectfully as *inge* (short for *ingeniero*, engineer) or *medio inge* (half-engineer), to indicate that lack of opportunity and real need had made them take jobs as simple workers. These young people facilitated my communication with women workers and made me appear less alien, since they included me in the network that they had developed during the six weeks they had worked together. The group also included five old men who performed tasks like carrying the plants out to the fields in wheelbarrows. The rest devoted their time to placing the plants in large trays to be taken to the fields, planting, cleaning, washing and watering. The greenhouse boss controlled the work. He was an experienced worker who had

been in charge for seven years, and received his orders from a technician and the owner. What interested me at that point was my concern with greenhouse organization and particularly the career of Alfonso, the department head, who had been the apprentice of another experienced worker. This greenhouse incorporated modern techniques, including a scientifically organized workday adapted from another company I call Rosa. A few days earlier a Leones company chemist (who participated in the course described in Chapter 5 and whose knowledge was well recognized by workers) had told me about a dialogue between company bosses and technical personnel on tomato diseases. They had concluded that the diseases were often due to the workers' bad habits, and that it was important to modify their conduct, however difficult that might be.

The Interaction
The heads of the company's technical department had to throw out many seedlings before they could be planted because women greenhouse workers' long fingernails had damaged the fragile stalks as they removed them from the trays. The company owner called upon Alfonso, the greenhouse manager, to make all the women who did this task cut their fingernails. Alfonso arrived and summoned his people. There were twenty-five women working in the four-metre-square room. The rest of the team was outside and came in. Alfonso began, 'I have received instructions from above that all female workers must have their fingernails cut, as they're damaging the plants.' Several women were furious, and screamed at him that it wasn't true. But Alfonso insisted that the command came from above and had to be obeyed. He explained that he and Paquita, a trusted worker who was also his *comadre* (co-godparent), would cut their nails, and that he already had the nail-cutters. The fact that Alfonso included his *comadre* and sister among the victims aggravated the situation.

There was a general uproar. Some women ran to get away, some hid behind the trays and others stayed to challenge him. Three women allowed their nails to be cut, but there were no other volunteers. Male workers were making the situation worse by clapping and demanding in chorus *¡otra, otra!* ('another!, another!'). Alfonso asked the men to help bring in the ones who had not yet had their nails cut. It took almost three hours of struggle. Yet in the process the women's tone shifted from genuine outrage and solidarity to mock resistance and mutual betrayal. The atmosphere turned almost festive, as women who were caught fell melodramatically to the floor and pointed out the ones who had not yet been caught; they even helped chase them. They later explained it had been a game for them.

Olivia was one of three who resisted until the end. She argued that their nails would look ugly and that it would be months before they would be long again. Olivia accused the others of being fools for having let their nails get cut, claiming that long nails are useful because they make it easy to pick up extra seeds from the hay in small tray compartments. In the end, she was the only one who refused to have her nails cut.

The worst part was having to make up the lost time. Alfonso made them work four extra hours and his mood changed radically: he screamed and scolded the workers over the smallest details. He insisted that they use a special saw to separate out each plant in the tray, rather than yanking them out or taking more than one at a time. Many complaints were heard around the room, especially from Paquita, Olivia and other women. Others began to say that they were not paid enough, especially for overtime. Then they began bantering about its being quitting time when it wasn't, pretending that they had done the last tray when there were at least twenty left and that the boss had sent them dinner from an expensive restaurant when he had sent nothing but nail-clippers.

None was following Alfonso's instructions very precisely. They were supposed to carry boxes of seedlings from the greenhouse to groups of five or six women. These women had to uproot and separate the plants, put them in boxes for the field, and take these boxes to the trucks. Everyone was expected to take great care with the plants, but they only did this when Alfonso was around. Olivia explained to me how the process should really be carried out, because in his absence the boxes were carelessly shoved about and the plants were yanked out by the dozen. It was getting late, and workers took advantage of the darkness to throw many plants they would normally have kept as replacements into the garbage bin.

After a little while, they devised an alarm to signal when Alfonso was approaching. They tied a long string to a tomato box located near one of the groups. The other end of the string was left on the floor of the passageway. If Alfonso approached, one of the men running up and down with the boxes could easily pull the string and make enough noise to alert everyone. When it was time to go, the owner sent two trucks to take the people home. This was unusual, since they normally walked: but it had been a long, difficult day. However, only ten people accepted the favour; the rest walked. Paquita, Carmen, Olivia and the five *inges* later said it was the worst day of the year and a real tragedy.

On another occasion the three women invited me to a party they were planning in the greenhouse to celebrate Alfonso's birthday. They had been collecting cash donations from other workers to provide for the music, gifts and drinks.[7] All the greenhouse workers and even people from other parts of the company were invited. The women prepared the food and the men bought beer and tequila.

The party took place at the greenhouse on a Sunday three months after the nail-cutting episode. All the victims were elegantly dressed. Several had gifts for Alfonso, and they had paid for a large cake that they decorated with red carnations. They summoned a professional photographer and posed for him behind the trays of plants or with their friends and relatives next to the musicians and dancing.

The women requested a special waltz from the musicians to dance with Alfonso, which was repeated so that he could dance with most of them. Only Olivia refused. As an extra gift for Alfonso, they had prepared a skit in which they imitated several famous artists on TV. Paquita was the master of ceremonies, and seven of the women, clad in miniskirts and low-cut dresses, danced and threw imaginary kisses to the audience. One man who did not want to let the opportunity pass went up to the stage pretending to be a fan so that he could hug and kiss the entertainer.

The women then asked Alfonso to climb the stage and accept a card Paquita had prepared for him with poetic thoughts about perseverance, morality and friendship. They handed it to him, but he was not allowed to return to his seat. Instead, Paquita offered the microphone to the men so that they could say something to Alfonso. One worker got up and said that he wished Alfonso all the best, that he would maintain unity among the workers and always be as happy as he was that day. Alfonso thanked them for the party and said that it was the best moment in his thirty-one years. During the chaos of the farewells, somebody asked him what time to get to work the next day. He said that he did not care what time people arrived after such a late party.

The Strike of the Burras

The Context

I first heard about the Teutlán[8] workers from Chimino, an experienced irrigation worker. During a course on irrigation for technicians, I had seen his practical expertise make an international expert look ignorant. Chimino claimed that Teutlán workers were *unos chingones* (formidable ones), because they managed to impose their rules on the tomato company, came and went to work whenever they felt like it, and worked by the job instead of by the day like the rest. That season the Teutlán group had up to ninety-two workers, most of them young and female. The group had been working ten straight years for the Rosa company on all facets of tomato work. It first got involved with the company through friendship with an old worker, who helped them find a house in the valley each year so that they would not have to travel six hours to and from their town every day. Instead, they spent the week in the valley and went home at weekends. However, the year I met them, group members decided that instead of renting a house they would persuade the company to provide them with transportation. They also went on a long strike to force the company to reduce their working day to six hours (7 a.m. to 1 p.m.).[9]

The group acknowledged a man named Jaime as their representative authority. They also had two *cabos* (overseers) leading the crews. On the day in question the Teutlán crews were divided into men's and women's groups. They were working on two neighbouring Rosa company farms where there was a major shortage of workers. It was immediately apparent that cultivation was far behind schedule: the company had only been able to cultivate 100 of the 180 hectares planted, and the plants were so top-heavy that some were dropping their fruit.

The Interaction

I had prepared a checklist focusing on previous conflicts over shortening the workday and changing the task-based payment system. I wanted to record all the organizational forms the group had developed to satisfy its demands, but the situation was a bit tenuous. Jaime, the group representative, and the *cabo* answered my questions politely enough while they worked; but the conversation centred on the difficulties of their particular tasks, particularly the *poceada* (boring of holes).[10]

It was not until later in the day that some of the young people working in the next furrow asked what I was doing, as I was conspicuous with my notebook and tape recorder. 'Hey', one asked, 'you earn wages like that, being a *catrincito* (little dandy) and coming in your car. What do you work at?' Another asked what political party I was from and if I knew anything about the *Cardenistas*, the new opposition party that was causing a commotion at that time. I simultaneously heard Jaime telling someone, 'One suffers and endures hunger to find people, and then they just sack them like this. It's screwed up (*está de la chingada*).' The Teutlán women's *cuadrilla* appeared, heading towards the men. Everybody stopped working, and one boy asked the *cabo* if he could go and see what was wrong; but the others were already on their way. Someone commented that the situation was hot, because 'When the broads get into it, the men can't cut out' (*cuando las viejas le entran los hombres no se pueden rajar*). A more communicative worker explained to me that on a similar occasions they had gone on strike to demand a special schedule. He joked that I should be a reporter and record everything. I offered the tape recorder to Chito, one of the youngest workers who was walking with us, and he accepted immediately. His friend advised him to hide it, so that the women would not get annoyed, or to pretend to listen to music. Chito quipped that he was a reporter from *Siete Días* (a TV news programme).

Jaime went up to the women and asked what had happened. They were extremely angry. Several of them began screaming that they would not work any more and one explained, 'Company representatives called us *burras* ['stupid donkeys']. They were saying our work is no good . . .'. Another woman interrupted, 'They got angry because Lorenzo, the *cabo* that the group had appointed, defended us and wouldn't pay attention to Maribel, a *cabo* imposed by the company. She went off to report to the *jefe* of the farm, and he came to scold us.' Jaime advised them to talk about what to do while he waited for the boss, and 'Then we get the hell out of here (*nos vamos a la fregada*); these people are unbearable.' The women found out that Chito had been recording and wanted to listen, although one of them said she would break the machine. Felipe, the head of the company personnel department, arrived in his truck. Someone voiced the idea that Jaime should go with the whole group rather than speak to Felipe alone. Felipe shouted that he wanted to speak to Jaime and the *cabos* at his truck, but the whole group surrounded the vehicle and Felipe could not even get out. I could not hear what they were saying, but the women were waving their hands and shouting indignantly.

Meanwhile I talked with the people who stayed by the furrows. One of them asked me if I wasn't going to get into trouble with the company bosses for being there. Then the conversation turned to the history of Teutlán and their coming *fiesta*, and I began to see many connecting threads.

We've fared badly in Teutlán ever since our grandfathers joined the *Cristeros*[11] and we received no land. The land that should be ours is controlled by the rich people of Tolimán, the county seat. There have been struggles for the land, but they killed the leaders, one twenty-two years ago and the other only two years ago. Don Trinito has been helping us, but the poor man is going a little crazy from so many years of strife. Recently we had a lot of hope, and even a well-intentioned priest was helping us. We got together with five other groups from the region, which is how we got the land we have on the hill slopes and why we were able to help reconstruct our houses after the earthquake. And now we're trying to get our man to the county seat, but when Don Salva was killed . . .

He then said that they had written a *corrido* (ballad) that told of their ordeals:

Year of '86, I wouldn't want to remember,
Because the town of Teutlán was dressed in mourning;
The Indian of the west died at the hands of a criminal.
From the day that he died all his people are blazing.
He had a struggle on his hands and a strong desire to win.
He wanted land and liberty for his *paisanos* [countrymen].
With this I say farewell landowners, sirs.
You put an end to the Indian and your worries are over.

The people who had gone to negotiate with Felipe had returned. They appeared satisfied, saying that they had agreed that Maribel, the company-imposed *caba* who had insulted them, would take another group. They were also promised more respect and that they would not be called names. The women reciprocated by inviting Felipe to the town *fiesta*, and informed him that they would be absent from work for a week. The fact that company representatives had not complained about their absenteeism in the high season was another important concession. Their satisfaction also derived from the feeling of freedom to celebrate the *fiesta*.

During one of my visits to Teutlán (when one of the woman strikers got married) I again asked about that day. I wanted to know if there had been any previous planning and how the women had decided to stop working. The issue proved difficult to discuss. One person mentioned that she had spoke informally to other women at the *tortillería* (tortilla bakery)[12] that morning before going to work; but it was during the workday that they negotiated the strike. Also, in the street in front of the school, two boys who had worked in other regions were talking about experiences that they had heard about from other workers.

But the wedding party conversation always drifted to other issues. I was told about their nice, peaceful town where everybody knows each other, is invited to weddings when someone gets married, and prays together when someone dies. They also talked about the divisions between Teutlán and the people on the other side of the river; the show-offs that return from the US different from how they left; their lack of land and the politicians' unkept promises.

The Theoretical and Methodological Implications of Ironic Practices

This section interprets the ethnographic situations described above in terms of legitimated profiles of collective behaviour. That is, these workers' tactics are collective actions despite the lack of coherent strategy and the difficulty of understanding how the social networks involved in these situations work. Even though there are class and ethnic dimensions, it is hard to accord them a central role, so I do not consider that uniform modes of conduct exist. Traces of class, gender and ethnic issues intermingle in the situations; but they do not account for all their complexity.

The three situations I present highlight an important methodological conclusion: researchers can only partially grasp their objects of study (cf. Habermas 1986 II:403), because research leads one to learn about more complex situations. These situations emerged not through articulated conceptions based on previous guidelines; they were triggered by games like Notes and Jokes, objects like the tape recorder and the snake, and behaviours like the forced fingernail cutting. These triggering events are embedded in chains of contexts.

The first situation highlights how groups create a special atmosphere. It also shows how the games augmented in the playing. One can also read a collective revenge in the workers' humorous detachment from company plans and interests. The situation also shows how boundaries and restraints emerge and how states of mind change according to emotional dispositions. For a moment we perceive states of mind as salient, but then they transform themselves. For example, at one moment the sociologist taking notes on workers' jokes represents the boundary between the inside and the outside of the group; but when the humorous climate spreads and a collective game is unleashed, the boundary is reconstituted and mixed with gender boundaries.

The figures of speech, jokes, riddles and *double entendres* have various implications. I could identify my doubts and the workers' mockery of me, but I felt uncomfortable with my repressive sexual morals when I observed the workers' revenge against linguistic conventions and refinements. The mockery of the woman worker's condition as a woman was overt; but she was apparently indifferent to being considered a sexual object. The situation also revealed successful forms of unplanned resistance triggered when workers found better ways of enduring their work. This highlights the fact that workers never surrender totally to bosses, even though their dreams of alternative life-worlds did not have them managing their own tomato farms.

The second situation destroys the dogmatic belief that humiliation and exploitation simply bring about more belligerence. Fingernails are sensitive symbols for women. To have them cut was a defeat, which they finally allowed to become a game or tragicomedy in order to save face. But they also tried to turn the tables and make the authorities suffer the consequences.

Challenging attitudes have three forms: (1) apparent resignation; (2) extreme carelessness in the face of technical warnings or administrative procedures; and (3) harsh criticism of impositions of extra hours, false promises or bosses' privileges. Olivia is an open but exceptional case of resistance. She gives a glimpse of a deeper dimension of resistance: how much creative genius a worker is willing to put at the boss's disposal. Olivia claimed that the boss lost by cutting nails, because he deprived himself of precision skills.

The subsequent party was an opportunity for workers to recover their self-reliance and express an alternative, autonomous style of tomato farm management or at least a pleasant escape from conflict. As they told Alfonso, they achieved this through the image of unity and good feelings. The workers appropriated the workplace on Sunday (when the companies find it difficult to get workers) and used it in a more relaxing way. Their self-reliance was ratified by the presence of a photographer, who was hired to represent the beautified women and to produce a new picture of a workspace transformed by party decorations.

The party was also a lesson for Alfonso and the other arrogant men. Clearly Paquita's and the other women's play-acting challenged the male bosses, in that the latter now had to see their female workers as unafraid of being considered sexual because they were secure in their condition as decent women. Also, the appropriation of television practices suggests both the extent of Televisa's hegemony and a critique of the inaccessibility of media which in principle should be open to everyone. The women started from an ideal situation and sketched their conditions in the same way that television does and felt as free and important as privileged artists.

The third case is the most ironic in my fieldwork. When it seemed that I would finally experience collective class resistance and be able to follow it closely as a trusted associate, it slipped through my fingers. Chimino had spoken of class behaviour in the Teutlán group's collective actions, and I was expecting to be involved; but the actions did not reflect a detailed strategic plan or preconceived process of change: they remained a circumstantial tactical project.

The affront to the women was associated with the historical memory of the communal defence: the women's perception of shared interests and boundaries was made operational at the moment of conflict. They interpreted the affront not only as the personal denigration of their own work, but as an insult to Teutlán itself. The fact that the insult came from a *caba* who was imposed on them from the outside to the detriment of their own *cabo* is an important aspect. The boundaries between external and internal are clearly defined here. However, my status as another kind of external agent demonstrates that I was ambivalently accepted and that boundaries are established differently than I had intended. There was an unspoken negotiation, in which I was assigned the role of a reporter who distils the moment to provide the group with the self-sustaining character it needs. There was also another mass media analogy, which may represent what they consider to be an ideal situation.

This case is explicitly linked to a complex chain of contexts and shows the heavy weight of accumulated local history in places like Teutlán. It also shows how the long-term is linked to the contingent: the grandfathers' fateful decision to join the Cristero movement and the contemporary townsmen's experiences encouraged the current resistance. The Teutlán group are predisposed to make claims and organize themselves; but their demands are not confined to the tomato fields of the region. They also extend to government institutions and the Church as bodies from which to claim services or land.

Utopias in a Contingent World

In this section I deepen the analysis of the collective profiles outlined above. Farmworkers' life projects are contingent and multifunctional activities. In practice many farmworkers become jacks-of-all-trades who enjoy not feeling trapped by specialized technical schemes. The motivation for young and old to undertake this seasonal activity is the multifaceted but violent need to survive. Thus they accept a kind of unalterable destiny, which they rationalize with *más vale hacer algo mal pagado que estar sin hacer nada y ganar nada* ('better to do something and be paid badly than to do nothing and earn nothing'). This does not keep them from their pleasure in pursuing life, which illustrates their preference for the present, because this is apparently the only time they can control, and in the last analysis they have nothing to lose. Therefore, in their multiple ways of thinking about their living conditions, workers perceive them as tolerable, but only temporarily: only until they find a better motivation that allows them to see those conditions as undesirable.

The uncertainties of tomato work lend themselves to contradictory interpretations. As Chapter 4 showed, a boss may call on worker sympathy when the survival of the tomato industry is at stake. On the other hand, economic uncertainty is not in itself an obstacle to maximizing profits: it can be given as a reason for not improving workers' living conditions.[13] For instance, a Labour Ministry official justified a 'non-interventionist policy' with respect to regulating rural labour relations because the industry faced extinction (Astorga Lira 1988:43). The boss can also argue in terms of security and convenience when he seeks to prescribe work duties legally and minimize human rights.

The uncertainties of tomato work point to interesting analytical problems: (1) heterogeneous, transient labour in the context of the industry's need for uninterrupted production; (2) tomato workers' changing living conditions in different crew and company production groupings; and (3) how to define the resulting emergent properties without slipping into reifications. A question I repeatedly asked myself was how to construct a sociological text about a philosophy of life communicated in the everyday attitudes and behaviour I observed in fieldwork situations.[14] To answer this question, de Certeau's (1984) concept of everyday life assesses the diversity of oral forms that workers use.[15] His perspective also interprets what Silverstone (1989:78) calls the 'pleasures of utopian thought and expression, both in the procedures and the narratives of the everyday'. However, for sociologists, writing down their understandings of workers' everyday verbal expressions is not without ironies and contradictions.[16] As Goody (1992) suggests, researchers interrupt the dynamism of (workers') oral expression by transforming themselves into tamers of the wild.[17]

The problem is that tomato workers are apparently embedded in the present, without any notion of utopia or at least without any documented utopian historical narrative. Following the methodology of Lorraine Nencel's (1990) study of the production of knowledge among Peruvian prostitutes[18] and the notion of utopia of Gorz (1989:8), who sees utopia as a vision of the future, my use of 'contingent utopias' similarly denotes momentary illusions, expectations of better conditions or pleas for more creative and realistic alternatives. This differs from idealized and unattainable social models. Gorz argues that fortunately such models have collapsed, but that we are still imprisoned in the wreckage, which limits future possibilities. I employ the term contingent utopia to characterize the association of actors and events and the paradox of seeking opportunities over a long time without being sure of the outcomes. This concept emphasizes the active and creative self-determination of workers, which does not require systematic rhetorical elaboration, only everyday forms of expression.

Workers' contingent utopias are their desires about how things could be better and how they see their prospects from the standpoint of their everyday affairs. They express these in domestic and working situations. They may do their jobs for years and achieve goals even though they are unhappy with their conditions. Thus one can follow workers' dramas, dreams and histories as those of social groups within disciplinary practices and plans. As Chapter 4 showed, there are multiple historical traces underlying tomato work, but no one history in which a preconceived utopia is triumphantly attained or tragically missed. Economic differences separating bosses and politicians from workers are contingent, mutable relations in specific local circumstances, where distinction, privilege and power reflect different living standards.

For some workers the hand of God is visible in the discrimination between or liberation of people. However, they attribute only individual misfortune to divine design. Variations in this religious interpretation can also legitimate class divisions. However, other workers interpret the subjection of the poor as caused by the rich (Stölcke 1988:171). Still, even here the outlook is fatalistic. Workers are familiar with death, and they attribute to it a double liberating effect: it removes the burden of work and it does justice. Stölcke observes that Brazilian workers' discourse on death has political significance: 'death is the great equalizer which knows no difference between rich and poor ... and serves to assert the common humanity of all people irrespective of worldly power' (1988:169).

I now look at a particular situation to analyse how contingent utopias operate and reflect workers' changing life-worlds. My argument is based on a story narrated to me at a large family party by Don Luis, the 87-year-old father of one of the workers, about his own father, who had been a day-worker for the Ahuacapan hacienda. Don Luis laughed to himself in anticipation before telling of this caper:

What I am about to tell happened during the days when there was revolution everywhere [c.1912]. It was a *travesura* (prank) played on a goat of the hacienda, a small prank that became a very big one. The goat was large, beautiful, well-formed. The *hacendado* treated it as a pet, and it was allowed to go from house to house, where the workers fed it rubbish and maize kernels. It was the day of the New Year *fiesta*, and at two in the morning my father went to help the butcher kill a bull for the banquet. The butcher kept the old dry bladders from other animals he had killed, and it was at that time of the night, when the whole town was asleep, that they thought of the prank. They wanted to do something memorable, so they filled the bladders with dry beans so that they would make a lot of noise and tied them to the hind legs of the goat, which happened to be sleeping nearby. The frightened animal fled, bellowing, through the small streets of the village, followed by an ever-increasing horde of dogs awakened by the noise. Seeking shelter, the poor goat went into several houses, knocking down chairs and awakening the whole town. In the confusion, someone yelled that the devil was loose, and it could have appeared as such, since the commotion and the animal's eyes shining in the dark night gave the incident an extraordinary tone. The commotion increased to the point where a terrified old man took a fall – which later caused his death – and a pregnant woman had a miscarriage. The rumour that the devil was loose reached the ears of the priest, who, agreeing that it probably had to do with the devil, performed some special exorcisms to rid the town of it. In the end the dogs killed the goat and the people who discovered the prank went into fits of laughter.

Don Luis ends his story by explaining that his father and the butcher had to flee the hacienda for fear of reprisals, although they both later returned to fight for the land as *agraristas*. The case shows how images of the future emerged and expressed contrasting meanings.

For most of the villagers the situation reproduced conditioned behaviour; but for a few it was a prophecy of change. That is, it could be seen as a mere prank or as a hacienda workers' game reflecting the plotters' predisposition to perceive change. They may not have verbally explained the revolution's strategic objectives, which in any case were experienced differently in different regions and by different people, but they could clearly understand that the *hacendado* had lost legitimacy. As the *hacendado's* pet, the goat was a symbol, and became an instrument that the pranksters chose to point to the weakness of the hacienda system.

Most of the villagers read the situation as the work of the devil. This reading was confirmed institutionally by the priest, who found it more in keeping with the *hacendado's* moral authority. After the hacienda disappeared most of the actors found the prophetic meaning of the contingent utopia.

The Power of the Subordinated

Among tomato workers I learned to understand irony as a discursive strategy and a strength of the subordinated. At least for fleeting moments certain incidents highlight poignant meanings, continuities and discontinuities in workers' life-worlds: the power of irony. Genovese showed that African-American slaves found a weapon in representing their lives as tragicomic, because oppressed people who can laugh at their oppressors have political potential: 'they bore their adversity so well because they never ceased to laugh at themselves. And by laughing at themselves, they freed themselves to laugh at their masters. Through their satire and behind their masks they asserted their rights as men and women' (Genovese 1974:584).

Tomato workers also know how to laugh at the power of the company. Their masks of subordination and apparent silences help restore dignity. Masks make it possible to counterbalance unfavourable forces despite the fact that they concede some advantages to the powerful. These workers' expressions of irony confirmed for me that their style of defying the powerful eschews open confrontation and may not even always be intelligible. Nor do they like to pretend to be powerful in order to be surrounded by people who believe in them and agree with their ideological preferences. They disdain power, as Zapata and Villa did, and rarely exercise it collectively. If they do so, they do it cautiously and in their own way. They prefer to act like the dripping water, which slowly but surely erodes the stone.

This leads me to look deeper into the style of power that these tomato workers like to exercise. Their power is reflected in routine situations and moments of conflict or rupture in the continuous process of daily life. It is interesting to link the analysis of different situations to understand what processes of domination mean. Even under circumstances in which passivity could seem hopeless, the workers never gave up; they made use of various mechanisms to preserve their dignity and ways of responding as a collective force. However, these responses are not definitive. In fact, the conflict and resistance I observed showed that after a break, new, more subtle forms of domination emerge.

To my surprise, the problem was how to interpret things in unexpected ways. Sometimes an insignificant offence appeared to provoke a very strong response, while what seemed like passive, resigned behaviour persisted in the face of a big offence. This observation leads me to ironize the rigidity of certain class conceptions and to look more deeply at the relativizing power of workers' irony. As happened with the jokers in the first situation, the border between irony and humour is unclear. In fact, the jokers' irony became an unbroken chain of humour. Irony and humour preserve a potential for social criticism, because they reinforce the scepticism that makes us see everything as less divine and more human. Therefore there is no enduring evil and all empires must fall.

Conclusion

The Teutlán workers allowed me to look more deeply into other dimensions of class consciousness. I take this to be a vigilant attitude that leads workers to demand respect for their dignity and to find solutions for their needs. Another expression of that consciousness was the capacity of the Ahuacapán hacienda *agraristas* of 1912 to intuit imminent change. These expressions make it possible to understand how workers use the power of their subordination to ready themselves and force change. The concern is less to know if such attitudes originate in pre-existing, violent, revolutionary social movements than it is to identify changes in groups and contexts. In such change, the actors reformulate beliefs and needs into a desire for justice and improved living conditions. Thus the power of the subordinated is a counterweight to fatalistic conceptions of history, despite the Marxist axiom that changing history to our taste is beyond our individual and group capacities.

The possibility of improving living conditions continues to be the basis for creating utopias. At times of crisis like now, promises of well-being can provoke more ire than hope, especially when the audiences for such discourses are social groups like the Teutlán workers, who are sick of promises. However, the masses are still generally inclined to listen to political promises of well-being. This may mean that the promise is not listened to so much for what it promises as for its capacity to intermingle with contingent utopias of peaceful alternatives and to control our overwhelming feelings of stress and pessimism. The complex thing for the analyst is to identify the determinants of living conditions, the real possibilities for meaningful social progress, propaganda that seeks to manipulate the masses, and desires for improvement and effective action.

This leads me to point out two other effects of analysing the power of the subordinated. First, up to a point the power of the subordinated is no different from other kinds of power, because it only has diffuse signs that are easily confused with the complexity of everyday circumstances. This means that it is almost impossible to measure the power of the subordinated in terms of the positivist mentality's hegemonic demand for precise conditions for generalizing hypotheses. However, this does not mean we should avoid analysing such power. Perhaps it only means that my collective profiles of these flesh-and-blood workers may not be universalizable.

Second, the power of the subordinated entails examining the researcher's preferences and dilemmas at the moment of producing a scientific text as determinants of the results. Therefore I have insisted on looking at the meaning of subordination in a different way. Faced with science's ambition for truth, one can ask if there are instruments precise enough to identify the traces of long fingernails on 300,000 plants or if there is an epistemology that can prove the irrationality of apparitions of the devil for centuries in Latin America, as the workers at the Ahuacapán hacienda remind us.

To resume, I assert that anywhere in the world it will continue to be frustrating to show why subordinated people keep consenting to representations of power that favour their oppressors and manipulators, like the majority of hacienda *peons* who believed the priest who defended the *hacendado*'s interests. On the other hand, there is reason for optimism, since there are also the punsters who know how to seek life and the jokers of both genders who are not motivated by the criteria of profit maximization and political efficiency currently in vogue. Lust for life will continue to have an important place in the analysis of collective behaviour.

Notes

1. For Goffman (1959:26): games are cathartic situations that embody knowledge and world-views.
2. In rural Mexico it is common for a young men to 'steal' or 'carry away' a woman, especially if her parents will not give her in marriage or have no money for the ceremony.
3. Apte (1992:67) reflects on how humour creates common feeling. Green (1992) observes that riddles are one of the oldest and most

widespread verbal genres, and that they constitute a distinctive group activity. Riddling has three features: (1) a question-and-answer structure with (2) sufficient information in the question to provide an answer; and (3) shared knowledge, world-view and tropes between performer and respondents. Each riddle is built on practices and objects commonly understandable to the group. Riddling is generally considered entertainment; but others have suggested it aids the cognitive development of children, manages social conflict, exhibits rules of conduct and conceptualizes the environment for adults as well as children. In some parts of Africa, riddles introduce ritual formulae to initiates.

4. Apte (1992:73) observed that in many societies women are more constrained than men in using and enjoying humour. The prescription of modesty and passivity for women can lead to their exclusion from public events; only men may engage in humour. As women get beyond reproductive age, however, these restrictions are often relaxed.

5. Work was not compulsory on Sundays. So that the workers would 'volunteer', the bosses made various promises.

6. They needed to make up for time lost due to rain, and there was the risk that all the work already invested in the forty hectares of tomatoes would be in vain. This put considerable pressure on the workers.

7. In three weeks, they collected $340. This was extraordinary considering that these people earned only US$4 a day. In addition, everyone contributed food.

8. The town of Teutlán is in the mountains about 100 kilometres from the Autlán-El Grullo irrigation district. It is only accessible by a small, rocky road.

9. Because of tomato production's high risks, a one-day work stoppage can mean big losses for a company. This potentially makes companies vulnerable and workers powerful, and in the region strikes are strongly criticized by company supporters. There are accounts of reprisals (including killings) against rebellious workers. This why some workers interpreted actions like those of the Teutlán group as typical working-class behaviour. This was also my initial impression when I tried to find out what happened in this first strike. Therefore, I was very interested in maintaining contact with this group.

10. Given the area's dense soil consistency, this is one of the heaviest jobs. Using an iron spear weighing five to eight kilograms, an eighty-centimetres hole is bored every seventy centimetres to hold rods, which are then connected by strong strings to support the tomato plants.

11. In the Cristero war (1926-9), most of Teutlán had favoured the

Catholic rebels, because of their close friendship with a priest who often came to town. However, after the war was lost to the *agraristas*, Teutlán became isolated. Whereas groups that had fought on the side of the government received land, they did not.

12. In rural Mexico women go to the *tortillería* early every morning to get hot corn tortillas or the dough to make them at home. Hence this is a common place for them to talk.

13. I observed two such extreme situations: (1) in order to avoid paying social security, a boss hid workers from federal social security supervisors for two hours on other farms; (2) in order to avoid paying indemnities, somebody stole two workers' medical records from a government hospital after they died from inhaling pesticides. Migrant workers led by a brother of one of the dead workers organized a massive demonstration against the company, forcing it to produce the records and make quick restitution (personal field notes, 1988, Report 154:14).

14. For Giddens reflexivity only partly operates at a discursive level: agents know what they do and why they do it, but their knowledgeability as agents is largely practical consciousness. Practical consciousness consists of everything actors tacitly know in order to carry on in social life without being able directly to express it discursively (Giddens 1984:xxiii; cf. Long 1989:255). More recently, Giddens insists that 'Discourse is not just what can be expressed propositionally, as stated beliefs. Humour, irony, sarcasm, expletives and even the calculated use of silences may form part of the discursive understanding of social circumstances' (Giddens 1990:314). James Scott (1990:xiii) refers to the hidden transcripts that save researchers in their task of decoding power relations. These hidden transcripts are typically disguised as rumour, gossip, jokes, etc. Subordinate groups employ these anonymous or innocuous forms to insinuate a critique of power.

15. De Certeau (1984) seeks to capture the creative essence of daily life. He rejects conceiving of ordinary people as a manipulated, inert and passive mass. Everyday practices no longer appear as merely the obscure background of social activity. On the contrary, practice always implies that social relations determine its terms and not the reverse. Thus, for de Certeau, the target of analysis should not be individual subjects but their modes of operation and schemes of action.

16. This is a challenge that has also been acknowledged by other authors. Goffman states that during the interaction there is not enough time or space for discovering the underlying reality (1959:14). Harre Secord (quoted in Habermas) also asserts that we cannot look at people's activities as simply eating, working, laughing or thinking.

And Habermas contends that no theoretical attitude can make life-worlds self-evident, because no social scientist can reach the totality of deep knowledge that determines their structure (1986 II:401).

17. Silverstone (1989:83) quotes Goody's (1977) assertion that writing provides the model for industry, the scientific laboratory and the modern city. In the realms of fashion, car design and food, bodies are defined, codified and controlled through writing. Also, in the production of folklore, history, the sciences of language and the definition of progress, voices are incorporated into the dominant discourse through writing.

18. Nencel (1990:9–10) describes her novel anthropological practice with prostitutes as 'feeling gender speak'. By sharing space, silence and discourse with prostitutes, she was able to understand their production of knowledge and status quo, fragile friendships and relationships, lack of confidence, floating alliances and momentary illusions when they asked to be treated as girlfriends.

CHAPTER SEVEN

Exploring the Opportunities of Social Change: A Theoretical Discussion

Despite technological and scientific developments, predicting the conditions for social change at a given place and unit of analysis is still beyond the capacity of social science theory. In the post-modern debate, social science is considered relativistic and social change is no longer explained with universal or unitary variables, but rather with a multiplicity of images in which different changes interact in concrete scenarios. In this book on the working and domestic lives of tomato workers, the main problem is not measuring the scale of change (whether revolutionary, evolutionary, ordinary or extraordinary), its quality or intensity. Nor is it a question of identifying privileged locations, domains or issues for observing change, because change occurs in different locations and aspects of life.

The question we must ask is how changes transform the farm-workers' lifestyles. This means locating feasible alternatives for improving tomato workers' living conditions, which implies a need to put this question in the specific context of a fragile system of agricultural production. In fact, the tomato industry provoked great transformations (new styles of organization, changes in pro-perty regimes, the creation of thousands of jobs and a constant restructuring process of domination) within the social formation of Autlán Valley. For workers it also meant securing more opportunities for survival and promotion. The difficulty with the tomato industry is that, although it is very profitable and quick to export capital and production in the short term, it is also prone to economic imbalances, and is disadvantageous to tomato workers in the long term. Despite twenty years of intensive tomato pro-duction, the industry has been practically dismantled without establishing a high economic level of development within the region. In addition, none of the workers have managed to receive a fair recompense in return for the efforts they have devoted to the tomato industry.

At stake is developing a rationale for change that addresses its uncertainties and subjectivities. Reflecting on theoretical approaches in a flexible way is a feature of good social science that should take account both of purposeful strategic action and the actor's emotional and affective dimensions. In this vein, S. B. Turner (1992) makes a plea for recognizing the full *embodiment* of social action. This may be seen as deductively or logically less powerful than the 'hard' sciences; but it should distinguish the social sciences. Thus, to explicate a rationale for social change, this chapter argues against Randall Collins' accusation that micro-sociologists are 'quite technical empirical researchers with an apolitical programme . . . [who become] some kind of anarchist radicals' (1992:79). This chapter is grounded in a dialogue between my ethnography and the sociological literature on farmworkers and the labour process.

The first section reviews theories of change in the life-world, including social movements theory and Habermas' (1987) meta-theory. I establish relations between these theoretical models and my own ethnographic material with a focus on structural change. The second section deals with the paradigm that is still used for studying the agricultural labour process. This scheme is a strait-jacket derived from the industrial shopfloor and adapted to the rural environment; it makes the agricultural labour process become not the twin but the bastard stepbrother of the industrial labour process. I also emphasize the need for a more flexible analysis of the workplace. The last section summarizes the political issues of tomato work raised in previous chapters, and more fully develops a counter-argument to Collins' criticisms. It also reviews Scott's approach to social change as the product of the resistance of subordinate groups (1985; 1990). My concluding remarks deal with the implications of these discussions for tomato workers' changing life-worlds.

Rethinking Agrarian and Social Change

In the literature on farmworkers social change is frequently seen to be caused by external forces of the capitalist system, the untheorized result of some exceptional boss's goodwill, shortened workdays and new economic practices. Danzinger (1988:6–11), who studied farmworkers in Britain, argued that without substantial improvements in material conditions one cannot talk about real change. Others see refining labour legislation and implementing progressive government measures as determinants of change. There is also optimism about technological innovations' capacity to change work routines. Another school holds that achieving economies of scale can improve workers' living conditions. Change and resistance to it are interpreted as predetermined or as reactions provoked by outside forces. These attitudes represent savage capitalism, government reform, heroic deeds, and the goodwill of technocrats, entrepreneurs and mediating groups as determinant.

There is little in the literature on farmworkers on how non-organized workers conceive and operationalize strategies of social change. None of these explanations of change holds open the possibility that workers can create the conditions for substantially improving their living standards and freeing themselves as a group from domination. Instead, the stress is on the complexity of domination and the weakness of unions, taken to be farmworkers' main institutional body. Successful legal reform movements require a constant accumulation of efforts by incipiently organized or non-organized workers.

The interpretation of social change cannot be momentary. As Barger and Reza's (1994) analysis of Mexican migrant labour organizations in the US shows, these are long-term historical practices. These authors connect the social struggles of the 1980s with strikes and other movements of earlier decades. Their detailed linking of historical events and current processes narrates the development of two unions: the United Farm Workers and the Farm Labour Organizing Committee. They claim that the 'social reform movement . . . has proven to be the most viable solution for eliminating the deprived conditions of farmworkers in America' (1994:43).

Barger and Reza add that 'the combined power of millions of American consumers counterbalanced the powerlessness of farm-workers . . .'. The sympathy of millions of consumers arose from a simple watchword: shift their gaze to the living conditions of the people who produce the food they eat. Here was a vision of social change associated with two factors: a chain of heroic founding actions that unleashed sympathy that reached wide social sectors. However, reproducing organizing experiences is problematic, and not a viable alternative in every case.

Verena Stölcke (1988:230-1) paints a penetrating picture of how Brazilian workers experience socioeconomic change and how change is informed by material facts, previous socioeconomic circumstances, and ideological and cultural values. She shows how changing situations have different meanings for different members of workers' families, and discusses in depth how family models and traditions reinforce exploitative practices. She also emphasizes that workers experience changing relations of production not as autonomous individuals but as actors enmeshed in relationships shaped by unequal power and gender divisions both inside and outside the household.

Although her exceptional depiction is perhaps unique, it reproduces an ideological orientation that assumes that farmworkers are defenceless because their employers, company administrators and agricultural distributors have economic advantages. This orientation privileges the economic meanings of social change despite the fact it highlights the embeddedness of the economic in the political. The weakness of this orientation is its presupposition that economic factors are determining. Indeed, the interrelationships between economics and politics have been obscured because of the fixed meanings attributed to indicators such as wages, housing and social security.

Mexican workers' movements are better at ameliorating bad treatment and transportation problems than at winning better salaries and housing (Paré 1980; Grammont 1986). This was confirmed in Chapters 4 and 6, where I observed a similar pattern of spontaneous local mobilizations winning the first kind of benefits. Posadas and García (1986) emphasize that in Mexico an important issue is to publicize farmworkers' exploitation. These authors also believe that to improve living conditions, independent workers' organizations must be consolidated by an intelligent group that can unselfishly direct the struggle to develop working-class and progressive alliances against capitalist hegemony. Danzinger, Posadas and García offer clear examples of strategies of enlightenment and intelligent parties, an issue to which I will return below.

The literature on farmworkers is still dominated by a structuralist, systemic approach that fails to interpret social change in everyday circumstances. As Long already stressed in his 1968 study of social change in rural Zambia, a structuralist approach 'cannot adequately deal with the problem of how change is generated' (1968:9). My own study has shown that a detailed observation of domestic and working routines is crucial in identifying excluding/ including mechanisms that result from diverse managerial styles and in going beyond the idea that if a system of exploitation cannot be totally overthrown, then there is nothing worthwhile about changes in workers' lives. In this chapter I appraise some theoretical foundations of social change in the light of my ethnography in order to see how change is generated and to situate it more concretely in the social process.

How Life-worlds Change

After the social movements of 1968, academics and political activists from around the world began focusing on abstract theories about intelligent parties and enlightening strategies. Touraine's (1981) theory of social movements and Habermas' (1986) critical theory of communicative action are good examples. Touraine's notion of social movements as the new motor of social change responded to the theoretical and political impasse of left-wing opposition parties and labour unions, which were ignored or bypassed in 1968. Touraine's concept of social movement stresses more flexible organizing principles, under which the objective is not to break the whole system and win total power but rather to meet specific demands. In social movements homogeneity is unimaginable, but alliances are not. Touraine (1981:77) defines a social movement as the 'organized collective behaviour of a class actor struggling against his class adversary for the social control of historicity in a concrete community'. Nevertheless, this idea still has shortcomings and rigidity, because it is based on a dichotomized image of society.

Recently, several tendencies have emerged in Europe, the US and Latin America that identify themselves as 'new social movements' (*nuevos movimientos sociales*). These emerged from disenchantment with abstract, academic Marxist models and psychological reductionist theories of collective action (Foweraker 1995). Reformulating action as central to collective identity in social movements has made intellectual tendencies from different continents converge. Ramírez Saíz (1994) discusses how, in concrete but globally related scenarios, the masses struggle for access to resources and against exclusion, how organizations and leaders are developed culturally, and how strategies to guarantee diverse interests are formulated.

Virginia Vargas (1991:7–15) has reinterpreted new Latin American social movements, and particularly women's movements. She emphasizes that 'these social movements make evident the complexity of social dynamics, highlighting the existence of many more areas of conflict than those related to social class and economics'. She also shows that the actors are diverse and not just from the privileged classes. Vargas' descriptions radically question how societies are structured, and they open new spaces for analysis and discussion; but her approach is tainted by vanguardism. Her alternative institutional model for change is problematic for understanding changes in groups both inside and outside of social movements. In a critical assessment of these theories, Foweraker suggests caution and even scepticism, to avoid making unprovable interpretations of social and historical situations (1995:3).

Habermas' theory of communicative action has a more complex and systematic definition of social change, which I cannot exhaustively discuss; I approach it from a specific angle to make explicit why Habermas' approach cannot deal with radical contingency and fragmentation like that found in the tomato industry. We should also explore why he restricts changes in the life-world to 'enlightening strategies' carried out by 'intelligent parties' in response to 'objective challenges'. I join Ryan's (1989) and Seur's (1992) critiques of Habermas.

Habermas claims that metatheory is necessary to grasp change in the life-world. He starts with Schutz' notion of life-world, and redefines it as the context that always remains in the background to represent unproblematic, taken-for-granted common convictions (1987:120). However, he dichotomizes the life-world by simultaneously confusing it with society at large and areas of social life that can be rationalized and mediated. Even when he accepts that fragmentation or circumstantial representations may occur within the life-world, he conceives of them as incidents emerging in the narrative presentation of historical events and social circumstances, but subordinated to the whole. He persistently denies their theoretical relevance. Although he recognizes that things in the life-world can change, he establishes fixed limits to this. Ryan (1989:28) criticizes this holistic conception as romantic metaphysics based on a rationality that separates abstract reason from empirical experience.

Habermas assumes that modernity and political order tend to organize themselves stably around the capitalist system. For Habermas money, markets, media and power are self-contained entities operated by systemically rational institutions 'out there' that can penetrate, regulate and colonize the life-world. For example, in this way the family becomes subject to legal supervision and schools become subject to bureaucratic administration (Ryan 1989). This view can either result in reification or lead one to conclude that there are enormous variations in meaning and representation in each of these entities, even though they are all affected by the same macro-level trends. In this book I have argued that power is not a self-contained entity, and, in particular, Chapter 5 affirms that power has no intrinsic explanatory capacity, but rather must itself be explained.

For Habermas systems are not contingent, material or socially and historically constructed; they are immanent and governed by agents who have learned to see rationality in the world. He understands rationality as the ability to transcend contingencies, and in this sense his concept of life-world is teleological because it locates meaning at a transcendental point beyond trivial everyday situations and the empirical contingencies of social struggle. Habermas' logic sees agents as operating on a macro level, because by definition agency is rational, and cannot secure a desired social order without having metatheoretical meanings.

In Habermas' conception, the social order is an imposition that contradicts physicality and emotionality. This is why his perspective is aligned with the political ideal of social democracy under an élite of rationalists who knows what the people want better than they themselves do (Ryan 1989:31). He believes that a social order can only be changed by organized, intelligent parties who understand how the system operates as a whole. For Habermas, these intelligent parties are superior to non-rational workers, who must accept the labour process organized by management. As a consequence intelligent parties subsume the material energies of exploited groups in the same way that reason subsumes material needs and desires.

Han Seur (1992:17) reinterprets Habermas by distinguishing overlapping personal life-worlds and shared life-worlds in Nchimishi, a rural area in central Zambia. There 'individuals assume that they share part of their personal lifeworlds with specific others', but 'some knowledge (for instance the language,

agricultural knowledge and knowledge related to kinship categories), values, norms and expressions were indeed seen as shared
by almost all inhabitants'(ibid.:xx). From this standpoint he offers
a flexible interpretation of how life-worlds change:

> it is through actions (including statements) that an actor intentionally
> or unintentionally constantly alters and/or recreates the external world
> that surrounds him. Therefore it is through motivated or unmotivated
> actions and the perception of these actions by others that an actor,
> intentionally or unintentionally, knowingly or unknowingly, becomes
> (at least temporarily) part of the personal lifeworld of other actors, in this
> way playing a role in recreating and changing their lifeworld (ibid.:23).

Analysing and precisely demarcating the boundaries of personal
and shared life-worlds is complex and perhaps impossible:

> at any given moment, a local community may consist of an indefinite
> number of shared lifeworlds. That is, individuals and groups may
> assume they share stocks of knowledge, practices, material resources,
> values, norms, discourses and expressions with a wide range of other
> individuals or groups. This means that during every communicative
> action an actor may for some reason feel the need to demarcate the
> boundary of the lifeworld s/he assumes s/he shares with others, or the
> boundaries between this shared lifeworld and what s/he considers to
> be other lifeworlds (ibid.:19).

Structural Constraints that Obscure or Illuminate Change

The ethnographic narratives in Chapters 2, 5 and 6 describe
how tomato workers' life-worlds are fragmented but interlocked.
Personal and shared life-worlds are embodied in people's everyday
lives and expressed through heterogeneous ideological phrases that
always exist in relation to other people's ideologies (Eagleton
1991).[1] Therefore, within changing life-worlds it is intriguing to
study the problematic points of causality established by the
researcher and the people researched in order to connect ideological expressions grounded in contingent daily interactions with
multiple elicited orders of everyday experience. This leads one
explore the relationships between structure and action (or contexts
and actors) and how structural constraints either obscure or
enlighten the meaning of change.

A typical structural constraint or ironic condition for tomato
workers like Rogelio and the Teutlán group (Chapters 2 and 6) is

that they cannot afford land or the resources needed to cultivate it (social security, credit and profitable harvests). However, looked at more positively, such constraints can enable people to develop contingent utopias by becoming *ejidatarios*, small farmers or simply more independent and by doing things on their own, even though only a few can do this successfully. Thus, structural constraints are dual.[2] Stressing only their constraining or enabling characteristics eliminates other possibilities, interrupts the flux of change, reduces the process to a single chain of cause and effect, and obscures the meaning of change.

The dynamics of social change have also been approached by analysing the relationship between the intended and unintended consequences of social action.[3] The notion of unintended consequences is ambiguous (Elster 1990:133) and not useful for clarifying fieldwork strategies. The terms perpetuate a dichotomized world, and lend themselves to circular arguments that do not clarify much. Boudon (1990) tries to sort out the circularity with reference to group theory. He analyses the concentration of educational opportunities in the upper class. He argues that it cannot be taken to mean that 'people are led by forces unconsciously regulating their level of aspiration, or simply to accept the idea that the level of aspiration is mechanically produced by the social environment' (Boudon 1990:124–5). For Elster the problem is to define precisely what is intended or unintended and for whom.

We can also interpret landlessness as the unintended consequence of actions by the tomato workers' predecessors such as hacienda *peons*. As was noted with the Teutlán workers in Chapter 6, the majority's involvement with the *Cristeros* in favour of the Church and landowners against the *agraristas* caused the repeated denial of their land petitions. As long as they remained landless, connections could be established between these events. Although the explanation may seem plausible, there are still difficulties in that the chain of actions connecting past and present is unprovable, and it is impossible to produce a general explanation for all of Teutlán.

In fact it is impossible to disentangle unintended from intended consequences and the past from the present. To take landlessness as an unintended historical consequence of ancestral actions is simply insufficient for explaining Teutlán's contemporary land struggles, because they seek land for many reasons, and are not denied it only for historical reasons. Teutlán tomato workers represent diverse social interests complexly interwoven with local events both there and in Autlán.

Teutlán tomato workers are differentiated by age, gender, religion, status and power, and their actions cross-cut the domestic and workplace domains. Weddings, strikes, migration and parties are meaningful within specific contexts and in relation to organizing practices and social interests both before and after the fact. For example, the strike shows how kinship and political ties in Teutlán encouraged communal solidarity among workers in conflict with the management. This solidarity was not random; it formed part of an ongoing tactical learning process for coping with resource scarcity and the remoteness of their village. These unique tactics are key to understanding how these workers extracted benefits from the company.

Thus tomato workers' behaviour and life-worlds cannot be grasped by simply isolating structural constraints; it requires a fine-grained analysis of the ongoing, intricate, ordinary, even trivial dynamics of everyday life. As I emphasized when discussing landlessness, the meaning of structural features is situational, and has no general value. As Long and van der Ploeg (1992:22) argue, it is more promising to see structural features as fluid, emergent properties resulting from the negotiations and struggles of people seeking survival, rather than fixed conditions that can only be changed by large-scale political action. This has both theoretical and practical implications. For example, faced with the uncertainty of the tomato industry in the region (as of 1994 it was collapsing), it would be absurd to claim permanent employment for all tomato workers, consider tomato work as an ideal livelihood or view it as an obligatory stage for all landless people of the region. The central challenge for the sociologist is to understand how workers and their families survive, advance their interests and struggle to secure better living conditions with many purposes in mind under difficult circumstances.

The Enlightenment Theory of Work

The literature on agricultural and industrial workers has traditionally had the ambitious political goal of focusing on the labour process in order to define the ideas and practices that empower workers and their organizations. Anything less would undermine this tradition's radical intent. Authors like Thompson (1983) conceive of the labour process as a tool for understanding the changing nature of work and workplace behaviour. Littler (1990) uses the theory to reveal the function of management and how workers' abilities are converted into capital accumulation. He argues that the labour process is a flexible concept that can order the great variety of economic and social activities in the workplace.

Labour process theory has been considered useful for analysing agricultural practices, and especially agro-industrial management (in the tomato industry among others). Anne Lacroix (1981) specifically conceptualizes the agricultural labour process.[4] Following Marx' schema, she underlines the peculiarities of agricultural as opposed to industrial labour: since labour time exceeds production time, and given the special nature of the agricultural means of production, she argues that the organization of agricultural work is more flexible and autonomous. Also, unlike industry, workers have the ability to transform the production process.

Jan Douwe van der Ploeg (1990:26) takes a similar view, but emphasizes that the modern agricultural labour process is part of wider technical and economic relations. Still, he does not go as far as Friedland and Barton, who argue that modern agriculture is now a 'factory in the field' as a result of technological changes (1976:40–1). They conclude that California tomato production is essentially industrial. However, Friedland and Barton acknowledge difficulties with their 'factory in the field' argument, because kinship and friendship networks influence commercial agricultural labour.

Unlike Marx, Knights and Willmott (1990) call for a critical theory that has no single conception of the labour process or its fundamental elements (Littler 1990:77). For example, Thompson (1983:101–5) recognizes that analysing the labour process for sets of interests generated within production cannot predict employer and worker behaviour. He also acknowledges that although managers are global agents of capital, this does not mean that there are no contradictions in that role or between strata or types of management. He recommends focusing on human agency as irreducible to labour units or modes of production. He points to the importance of choices made within structural constraints. Consequently, he proposes that changes in the labour process have to be established empirically rather than read from general categories.

Still, it would be unfair to conclude that labour process theory was worthless, as some sceptics suggest. Baudrillard (1975) helps clarify one of labour process theory's weaker points: its association with the Marxist theory of value. He argues that Marx essentially failed because he took contemporary concepts of political economy for granted and projected them as universals. He also asserts that Marx unsuccessfully differentiated use and exchange value, and that his notions of abstract and concrete labour are mirror images of Western rationalistic categories of labour and wealth. In other words, Marx takes labour to be a human essence. The distinction between abstract and concrete labour is inadequate for dealing with labour practices considered unessential. Marx passes this failure on to the workers by claiming that their labour power could produce a radical alternative to the present system, but never did. So, if the theory no longer offers a general explanation and cannot fully understand labour practices or empower workers' organizations, what remains of this sociological research tradition? Using concepts more flexibly and grounding them empirically may renew the paradigm.

Some of this tradition's concerns encourage more critical scrutiny. One such concern is to define exploitation and determine whether it can ever repeat itself. One way to reassess power is to examine its specific meanings in the connections between domains and issues that cross-cut work scenarios. Novel, discontinuous, progressive and transformative features of work may offer a dynamic, but the problem is still complex: power and political inequality constantly but asymmetrically provide and deprive workers of opportunities. Another issue is how these asymmetries are created.

A second concern is technological and external change. Again, the meanings and interactions of local actors dealing with these changes must be reconsidered.[5] This means studying cultivation patterns, the introduction of new equipment and other innovations, property regimes and regulations, and government policy changes not in formal terms but as flexible patterns reshaped by local actors. Reshaping concepts of the labour process means exploring forms of worker discipline and self-discipline in unpaid domestic work and paid labour contexts where the specifics of gender, class and age combine. This was the perspective used for describing tomato work in Chapter 3.

Micro-Sociological Anarchism

In the last section of Chapter 6 I explored how irony allowed me to interpret changes in tomato workers' life-worlds more optimistically and contradicted theoretical positions that deny that workers can develop their own strategies for change. I now focus on what tomato workers' verbal and contingent strategies mean politically and how politics intertwines company and worker strategies, domains and issues. Micro-level analysis sheds light on how politics, stratification or power differentials, social conflict and local movements apply in specific circumstances without making these out to be objective, universal phenomena.

I have also referred to the extensive repertoire of motives, in which pleasure and joking are important. For believers in rational social science, the collective practices of irony described in Chapter 6 may be frivolous, individualistic, anarchistic and sociologically of little value. However, by including past experiences, one can show that tomato workers do not act in a social vacuum; their behaviour reflects wider social processes in space and time.

In complex micro-situations, I identified how the ordinary intertwines with the extraordinary. Unlike Danzinger's study of British farmworkers from 1920 to 1950 (1988:81), we should not take protests like arson, stealing company supplies, hostile letters, destroying fences and maiming farm animals to be 'highly individualistic forms'. Danzinger concludes that such protests fail to gain workers better living conditions or consolidate their organization.

Collins (R. Collins 1992)[6] takes this point further by claiming that ethnomethodology and micro-sociology misinterpret how change comes about. He criticizes conservative and romantic tendencies for conceiving of social change as driven by cognitive schemata instead of episodically in everyday life. In contrast, my interpretation is concerned with avoiding deterministic interpretations of changing circumstances. Even though my results can only offer fleeting glimpses of workers transformed from the dominated into the dominant, this was reason enough to examine critically the political and theoretical implications of various kinds of everyday behaviour that put domination into question. The initiatives of both weak, unskilled and powerful, skilled workers reveal the instability of control, power games, authority and knowledge in the workplace.

The passages about tomato workers like Rogelio, Polo and Alejandro (Chapter 3); Ricardo and Chimino (Chapter 5); the Teutlán group, the Leones Company greenhouse workers and the jokers (Chapter 6) show us that workers can exert power, not as a fantasy (which Collins takes to be the typical outcome), but as an effective way to force companies to shift their organizational schemes, as in Chapters 5 (the reinstated worker) and 6 (the Teutlán strike). To put it more provocatively, tomato workers' 'fantasies' or contingent utopias allow us to see beyond the status quo. Without these workers' images and concomitant unpredictability, the bosses' and managers' caution and flexibility are not readily understandable.

Scott's Theory of Social Change

I agree with Collins that the extraordinary reflects people's ordinary lives. However, this implies that the extraordinary has to be understood in terms of local circumstances, and not as an alternative social model. This is critical for assessing Scott's theory of social change (1985; 1990), which aims at modelling 'everyday forms of resistance of subaltern groups', but is flawed by circular reasoning.

Scott defines everyday forms of resistance as a permanent process of ordinary, undramatic change. It is misleading to expand this into a general explanation in which ordinary situations explain or even replace revolutionary transformations. Scott cannot be accused of deliberately overstressing everyday, less defiant events, because no one can predict when major events will happen; but the meanings he attributes to small, specific events remain problematic. Indeed, if revolutions or other important conflicts are unjustifiably generalized to whole nations and masses of mobilized people,[7] it is also true that fleeting downturns or momentary collapses of political systems in revolutionary episodes emerge from extensive/intensive everyday situations. That is, extraordinary circumstances underlie ordinary people's struggles, in which they become temporarily polarized defending their interests.

Hobsbawn and Rudé (1969) reinterpret the massive farmworkers' riots in England around 1830 from the perspective of everyday life.[8] Everyday forms of resistance like arson, threatening letters, inflammatory handbills and posters, robbery, meetings and sabotage, which could be described as major events, only took place two or three times, and usually were aimed at a single goal: to earn a living wage, and in some localities to end unemployment (1969:195). In different historical contexts, occasionally severe conflicts and revolutions were built upon infinitesimal, hetero-geneous resistances.

Scott's model has two premises: (1) the powerful must always dominate (or else dominated people's everyday forms of resistance would be inappropriate and meaningless); and (2) the subaltern classes must be homogeneous at least in terms of a common subversive strategy. Some parts of my ethnographic narrative, such as the subversive network around the reinstated worker in Chapter 5, may convey a similar tone. However, I present such cases as local practices, not as examples of extended patterns. In the same chapter, I also discuss power games in the workplace, where company interests and official truths intertwine with workers' images of power and skills. Hence workers' consent is a complex political arrangement. This is confirmed by the workplace des-criptions in Chapter 3 and the three situations related in Chapter 6. The definition of tasks reveals workplace values implicitly shared by both bosses and workers. As Marx rightly emphasized, 'workers accept with "good reasons" their exploitation' (quoted in Boudon 1990:124). That is, they translate capitalist reason into their own words and internalize it into their own worlds, and they do so by using arguments that reflect the consequences of their actions.

Rethinking the Ethics and Politics of Tomato Work

Workers studies are full of moral considerations like justice and equity with respect to economic, social and political resources. However, abstract proposals that never fit with local conditions are rhetorics more akin to politicians and mediators than workers. My micro-sociological experience has allowed me to identify with tomato workers' sceptical view of political issues, activities and rhetorics (like Rogelio and the students in Chapter 2). This point of view may enlighten my discussion of ethical issues as they present themselves in local contexts and in the literature. In this sense, I also regard ethics and politics with pragmatism, cynicism and mistrust (cf. Held 1989:243-7).

In Chapter 4, I characterized the tomato industry in terms of changing relationships between workers, managers and bosses in a relativistic legal and moral environment. I emphasized the complex intersection of local and global practices that affect and depend on political equilibria in which workers, managers and other parties constantly negotiate their rights, demands and interests. In Chapter 6, I reflected on workers' and companies' shared collective identities based on the contingencies and uncertainty of tomato work (enterprises on wheels and workers on the move). I showed how this leads to a legal and moral relativism in which government actors justify non-intervention because of that uncertainty.

The contingent nature of tomato work presents ethical questions as to what moral authority institutions and actors have to dictate solutions as neutral arbiters; these questions are difficult to address with general formulae. Although the circumstances are constantly changing, they must nevertheless fall within the symbolic category of human action to avoid despair. Thus unsatisfactory wage agreements or housing conditions may be interpreted as tolerable if they temporarily avert situations that could break the tomato industry.

Moral or legal formulae cannot wait for ideal conditions. Faced with the improbability of a better life for everybody and in order to keep from damaging the regional tomato industry with environmental controls, accepting less so that family needs can continue to be met and the regional economy can grow may be the appropriate response. Thus, it is difficult to invoke general criteria for improving workers' living conditions and conserving the local environment. Negotiations take two general routes: establishing a balance between family survival and quick corporate profits; and finding new ways of managing scarce resources (credit, land, etc.). Solutions must take account of the ecological consequences of intensive tomato production (land exhaustion and water pollution).

To reach a sustainable situation implies avoiding one party's interests subsuming another's. This leads one to assert that in dealing with these contingencies the ethics of tomato work privilege the political realism of negotiated settlements in conflictive or peaceful circumstances. However, the expected outcome will be mostly unfavourable to workers' interests. In this vein, the literature on farmworkers has correctly regarded the tomato industry as immorally preying on local resources for transnational interests that always gain more than local people. Issues like the exhaustion of local water, land, capital, labour, knowledge and skills are important questions; but they can be examined in the local context to avoid the reification of applying universal moral standards.

In this respect, the notion of local justice advanced by Elster (1992) sounds promising. Elster's approach to justice is a non-normative but explanatory one that takes justice and its components as scarce resources to be allocated and negotiated by institutions and different actors. He refers to specific issues, such as redistributive criteria and the interpretations of equity involved in political decision-making processes, as important points for explaining how justice is globally/locally constructed. Within this framework Elster discusses whence and how it can acquire authority, principles and procedures to compensate denied rights and the unmet claims of labour. He analyses different theories of justice (utilitarianism, Rawls and Nozick) and concludes that 'it is not possible to create economic equality once and for all, and to expect it to maintain itself without further interventions' (1992:204).

Elster defines his conception as common-sense justice, which includes the visions of first-order authorities (decision-makers), second-order authorities (doctors, preachers, officers) and public opinion. Common-sense conceptions are at an intermediate level of generality and abstractness. They are located between two axes: the inhuman character of maximizing total welfare and the inefficiency of maximizing minimum welfare. However, for the Mexican circumstances we have to apply Elster's approach with caution, because his notion of local justice takes for granted a healthy democratic practice. It is clear that Mexican politics are under suspicion in terms of their democratic functioning. The Autlán valley experiences left us with two unresolved ethical issues: (1) how to deal with cumulative debts of justice consisting of unpaid labour and unfairness that will be transferred to other productive regions and activities; and (2) how to analyse the claims and liberating efforts of workers and other social groups that obey diverse interests that can not be elucidated within the legal constraints of a particular social formation. In this sense, the Chiapas uprising (cf. introductory chapter) illustrates the multiplying effects of postponed justice. It also expresses the radicalism of the interweaving of local demands and organizational processes, which leads to a critical revision of democratic practices all over the country.

Bringing Absent Characters Back Into History

Rereading the literature on workers, I realized the pertinence of Kundera's phrase 'things are looser than they seem' (quoted at the beginning of this book). Still, I did not find it so easy to detach myself from 'their gravity that oppresses us' when I got involved in these arguments. Two aspects of my fieldwork that were satisfying in retrospect convinced me that it was useful to look beyond conventional approaches.

The first was Chimino (the absent worker) of Chapter 5. After his altercation with the Israeli professor, Chimino strongly criticized the official truth. This showed me how official truth reinforces privileges, commercial interests and moral values. In the second case, described in Chapter 6 as my most ironic fieldwork moment, the Teutlán strike, I lost and then recovered the possibility of analysing class behaviour. I had expected to use a fixed class model for locating workers following a common anti-company strategy, but instead reflected on how meanings were transformed. I discovered the complex ways in which the group's personal and shared life-worlds fit together and how economic and cultural interpretations of class offer flexible alternatives for changing their working conditions. How these workers spontaneously decoded their experiences and internalized values and knowledge from their households, their town and the tomato fields made me question whether social change is best understood from institutional patterns and planned strategies.

The scant improvement in workers' conditions over one hundred years of social policy and legislation in advanced countries like the United States (Friedland and Barton 1976:42) or England (Newby and Danzinger) can hardly strengthen the belief that social change will come from external organizations and government bodies. This scepticism about institutional social change leads to the realization that change cannot be imported into a vacuum from another territory.

This also leads us to ask where and how will feasible alternatives come from? This question is more vexing when change seems more difficult to conceive because of structural constraints and contradictory interests. Ultimately moral authority and feasible alternatives do not follow centralized patterns; they result from the ability to solve acute conflicts and offer new opportunities. This is to acknowledge that actors, whether part of the institutional apparatus or not, can exert moral authority, and that it does not reside within a specialized body. The possibilities for change are open and take on various forms, which can include a mixture of social forces, institutions and other actors promoting better living conditions for workers. In this mixture workers' efforts at self-liberation (whether through unions or spontaneous organizations) can play an important role. In any case, an enduring problem is highly differentiated tomato workers' consistent disadvantage with respect to the company and its demands. Does one have to attribute moral authority to some institutional body or agent who can force the amelioration of workers' living conditions?

Nozick (1974) deals with a similar problem in more abstract terms. He identifies the minimal practices of the state developed by agencies capable of guaranteeing human rights. He distinguishes between minimal and extensive state formations in terms of their functions. Nozick's minimal state provides for national defence and protection against violence, theft and fraud, and it enforces contracts and general sanctions to protect these basic rights. The minimal practices of state intervention in turn define the extended state and show how agents acquire different meanings. However, Nozick's dual conception of the state has problems with concretely establishing precise boundaries between these basic functions. Another point concerns the conditions that justify forceful intervention to preserve human rights, and who will intervene.

Chapter 4 showed how the state can reinforce the company in the face of worker claims for indemnifications. Workers acknowledge that constant surveillance and the threat of violence from companies and their allies are more effective than resistance. However, worker resistance combined with collaboration and negotiation can render this surveillance ineffective. Support from progressive government agents and other sectors can help win minimal concessions. Work patterns and living conditions refer to specific human rights. These rights were influenced by past experience; but there were dangerous occasions when past experience was of no help. Such was the case when workers started denouncing mistreatment and worsening economic conditions, but did not get what they wanted. Companies lose some conflicts, but workers lose more, since companies can coopt leaders and skilled workers or they can confound workers' interests. Cooptation can be more effective than coercion for containing worker reactions. The question of who defines minimum rights and who benefits most from them is a complex matter transformed at the negotiating table.

Conclusion

I close this chapter with some remarks on the paradoxes and tensions in the analysis of social change. The issue is how to understand variations of social change. That is, whether to interpret social change as a series of concrete, fleeting opportunities, or as a general, more permanent process. Change can be, in fact, simultaneously permanent and ephemeral. Events have profound and differentiated effects. For instance, the arrival of the tomato companies unfolded many changes, but these did not transform substantially the living standards of tomato workers.

A question increasingly considered fundamental for overcoming the gap between the theoretical and the empirical is that workplace changes cannot be isolated from other domains, because change cannot be read off from people's life-worlds; it must be demonstrated empirically in the interconnected situations of everyday life. This is consistent with how agents intervene in social change. The point is not to affirm generally that human agents can change the state of affairs, but to explore the concrete possibilities for doing so.

A related point is the relevance of the subjects of social change, a recurrent topic in sociological debates on methodological individualism and the political significance of everyday 'trivia'. One interpretation identifies the subjects of change as individual agents pursuing their own interests over those of the community or those of structural change. As stressed in Chapter 6 and in the preceding section, the meanings attributed to change intermingle with radical *(agrarista)*, liberal *(cardenista)* or conservative *(cristero)* political ideologies. Moreover, if anarchism submits to or justifies exploitation, then this does not square with my micro-sociological experience either. I used the notion of contingent utopia to expose conventional models of domination and work, the instabilities of the status quo and the fluidity of power. Following farmworkers into different social contexts makes it abundantly clear that individuals are never isolated, and are basic to power mechanisms that inform political issues and organizing strategies.

A last question is whether we conceptualize change as it actually occurs or in terms of ideal conditions or models. The first approach lets us trace social processes that simultaneously promote change and are transformed by countervailing actions and powers, without assuming that the individuals and groups involved have loyalties or institutional commitments. Exploring everyday struggles aimed at solving problems or meeting needs can help produce alternative views of social processes far removed from 'intelligent parties' in institutional frameworks who consider themselves to be fighting for justice.

Notes

1. Eagleton (1991:45-6) argues that ideologies are complex, differentiated formations with internal conflicts that must be continually renegotiated. He assumes that ideology is an action-oriented, practical operation, thus subscribing to Macherey's conception of ideology 'as the invisible colour of daily life . . . in which we move like a fish in water with no more ability than a fish to grasp this elusive environment as a whole'.
2. Giddens (1984) understands that structural constraints simultaneously enable and constrain social action.
3. It is always difficult to define the 'unintended' consequences of action. The aim of the concept is paradoxical, because it tries to explain not obvious but accumulated social disadvantages. In the Marxist and Weberian literature the term is used as 'unanticipated', to indicate people's propensity to undermine the spirit of capitalism (Ritzer 1983:75). Boudon (1990) makes this idea into a paradigm in which social phenomena are considered unintended consequences of individual actions, and he reviews philosophers, economists and sociologists like Mandeville, Adam Smith, Hayek and Popper who employ it. Boudon especially cites Merton for addressing specific questions like racism and scientific developments as unintended consequences of individual actions. Giddens (1984:14) makes the argument more sociological by referring to 'a social life full of different kinds of unintended consequences with varying ramifications' (in Long and van der Ploeg 1992:6).
4. For Lacroix (1981:15), the agricultural labour process is the human appropriation of nature to produce goods (use values) that satisfy needs. This process is articulated and includes labour, its means and its objects. She believes that this theory allows her to analyse articulations in human relationships with nature and the social context.
5. In Chapter 5, I demonstrate the ambivalence of technological change.
6. This reformulates his idea of systematic micro-translation (R. Collins

1981). For a detailed critique of Collins' programme see Long (1989: 227-30).

7. Newby (1977:78) explains that the 1870s English 'revolt in the field' was minor, despite its symbolic importance and the national attention it received. There were over 980,000 agricultural workers in England and Wales at that time, but at no point did the farmworkers' unions attract more than 12 per cent. For Knight (1990:169) the Mexican Revolution was an amalgam of numerous revolutionary experiences. Many Mexicos bred many revolutions. Masses of people were involved, but intermittently and differently, from region to region. Revolutionary activists were always a minority, and the peasants' and farmworkers' responses to the revolution ranged from hostility to indifference to heroic sacrifice. Still, for Knight this variability does not invalidate the importance of radicalism and revolutionary transformations: land and labour reform, mass public education and social security.

8. The story of Don Luis in Chapter 6 makes the same point.

Epilogue: Who Are They?

The Centrality of the Notion of Human Agency

To paraphrase E. P. Thompson's *The Poverty of Theory* (1979:198), how do I know that you exist, and, if you do, how do I know that my concept represents your real existence? This question leads me to assess tomato workers' human agency in terms of the interplay between their social experience and consciousness. Thompson claims that this interplay is manifold, because 'if a social being is not an inert table which cannot refute a philosopher with its legs, then neither is social consciousness a passive recipient of "reflections" of that table' (1979:201).

In short, human agency is continuously and mutually constructed by researchers and the people they research in varied dialogical situations. This notion can lead to an epistemological break by critically reviewing the literature on industrial workers and farmworkers. It is no exaggeration that denouncing exploitative practices in order to defend workers has the opposite effect, because the denunciations portray workers as powerless and virtually imprisoned under 'structural conditions'. On the contrary, my research verifies Rosaldo's (1990:114) suggestion that in Thompson's concept of class, 'human agency always transcends conditioning'. My text is the result of a long process of research and reflection, which overcame many obstacles, tried various procedures, and does not seek to construct a totalizing model of workers' lives. Even if such a model were theoretically possible, the research timetable precluded following workers into every aspect of their working and domestic lives.

However, constraints are not only obstacles. They can also challenge us to seek new ways of understanding. Therefore examining practices of domination is key to analysing tomato workers' everyday lives. By going beyond stereotypical images of power and authority, I could compare hierarchies at work and at home. One of this book's corollaries is to present social actors' contingent, changing circumstances as free from feelings of inferiority and fear of superiors.

The Distinctiveness of Human Agency

For Taylor (1985) human agency is distinguished by its capacity to evaluate motives. For Giddens (1979) it is people's transformative capacity to act in alternative ways at any time. Turner (S. B. Turner 1992) emphasizes that these transformative capacities are not mere discursive knowledge, intention and consciousness, but social action (cf. Long and van der Ploeg's 'interlocking projects' (1992)). Turner (1992:87) further observes that for Giddens, 'the actor is essentially a thinking and choosing agent, not a feeling and being agent'. Turner also criticizes sociology's failure to theorize the human body, despite the fact that much social action is grounded in biological events like birth, sex and death and expressed corporeally in pain, joy and suffering (ibid.:92).

Defining transformative capacities in terms of meaningful social change is problematic. Indeed, they cannot be defined without also analysing those capacities' concrete social embodiments and related contexts. At the end of his study of peasant–state relations in Costa Rica, de Vries (1992b:233–4) shows how agency is differentially constructed in relationships between peasants and authority-holders. Experts, frontline workers and peasants reshape their notions of agency in terms of representation and boundary-marking.

Long (1992) goes further. He distinguishes two kinds of conceptualizations and social constructions: 'First, [those] which [are] culturally endogenous in that [they are] based upon the kinds of representations characteristic of the culture in which the particular actor is embedded; and second, [those] which arise from the researchers' or analysts' own categories and theoretical orientation' (ibid.:25).' He calls for grounding these conceptualizations culturally in order to avoid a universalizing interpretation of agency across all societies. Although Long is clear, this does not mean we can altogether avoid ambiguities and contradictions. Instead, the emergent, circumstantial nature of transformative capacities is a constant.

The Ambiguity of 'Passive Agents'

The humiliation of women workers described in Chapter 6 illustrates that transformative capacities overlap with the practices of domination in complex ways. This leads me to question how much managers instrumentalize workers and create passive agents (cf. Law 1986): the women whose fingernails were forcibly cut both resisted and transformed the conditions of their humiliation. To make the notion of passive agents more problematic, I draw upon Inden's (1990:217) suggestion that we adopt a less Western meaning of 'patient' from Indian philosophy and history. That is, passivity and humiliation may not be definitive, extreme conditions and the people being humiliated may not be mere instruments, as theories of repression and domination have assumed.

Also, María in Chapter 2, the avoidance behaviour in Chapter 3 and the jokers of Chapter 6 were all ostensibly cases of subordination; but this apparent passivity and obedience does not mean that they lack the capacity to act otherwise. María only worked fast until she got close to finishing her task; then she took time for herself. Even though the jokers were asked to work on Saturday, they stayed away and did their own work. Other workers avoided difficult working conditions and other problems. If they complied with company instructions, they did not do exactly what the managers wanted. Hence so-called passive, subordinated agents are more active than they may appear to be at first.

Emergent Transformative Capacities

Focusing on actor-oriented human agency (cf. Long 1992) may be a paradigmatic ideological stance, but it is not closed, as Collins supposes (R. Collins 1981). Taking human agency seriously led me to interpret the party after the women's humiliation as a context for analysing embodied action and how transformative capacities emerge and function. The women's retaking of the site of their humiliation reveals several contingent transformations. These were not mere symbols, because they affected what the company considered to be structural components of their operation: work timing, discipline and roles. The women transformed themselves through speech and dress into organizers capable of enlisting other workers into extra work, collecting money and performing theatrically – activities which allowed them to recover face.

The importance I assign to these transformative capacities may be questioned, since nothing has 'really' changed; further collective humiliations could still occur. However, if we thoroughly follow up on the actors, we can grasp their significant social action, as when I recognized the connection between the women's humiliation and later festive transformation as part of an ongoing process. This allows one to go beyond interpreting events as separate from the processes underlying them.

Images produced by others are important for constructing agents and their transformative capacities. Strathern goes further, arguing that 'an agent is one who acts with another in mind, and that other may in fact coerce the agent into so acting' (1988:272). This is why individuals cannot be seen as isolated agents. Agency is socially constructed in organizing practices involving persuasion and charisma. These are effective ways of exerting power, translating interests and enrolling others in projects (Long 1992:23).

As we observed in Chapter 5, power and skills became understandable through the actions of others. Skilful practice and the exercise of power depended on a network of co-workers (who made a hero out of Ricardo for defeating the boss), even though this may have been done in the name of the company. Hence, as demonstrated by the Teutlán group, 'unos chingones who got what they wanted from the company', workers also have agency.

Analysing images of agency created by other interlocutors like sociologists and co-workers can be complicated by overlapping interpretations. One must see whether images correspond to real capabilities, actions and events. This is further complicated by people's contingent utopias and by propaganda, 'official truths', stereotypes and fictions in the media. The caricatures described in Chapter 1 depict some real behaviour. Slater (1990:29) suggests that Long's 'culturally endogenous' notions of agency should include externally-produced mass media culture. For instance the women and the Teutlán group discussed in Chapter 6 used media images to promote self-reliance. Of course, this does not exhaust the external influences that merit empirical research. Considering these influences avoids assuming that the media are omnipotent and the audience is weak and passive. This interconnection of external and internal images with multiple sources could be researched in relation to more locally grounded images found in rumour, bias and gossip.

To return to the issue of passivity, absent characters and the dissolution of group agency, when people are part of a network, analysts regard the leader as the agent and the rest as passive, obedient, less important followers. I have already discussed how invisibility and derogatory labels can influence descriptions and processes of change. I have also described how stereotypes of workers that neglect their capabilities are disseminated. But this cannot be taken as definitive: it is also worth analysing how pre-conceived images of passivity are assigned to people who join networks when in fact they may do so to use the power of the actor who recruited them for their own purposes. It may also be the case that there is the promise of upward mobility for new members within the network.

Future Research Agendas

Normally books conclude by summarizing all the features and implications presented in the preceding chapters. But I am also concerned about the possibilities that lie beyond this academic journey for analytic summaries. This is not because I think quest-ions for the future are a literary alternative to final summary statements; I am convinced that our knowledge of the social actors we interact with is limited. It is monstrous to believe that a researcher can sort out all the research problems he aims to deal with.

Researchers must come to terms with the ironic outcomes of their work, and, because of this, contact with a wider audience is challenging. How then do I summarize the findings of this book? This ethnography of apparently quiescent farmworkers in western Mexico demonstrates the indeterminacy of the objective macro-structural variables that other authors have pointed to as the cause of social action, as well as the impossibility of analytic closure imposed by observers implicated in the processes they study. Instead, the data point to 'contingent utopias' as motivating farm-workers' spontaneous, creative, ironic acts, which should therefore be seen as part of a subtle but active strategy of resistance. Still, such reductive summaries can obliterate the reader's opportunity to judge the relationship between social scientific findings and data. An ironic outcome of my research is that by trying to answer my initial questions, I ended up with more questions than I began with. I will close by considering some possibilities for future research on the most recurrent and intriguing question: human agency.

First, one must define agents and subjects. This entails thinking through tomato workers' contingency, their overlapping personal and shared life-worlds, and the connections between the home and workplace as domains of action. There is a general contention that people are defined by what they do. I also define tomato workers by their tomato work; but many of them (especially women) have several jobs, which connect different domains. These people are defined by and define themselves with images and notions that lead to intriguing questions: how do the exceptional workers who express their transformative capacities through skills at work do so at home? Does their behaviour at work contrast with their behaviour at home? Are they absent and invisible in one domain and active and visible in the other?

Another set of questions deals with gender, class, age and ethnicity in the domains where people act with different ideas and with individual as well as collective identities – aspects of agency I have frequently mentioned, but not systematically addressed. Agency differentially interconnects these features according to circumstances for particular workers, families, crews and companies. Power/knowledge inequalities are intimately related to locally-grounded cultural expressions of such features. I touched upon these inequalities when I compared contexts in which worker and manager imagery clashed with the imagery in the literature. One example was the case of the apparently disadvantaged indigenous migrant workers, who lived segregated in isolated camps, but extracted more of certain economic benefits and were more prone to rebel than local workers. Another example was the gender links to company authority, which both conformed to and contrasted with household patterns.

A final set of questions involves effective agency or the quality of agency. When and for whom is it effective? Since other people like observers, co-workers and counterparts usually define what is effective, what is social agency? Although individual expressions of agency are more noticeable than institutional expressions, they are tied to the powerful institutional agents who promote effective agency and change. That is, where is the effectiveness of agency located, and can it be measured in time? The problem is that contingent, context-specific expressions require detailed examination of issues related to this analytical perspective. Thus we can extend the question of effective agency to both internal and external institutional initiatives, and see if they represent, promote or generate workers' agency in unions and other local organizations. That is, we can explore whether institutional initiatives offer as little hope as they appear to, and whether effective agency must rely upon self-organizing.

Appendix

Weekly bulletin for international students in The Netherlands

NL. 6/92 - 13 February 1992

JOBS FOR IMMIGRANTS

Unemployment among minority groups is 31%, compared to 7% among the ethnic Dutch. A report by *Stichting van de Arbeid* has concluded that voluntary agreement between labour and management that employers would hire more members of the minorities has had little effect. Three companies out of four have never even heard of the agreement, and only 3% have made any effort.

According to *NRC Handelsblad*, it will probably become mandatory for employers to keep a register of their employees' ethnic backgrounds as a way of pressuring them into hiring more members of minority groups. A majority in parliament favours this, although the Christian Democrats and the management organisations continue to oppose any such legislation of employment policy.

Meanwhile, reports about employment in the horticulture industry reveal that illegal immigration puts many legal immigrants out of work. Police in The Hague estimate that between 15,000 and 30,000 illegal immigrants work in the nearby glasshouses. Many growers would rather pay ƒ 5 to ƒ 10 an hour to workers who have no rights than pay ƒ 35 an hour to legal workers. A social affairs ministry official told *NCR*, "If we do nothing to stop this, we are legalising social exploitation." Police and labour inspectors have promised to intensify their investigations in 1992. This caused a brief scare in the glasshouses; within two weeks in January the number of registeres job vacancies jumped from 40 to 476.

There is demand for illegal immigrants mainly for irregular, heavy and/or dangerous work; in agriculture, the garment industry, hotel and restaurants, and cleaning.

Annexe 1.

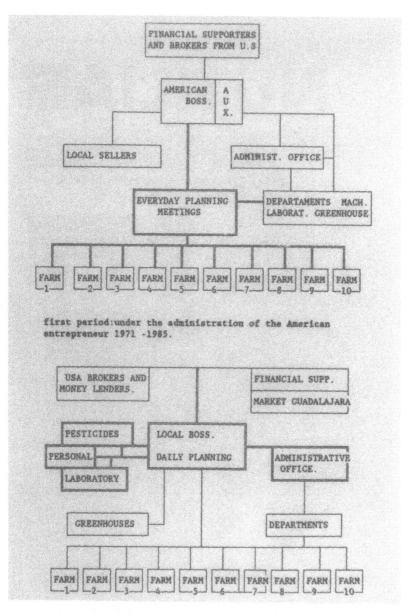

first period: under the administration of the American entrepreneur 1971 -1985.

Second period: under the Mexican ownership 1985–1988

Annexe 2. Organizational chart of the Rose Company

AÑO XIV   **AUTLAN, JAL.,**   **OCTUBRE 16 DE 1988**   **NÚMERO 481**

AHORA SI SE APLICARA DEBIDAMENTE EL SISTEMA DE RIEGO POR GOTEO

La competencia mundial de la comercialización de hortalizas y frutas está muy dura, por lo tanto los agricultores mexicanos requerimos actualizarnos en el rengión tecnológico, señaló lo anterior el Lic. Mario Haroldo Robles Escalante, Gerente General de la Unión Nacional de Organismos de Productores de Hortalizas y Frutas, al terminar el curso de riego por goteo y fertilización que se efectuó en esta ciudad durante cuatro semanas en un programa conjunto entre México-Israel con la participación de productores de varios estados del país.

También dijo que este programa de trabajo es parte de los objetivos que la Unión Nacional está buscando de incorporar las mejores tecnologías para aumentar la producción y la eficiencia de los productores para rescatar la posición en el mercado de Estados Unidos y de otros lugres del mundo a donde llegan productos de América que han desplazado a lo nuestro.

Dijo sentirse satisfecho de que en este lugar se estén haciendo esfuerzos decididos para incorporar nuevas tecnologías como el riego por goteo lo que demuestra que hay una mentalidad progresista de los agricultores de hortalizas y frutas que redituaran en producción.

Por su parte, el Ingeniero Agrónomo Daniel Michel Padilla, uno de los alumnos que vinieron del Estado de Colima, dijo que el curso le pareció muy provechoso porque permitía diseñar sistemas de riego por goteo para el cultivo de hortali-

Los dirigentes locales José Llamas Medina, Francisco Simón Miranda y Gabriel Castro Cavazos, junto con el Lic. Mario Haroldo Robles en la clausura del curso de riego.

zas y frutas para aumentar la producción por hectárea.

Asegura que en la actualidad se cosecha unas 25 toneladas de melón por hectárea y con el sistema de riego se producirían el doble para exportación aplicando la nueva tecnología.

Aclaró que el sistema de riego por goteo se utiliza desde hace tiempo en el país, pero de acuerdo a los conocimientos obtenidos en el curso, nunca se ha aplicado debidamente la tecnología requerida, culpando por ello a vendedores que solo venden el equipo y ahora los expositores israelita nos han enseñado la tecnología para aplicarla en el campo mexicano.

El curso de riego por goteo y fertilización fué organizado por la Asociación Agrícola Local de Productores de Hortalizas de Autlán con el apoyo de la S. N. P. H. Unión Nacional de Organismos productores de hortalizas y frutas, como consecuencia de un estudio realizado por estas instituciones que fueron apoyadas por el Ing. Abi Sade, Director del Campo Experimental del Departamento de Comercio vegetal del Instituto Científico Neisman de Israel, explicó Gabriel Castro Cavazos, Gerente de la Asociación Local.

Los alumnos que asistieron vienen de la zona de Casimiro Castillo, Jalisco; de los Estados de Colima, Baja California, Sinaloa, Michoacan y Guanajuato: fueron 23 Ingenieros Agrónomos y un médico alópata que por circunstancias especiales y personales aprovechó la oportunidad

El Ing. Abi Sade, científico israelita que dirigió al curso junto con el ingeniero Mata que también asistió al importante curso.

Annexe 3.

Annexe 4.

Bibliography

Agnew, John and Duncan, James S. (1989). *The Power of Place: Bringing Together Geographical and Sociological Imaginations.* Cambridge: Cambridge University Press.

Apte, Mahadev L. (1992). 'Humor', in: Richard Bauman (ed.), *Folklore, Cultural Performances, and Popular Entertainments: A Communications-Centered Handbook.* New York and Oxford: Oxford University Press.

Arce, Alberto (1989). 'The Social Construction of Agrarian Development: A Case Study of Producer–Bureaucrat Relations in an Agrarian Unit in Western México', in: Norman Long (ed.), *Encounters at the Interface.* Wageningen: The Agricultural University.

Arce, Alberto (1990). 'The Local Effects of Export Agriculture: A Case Study from Western México'. *Hull Papers in Developing Area Studies*, No. 3. Hull: The University of Hull.

Arendt, Hanna (1958). *The Human Condition.* New York: Garden City and Doubleday.

Astorga Lira, Enrique (1985). *Mercado de Trabajo Rural en México.* México: Era.

Astorga Lira, Enrique (1988). 'Los Jornaleros Agrícolas y Sus Organizaciones', in: Jorge Zepeda Paterson (ed.), *Las Sociedades Rurales Hoy.* México: Colegio de Michoacán.

Barger, W. K. and Reza, Ernesto M. (1994). *The Farm Labor Movement in the Midwest: Social Change and Adaptation among Migrant Farmworkers.* Austin: University of Texas Press.

Barnes, Barry (1986). 'On Authority and its Relationship to Power', in: John Law (ed.), *Power, Action and Belief: A New Sociology of Knowledge.* London: Routledge & Kegan Paul.

Baudrillard, Jean (1975). *The Mirror of Production.* St Louis: Telos Press.

Baudrillard, Jean (1988). *Selected Writings*, edited and introduced by Mark Poster. Stanford, California: Stanford University Press.

Bauman, Zygmunt (1992). *Intimations of Post-modernity.* London and New York: Routledge.

Boudon, Raymond (1990). 'The Two Facets of the Unintended Consequences Paradigm', in: Jon Clark, Celia Modgil and Sohan Modgil (eds),

Robert K. Merton: Consensus and Controversy. London, New York and Philadelphia: The Falmer Press.

Bourdieu, Pierre (1977). *Outline of a Theory of Practice*. Cambridge: Cambridge University Press.

Bourdieu, Pierre (1981). 'Men and Machines', in: K. Knorr-Cetina and V. Cicourel (eds), *Advances in Social Theory and Methodology: Toward an Integration of Micro and Macro Sociologies*. Boston, London and Henley: Routledge & Kegan Paul.

Brass, Tom (1989). 'Unfree Labour and Capitalist Restructuring in the Agrarian Sector: Peru and India'. *Journal of Peasant Studies*, 1: 51–77.

Brass, Tom (1990). 'The Latin American Enganche System: Some Revisionist Reinterpretations Revisited'. *Slavery Abolition: Journal of Comparative Studies* 11 (1): 73–103. London: Frank Cass.

Brown, Richard Harvey (1977). *A Poetic for Sociology: Towards a Logic of Discovery for the Human Sciences*. Cambridge: Cambridge University Press.

Brown, Richard Harvey (1987). *Society as Text: Essays on Rhetoric, Reason and Reality*. Chicago and London: The University of Chicago Press.

Brunt, Dorien (1992). *Mastering the Struggle: Gender, Actors and Agrarian Change in a Mexican Ejido*. Wageningen: The Agricultural University.

Bulmer, Martin (ed.) (1975). *Working Class Images of Society*. London and Boston: Routledge & Kegan Paul.

Burawoy, Michael (1979). *Manufacturing Consent*. Chicago and London: The University of Chicago Press.

Burawoy, Michael (1985). *The Politics of Production*. London and New York: Verso.

Calagione, John and Nugent, Daniel (1992). 'Workers' Expressions: Beyond Accommodation and Resistance on the Margins of Capitalism', in: John Calagione, Doris Francis and Daniel Nugent (eds), *Workers' Expressions: Beyond Accommodation and Resistance*. Albany: State University of New York Press.

Callon, Michel (1986a). 'The Sociology of an Actor Network: The Case of the Electric Vehicle', in: Callon Michel, Law John and Rip Arie (eds), *Mapping the Dynamics of Science and Technology*. London: Macmillan.

Callon, Michel (1986b). 'Some Elements of a Sociology of Translation: Domestication of the Scallops and the Fishermen of St Brieuc Bay', in: John Law (ed.), *Power, Action and Belief: A New Sociology of Knowledge*. London and Henley: Routledge & Kegan Paul.

Camp, Roderic Ai (1992). *Generals in the Palacio: The Military in Modern Mexico*. New York and Oxford: Oxford University Press.

Carlos, Manuel L. and Anderson, Bo (1981). 'Political Brokerage and Network Politics in Mexico: The Case of a Dominance System', in: David Wiler and Bo Anderson (comps.), *Networks, Exchange and Coercion*. New York and Oxford: Elsevier.

Castañeda Jiménez, Héctor F. (1987). *Marcelino García Barragán: Una Vida al Servicio de México*. Guadalajara, México: Unidad Editorial Gobierno de Jalisco.

de Certeau, M. (1984). *The Practice of Everyday Life*. Berkeley: University of California Press.

Cockcroft, James D. *et al.* (1982). *Trabajadores de Michoacán: Historia de un Pueblo Migrante*. Morelia, México: IMISAC.

Collins, Jane L. (1993). 'Gender, Contracts and Wage Work: Agricultural Restructuring in Brazil's Sao Francisco Valley'. *Development and Change*, 24: 53–82. London: Sage.

Collins, Randall (1981). 'Micro-Translation as a Theory-building Strategy', in: K. Knorr-Cetina and A. V. Cicourel (eds), *Advances in Social Theory and Methodology*. Boston, London and Henley: Routledge & Kegan Paul.

Collins, Randall (1992). 'The Romanticism of Agency/Structure versus the Analysis of Micro/Macro'. *Current Sociology*, 40 (1): 77–97. London: Sage.

Cornelius, A. Wayne and Craig, Ann L. (1988). *Politics in México: An Introduction and Overview*. San Diego: Center for US Mexican Studies, The University of California.

Danzinger, Rene (1988). *Political Powerlessness: Agricultural Workers in Post-war England*. Manchester and New York: Manchester University Press.

Deleuze, Giles and Foucault, M. (1977). 'Intellectuals and Power', in: Michel Foucault (ed.), *Language, Counter-Memory, Practice*. Oxford: Oxford University Press.

Eagleton, Terry (1991). *Ideology: An Introduction*. London and New York: Verso.

Elias, Norbert (1978). *The History of Manners: The Civilizing Process*, Vol. I. Oxford: Basil Blackwell.

Elias, Norbert (1982). *State Formation and Civilization: The Civilizing Process*, Vol. II. Oxford: Basil Blackwell.

Elster, Jon (1990). 'Merton's Functionalism and the Unintended Consequences of Action', in: Jon Clark, Celia Modgil and Sohan Modgil (eds), *Robert K. Merton: Consensus and Controversy*. London, New York and Philadelphia: The Falmer Press.

Elster, Jon (1992). *Local Justice: How Institutions Allocate Scarce Goods and Necessary Burdens*. New York: Russel Sage Foundation.

Fielding, Nigel G. (1988). 'Introduction: Between Micro and Macro', in: Nigel G. Fielding (ed.), *Actions and Structure*. London, Beverly Hills: Sage.

Foucault, Michel (1972). *The Archeology of Knowledge*. London and New York: Tavistock and Pantheon books.

Foucault, Michel (1977). *Discipline and Punish: The Birth of the Prison*. London: Penguin Books.

Foucault, Michel (1981). *The History of Sexuality*. New York: Vintage Books.

Foucault, Michel (1991). 'Questions of Method', in: Graham Burchell, Colin Gordon and Peter Miller (eds), *The Foucault Effect: Studies on Governmentality*. London and Chicago: The University of Chicago Press.

Foweraker, Joe (1995). *Theorizing Social Movements*. London: Pluto Press.

Friedland, William H. and Barton, Amy (1976). 'Tomato Technology: The Harvesting Machine Saved Tomatoes for California'. *Society*, 13 (6) (Sept./Oct.): 35–42.

Garfinkel, Harold and Sacks, Harvey (1986). 'On Formal Structures of Practical Actions', in: Harvey Garfinkel (ed.), *Ethnomethodological Studies of Work*. Berkeley: University of California Press and London: Routledge & Kegan Paul.

Genovese, Eugene D. (1974). *Roll Jordan Roll: The World the Slaves Made*, 2nd edn. New York: Pantheon.

Ghai, Dharam, Kay, Cristobal, and Peek, Peter (1988). *Labour and Development in Rural Cuba*. Hong Kong: Macmillan Press for ILO.

Giddens, Anthony (1979). *Central Problems in Social Theory*. London: Macmillan.

Giddens, Anthony (1984). *The Constitution of Society*. Cambridge: Polity Press.

Giddens, Anthony (1987). *Social Theory and Modern Sociology*. Oxford: Polity Press.

Giddens, Anthony (1990). 'Structuration Theory and Sociological Analysis', in: Jon Clark, Celia Modgil and Sohan Modgil (eds), *Anthony Giddens: Consensus and Controversy*. London, New York and Philadelphia: The Falmer Press.

Gledhill, John (1973). Optimisation Models in Economic Anthropology. Unpublished B. Litt. Thesis, Oxford University.

Goffman, Erving (1959). *The Presentation of Self in Everyday Life*. London: Penguin Books.

Goffman, Erving (1961). *Asylums*. London: Penguin Books.

González, Humberto (1991). 'Los Empresarios en la Agricultura de Exportación en México: Un Estudio de Caso'. *Revista Europea de Estudios Latinoamericanos y del Caribe*, 50: 87–114. Amsterdam: CEDLA.

González, Humberto (1994). *El Empresario Agrícola en el Jugoso Negocio de las Frutas y Hortalizas de México*. Wageningen: The Agricultural University.

Goodman, David (1991). 'The Global Fresh Fruit and Vegetable System: Stylized Facts and Some Half-Full Shelves'. Working Paper. Santa Cruz: University of California.

Goody, J. (1977). *The Domestication of the Savage Mind*. Cambridge: Cambridge University Press.

Goody, Jack (1992). 'Oral Culture', in: Richard Bauman (ed.), *Folklore, Cultural Performances, and Popular Entertainments: A Communications-Centered Handbook*. New York and Oxford: Oxford University Press.

Gorz, André (1980a) 'Técnicos, Especialistas y Lucha de Clases', in: *La División Capitalista del Trabajo*, Cuadernos de Pasado y Presente No. 32. México: Siglo XXI.

Gorz, André (1980b). *Adieu aux Proletariat*. Paris: Editions Galilée.

Gorz, André (1989). *Critique of Economic Reason*. London: Verso.

Grammont, Humberto (ed.) (1986). *Asalariados Agrícolas y Sindicalismo en el Campo Mexicano*. México: Ed. Juan Pablos–Instituto de Investigaciones Sociales UNAM.

Graumans, Adriënne (1989). 'Soy Mayordoma: Un Estudio de las Relaciones entre Mayordoma, Patrones y Jornaleras', Unpublished MSc. thesis. Wageningen: The Agricultural University.

Green, Thomas A. (1992). 'Riddle', in: Richard Bauman (ed.), *Folklore, Cultural Performances, And Popular Entertainments: A Communications-Centered Handbook*. New York and Oxford: Oxford University Press.

Guzmán Flores, Elsa (1995). *The Political Organization of Sugar-Cane Production in Western México*. Wageningen: The Agricultural University.

Habermas, Jurgen (1986). *The Theory of Communicative Action*. London: Heinemann Educational.

Harvey, Neil (1994). *Rebellion in Chiapas: Rural Reforms, Campesino Radicalism, and the Limits to Salinismo*. San Diego: Center for U.S.–Mexican Studies, University of California, San Diego.

Held, David (1989). *Political Theory and the Modern State*. Cambridge and Oxford: Polity Press.

Hernández, Luis (1994). 'The Chiapas Uprising', in: Neil Harvey (ed.), *Rebellion in Chiapas: Rural Reforms, Campesino Radicalism, and the Limits to Salinismo*. San Diego: Center for U.S.–Mexican Studies, University of California, San Diego.

Hirata, Jaime F., Trujillo, Felix, Romero, A. and Meza, C. H. (1986). 'La Corriente Migratoria de los Altos hacia la Costa y los Valles de Sinaloa', in: Humberto Grammont (coord.), *Asalariados Agrícolas en el Campo Mexicano*. México: Juan Pablos ed.–IIS, UNAM.

Hobsbawm, E. J. and Rudé, G. (1969). *Captain Swing*. London: Lawrence and Wishart.

Inden, Ronald (1990). *Imagining India*. Cambridge and Oxford: Blackwell.

Jessop, Bob (1990). 'Regulation Theories in Retrospect and Prospect'. *Economy and Society*, 19 (2): 153–216. London: Routledge.

Kierkegaard, Soren (1965). *The Concept of Irony*. Bloomington: Indiana University Press.

Knight, Alan (1990). 'Revisionism and Revolution: Mexico Compared to England and France'. *Past and Present*, 134: 159–99.

Knights, David and Willmott, Hugh (1990). *Labour Process Theory*. London: Macmillan.

Knorr-Cetina, Karin (1988). 'The Micro-Social Order: Towards a Reconception', in: Nigel G. Fielding (ed.), *Actions and Structure*. London and Bevery Hills: Sage.

Kundera, Milan (1980). *The Book of Laughter and Forgetting*. London: Penguin Books.

Lacroix, Anne (1981). *Transformations du Procès de Travail Agricole: Incidences de l'Industrialisation sur les Conditions de Travail Paysannes*. Paris: Institut National de la Recherche Agronomique & Institut de Recherche Economique et de Planification.

Lara, Sara (forthcoming). 'La Feminización del Trabajo Agrícola en México'. Paris: Institut des Hautes Etudes.

Latour, Bruno (1986). 'The Powers of Association', in: John Law (ed.), *Power, Action and Belief: A New Sociology of Knowledge*. London and Boston: Routledge & Kegan Paul.

Latour, Bruno (1988). 'The Politics of Explanation: An Alternative', in: Steve Woolgar (ed.), *Knowledge and Reflexivity: New Frontiers in the Sociology of Knowledge*. London: Sage.

Latour, Bruno (1991). 'Technology is Society made Durable', in: John Law (ed.), *A Sociology of Monsters: Essays on Power, Technology and Domination*. Routledge: London and New York.

Law, John (1986). 'On the Methods of Long-Distance Control: Vessels, Navigation and the Portuguese Route to India', in: John Law (ed.), *Power, Action and Belief: A New Sociology of Knowledge*. London and Boston: Routledge & Kegan Paul.

Law, John (1991). 'Power, Discretion and Strategy', in: John Law (ed.), *A Sociology of Monsters: Essays on Power, Technology and Domination*. London and New York: Routledge.

Liffman, Paul (1996). 'Reivindicación Territorial y Convergencia Democrática de los Wixáritari (Huicholes)', in: Jorge Alonso and Juan Manuel Ramírez Sáiz (comps.), *La Democracia de los de Abajo en Jalisco*. Guadalajara, México: Universidad de Guadalajara–CIESAS–CIICH (UNAM)–CEEJ.

Littler, Craig R. (1990). 'The Labour Process Debate: A Theoretical Review 1974-1988', in: David Knights and Hugh Willmott (eds), *Labour Process Theory*. London: Macmillan.

Long, Norman (1968). *Social Change and Individual: A Study of the Social and Religious Responses to Innovation in a Zambian Rural Community*. Manchester: Manchester University Press.

Long, N. (1984). 'Creating Space for Change: A Perspective of the Sociology of Rural Development'. Working Paper. Wageningen: The Agricultural University.

Long, N. (1986). 'Contrasting Patterns of Irrigation Organisation: Peasant Strategies and Planned Intervention'. A Research Proposal, Department of Sociology of Rural Development. Wageningen: The Agricultural University.

Long, Norman (1988). 'Sociological Perspectives On Agrarian Development and State Intervention', in: A. Hall and J. Midgley (eds),

Development Policies: Sociological Perspective. Manchester: Manchester University Press.

Long, N. (1989). *Encounters at the Interface: A Perspective on Social Discontinuities in Rural Development*. Wageningen: The Agricultural University.

Long, N. (1992). 'From Paradigm Lost to Paradigms Regained: The Case for an Actor-oriented Sociology of Development', in: Norman Long and Ann Long (eds), *Battlefields of Knowledge*. London and New York: Routledge.

Long, Norman and van der Ploeg, Jan Douwe (1992). 'Heterogeneity, Actor and Structure: Towards a Reconstitution of the Concept of Structure'. Working Paper. Wageningen: The Agricultural University.

Long, N. and Long, A. (1992). *Battlefields of Knowledge: The Interlocking of Theory and Practice in Social Research and Development*. London and New York: Routledge.

Long, Norman and Villarreal, Magdalena (1993). 'Exploring Development Interfaces: From Knowledge Transfer to the Transformation of Meaning', in: F. Schuurman (ed.), *Beyond the Impasse: New Directions for Development Theory*. London: Zed Press.

Lycklama à Nijeholt, G. Thomas (1980). *On the Road of Work: Migratory Workers on the East Coast of the United States*. The Hague: ISS–Nijhoff publishing.

Marsden, Terry and Murdoch, Jonathan (1990a). *'Restructuring Rurality: Key Areas for Development in Assessing Rural Change'*. Countryside Change Working Paper series, 4, London: South Bank Polytechnic.

Marsden, Terry, Lowe, Philip and Whatmore, Sara (1990b). *Rural Restructuring: Global Processes and their Responses*. London: David Fulton Publishers.

Marsden, Terry, Lowe, Philip and Whatmore, Sara (1992). 'Introduction: Labour and Locality: Emerging Research Issues', in: Terry Marsden, Philip Lowe and Sara Whatmore (eds), *Labour and Locality: Uneven Development and the Rural Labour Process*. London: David Fulton Publishers.

Martínez-Alier, Juan (1971). *Labourers and Landowners in Southern Spain*. Oxford Studies. London: Allen & Unwin.

Mestries, Francis (1991). 'Testimonios del Congreso Indígena de San Cristobal de las Casas', in: Julio Moguel (coord), *Historia de la Cuestión Agraria Mexicana*. Vol. IX, pp. 473–89. México: Siglo XXI-CEHAM.

Middleton, Chris (1988). 'The Familiar Fate of the Famulae: Gender Divisions in the History of Wage Labour', in: R. E. Pahl (ed.), *On Work: Historical, Comparative & Theoretical Approaches*. Oxford and New York: Basil Blackwell.

Muriá, J. Maria (1982). *Historia de Jalisco*. Guadalajara, México: Gobierno del Estado de Jalisco.

Nencel, Lorraine (1990). *Feeling Gender Speak : Sharing Space with Female*

Prostitutes in Lima Peru. Amsterdam: CEDLA-The University of Amsterdam.

Newby, Howard (1977). *The Deferential Worker: A Study of Farm Workers in East Anglia.* London: Allen Lane and Penguin Books.

Nozick, Robert (1974). *Anarchy, State and Utopia.* Oxford: Basil Blackwell.

Orwell, George (1961). *1984.* New York: New American Library of World Literature.

Paré, Luisa (1980). *El Proletariado Agrícola en México,* 3rd edn. México: Siglo XXI.

(De La) Peña, Guillermo (1986). 'Poder Local y Poder Regional: Perspectivas Socio-Antropológicas', in: J. Padua and Alain Vanneph (comps), *Poder Local, Poder Regional.* México: El Colegio de México CEMCA.

(van der) Ploeg, Jan Douwe (1990). *Labor, Markets, and Agricultural Production.* Boulder, San Francisco and Oxford: Westview Press.

(van der) Ploeg, Jan Douwe (1992). 'The Reconstitution of Locality Technology and Labour in Modern Agriculture', in: Terry Marsden, Philip Lowe and Sarah Whatmore (eds), *Labour and Locality: Uneven Development and the Rural Labour Process.* London: David Fulton Publishers.

Polier, Nicole and Roseberry, William (1989). 'Tristes Tropes: Post-modern Anthropologists Encounter the Other and Discover Themselves'. *Economy and Society,* 18 (2): 245–64. London: Routledge.

Posadas, S. Florencio and García, Benito (1986). 'El Movimiento de los Obreros Agrícolas en Sinaloa: 1977–1983', in: Humberto Grammont (coord.), *Asalariados Agrícolas y Sindicalismo en el Campo Mexicano.* México: Juan Pablos Editor/IIS–UNAM.

Pusey, Michael (1987). *Jürgen Habermas.* Chichester and London: Ellis Horwood and Tavistock.

Ramírez Sáiz, Juan-Manuel (1994). *Los Caminos de la Acción Colectiva.* Guadalajara, México: El Colegio de Jalisco.

Redclift, M. (1990). 'Book Review on: Labour and Development in Rural Cuba'. *Journal of Peasant Studies* 17 (2): 315–16. London: Frank Cass.

Ritzer, George (1983). *Sociological Theory.* New York: Knopf.

Robertson, Roland (1990). 'Mapping the Global Condition: Globalization as the Central Concept', in: Mike Featherstone (ed.), *Global Culture: Nationalism, Globalization and Modernity: A Theory, Culture and Society Special Issue.* London, Newbury Park and New Delhi: Sage.

Roldán, Martha (1980). 'Trabajo Asalariado y Condición de la Mujer Rural en un Cultivo de Exportación: El Caso de las Trabajadoras del Tomate en el Estado de Sinaloa, México', Informe final de investigación. Amsterdam: The Amsterdam University.

Rorty, Richard (1989). *Contingency, Irony and Solidarity.* Cambridge: Cambridge University Press.

Rosaldo, Renato (1990). 'Social Analysis in History and Anthropology', in: Harvey J. Kaye and Keith McClelland (eds), *E. P. Thompson: Critical Perspectives*. Cambridge: Polity Press.

Rubín, Ramón (1987). *El Valle de Autlán: Monografía*. Guadalajara, Jalisco, México: Unidad Editorial Gobierno del Estado de Jalisco.

Ryan, Michael (1989). *Politics and Culture: Working Hypotheses for Post-Revolutionary Society*. London: Macmillan.

Sayer, Andrew (1984). *Method in Social Science: A Realist Approach*. London: Hutchinson.

Schutz, Alfred (1962). *The Problem of Social Reality*. The Hague: Nijhoff.

Schutz, Alfred and Luckmann, Thomas (1973). *The Structures of the Life-World*. Evanston, Illinois: Northwestern University Press. Republished 1974, London: Heinemann.

Scott, James C. (1985). *Weapons of the Weak: Everyday Peasants' Forms of Resistance*. New Haven and London: Yale University Press.

Scott, James C. (1990). *Domination and the Arts of Resistance: Hidden Transcripts*. New Haven and London: Yale University Press.

Seur, Han (1992a). 'The Engagement of Researcher and Local Actors in the Construction of Case Studies and Research Themes: Exploring Methods of Restudy', in: N. Long and A. Long (eds), *Battlefields of Knowledge*. London and New York: Routledge.

Seur, Han (1992b). 'Sowing the Good Seed: The Interweaving of Agricultural Change, Gender Relations and Religion in Serenje District, Zambia'. Ph.D. Thesis, Wageningen: The Agricultural University.

Silverman, David and Gubrium, Jaber F. (1989). *The Politics of Field Research: Sociology Beyond Enlightenment*. London: Sage.

Silverstone, Roger (1989). 'Let Us Return to the Murmuring of Everyday Practices: A Note on Michel de Certeau, Television and Everyday Life'. *Theory, Culture and Society*, 6: 77–94. London, Newbury Park and New Delhi: Sage.

Slater, David (1990). 'Fading Paradigms and New Agendas: Crisis and Controversy in Development Studies', in: *Revista Europea de Estudios Latinoamericanos y del Caribe*, 49: 25–32. Amsterdam: CEDLA.

Stölcke, Verena (1988). *Coffee Planters, Workers and Wives: Class Conflict and Gender Relations on Sao Paulo Plantations, 1850–1980*. London: St Antony's/Macmillan Press.

Strathern, Marilyn (1988). *The Gender of the Gift*. Berkeley and Los Angeles: University of California Press.

Summers, Gene F., Horton, Francine and Gringeri, Christina (1990). 'Rural Labour-Market Changes in the United States', in: Terry Marsden, Philip Lowe and Sarah Whatmore (eds), *Rural Restructuring: Global Processes and their Responses (Critical Perspectives in Rural Change)*. London: David Fulton Publishers.

Taylor, Charles (1985). *Human Agency and Language*. New York: Cambridge University Press.

Thompson, E. P. (1979). *The Poverty of Theory and Other Essays*. London: Merlin Press.

Thompson, P. (1983). *The Nature of Work*. London: Macmillan.

Torres, Gabriel (1992). 'Plunging into the Garlic: Methodological Issues and Challenges', in: N. Long and A. Long (eds), *Battlefields of Knowledge*. London and New York: Routledge.

Torres, Gabriel (1997). 'El Derecho de Barzonear y sus Efectos Políticos', in: Jorge Alonso and Juan Manuel Ramírez Sáiz (coords.), *La Democracia desde Abajo*. México: Ed. La Jornada–UNAM.

Torres, Gabriel and Rodríguez Gómez, Guadalupe (1996). 'El Barzón y COMAGRO: la Resistencia de los Agroproductores a la Política Neoliberal', in: Hubert C. de Grammont and Héctor Tejera Gaona (coords.), *La Sociedad Rural Mexicana Frente al Nuevo Milenio*. México: Plaza y Valdés Editores.

Touraine, Alain (1981). *The Voice and the Eye: An Analysis of Social Movements*. Cambridge and New York: Cambridge University Press.

Turner, Roy (1989). 'Deconstructing the Field', in: David Silverman and J. F. Gubrium (eds), *The Politics of Field Research*. London: Sage.

Turner, S. Brian (1992). *Regulating Bodies: Essays in Medical Sociology*. London and New York: Routledge.

Vargas, Virginia (1991). 'The Women's Movement in Peru: Streams, Spaces and Knots'. *Revista Europea de Estudios Latinoamericanos y del Caribe*, 50: 7–50. Amsterdam: CEDLA.

Verhulst, Yikke (1988). 'Agrarian Change and Household Strategies: A study of the Role of Export-oriented Tomato Production in Western México'. Unpublished MSc. Thesis, Wageningen: The Agricultural University.

Vernooy, Ronnie (1992). *Starting All Over Again: Making and Remaking a Living in the Atlantic Coast of Nicaragua*. Ph.D. Thesis, Wageningen: The Agricultural University.

Villarreal, Magdalena (1992). 'The Poverty of Practice: Power, Gender and Intervention from an Actor-oriented Perspective', in: N. Long and A. Long (eds), *Battlefields of Knowledge*. London and New York: Routledge.

Villarreal, Magdalena (1994). *Wielding and Yielding: Power, Subordination and Gender Identity in the context of a Mexican Development Project*. Wageningen: The Agricultural University.

Vries, Pieter de (1992a). 'A Research Journey: On Actors, Concepts and the Text', in: N. Long and A. Long (eds), *Battlefields of Knowledge*. London and New York: Routledge.

Vries, Pieter de (1992b). *Unruly Clients: A Study of How Bureaucrats Try and Fail to Transform Gatekeepers, Communists and Preachers into Ideal Beneficiaries*. Wageningen: The Agricultural University.

Wickham, Gary (1983). 'Power and Power Analysis: Beyond Foucault'. *Economy and Society*, 12 (4): 468–97. London: Routledge.

Willener, Alfred (1975). 'Images, Action, "Us" and "Them"', in: Martin Bulmer (ed.), *Working-Class Images of Society*. London and Boston: Routledge & Kegan Paul.

Wilson, Fiona (1986). 'Commodity Production and Labour Systems: Alcohol in the Peruvian Central Sierra 1860s–1930s'. Copenhagen: Centre for Development Research.

Woolgar, Steve (1983). 'Irony in the Social Study of Science', in: K. D. Knorr-Cetina and M. Mulkay (eds), *Science Observed: Perspectives on the Social Study of Science*. London: Sage.

Zaag, van der, Pieter (1992). *Chicanery at the Canal: Changing Practice in Irrigation Management in Western México*. Amsterdam: CEDLA.

Index